D1472258

THE NEW TALENT ACQUISITION FRONTIER

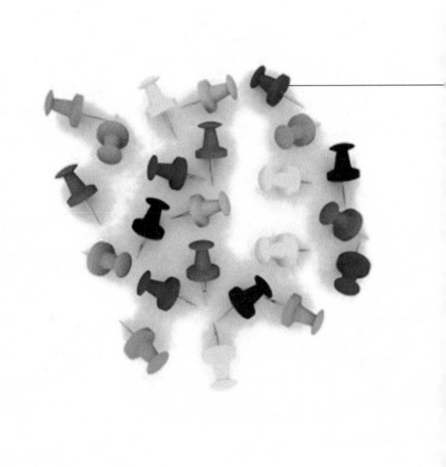

THE NEW TALENT ACQUISITION FRONTIER

Integrating HR and Diversity Strategy in the Private and Public Sectors and Higher Education

Edna Chun and Alvin Evans

Forewords by Andy Brantley and Benjamin D. Reese Jr.

STERLING, VIRGINIA

Published by Stylus Publishing, LLC
22883 Quicksilver Drive
Sterling, Virginia 20166-2102

Library of Congress Cataloging-in-Publication Data
Chun, Edna Breinig.
The new talent acquisition frontier : integrating HR and diversity
strategy in the private and public sectors and higher education /
Edna Chun and Alvin Evans ; forewords by Andy Brantley and
Benjamin D. Reese Jr. -- First edition.

    pages cm
Includes bibliographical references and index.
ISBN 978-1-62036-084-2 (pbk. : alk. paper)
ISBN 978-1-62036-083-5 (cloth : alk. paper)
ISBN 978-1-62036-085-9 (library networkable e-edition)
ISBN 978-1-62036-086-6 (consumer e-edition)
1. Diversity in the workplace.
2. Personnel management.
3. Universities and colleges--Personnel management.I. Evans,
Alvin. II. Title.
HF5549.5.M5C48 2014
658.3008--dc23   2013019647

13-digit ISBN: 978-1-62036-083-5 (cloth)
13-digit ISBN: 978-1-62036-084-2 (paperback)
13-digit ISBN: 978-1-62036-085-9 (library networkable e-edition)
13-digit ISBN: 978-1-62036-086-6 (consumer e-edition)

Printed in the United States of America

All first editions printed on acid-free paper
that meets the American National Standards Institute
Z39-48 Standard.

Bulk Purchases

Quantity discounts are available for use in workshops and for
staff development.
Call 1-800-232-0223

First Edition, 2014

10   9   8   7   6   5   4   3   2   1

CONTENTS

ILLUSTRATIONS

Figures

Tables

Exercises

D iversity and inclusion is so much more than affirmative action. Human resources professionals play a key role.

From a 2011 *New York Times* article regarding mixed-race growth across the country,

> In North Carolina, the mixed-race population doubled. In Georgia, it expanded by more than 80 percent, and by nearly as much in Kentucky and Tennessee. In Indiana, Iowa and South Dakota, the multiracial population increased by about 70 percent. . . .
>
> Census officials were expecting a national multiracial growth rate of about 35 percent since 2000, when seven million people—2.4 percent of the population—chose more than one race. (Saulny, 2011)

The College and University Professional Association for Human Resources (CUPA-HR) national board members and national office staff are working with higher education HR leaders from across the country to more clearly emphasize the important role these leaders have in creating diverse and inclusive working environments. Regarding the following comment made to me, "Our institution has wonderful diversity programs and our student population has become increasingly diverse," this institution deserves congratulations and those are great accomplishments, but these types of programs typically have little to no impact on the higher-education workforce, that is, members of the faculty and *all* staff.

Why is this greater emphasis important for higher education HR professionals?

- A changing higher education environment:
    - The workforce is changing.
    - Our higher-ed employees are becoming more diverse on a broad range of dimensions (e.g., gender, sex, sexual orientation, language,

age, ability status, national origin, religion, as well as race and
ethnicity and heritage).
- ○ Those who manage and develop the workforce need to be prepared
  to address the environmental factors that influence performance
  and affect employees' overall well-being.
- The changing role of higher education HR professionals:
  - ○ At every institutional level, leaders who manage and develop the
    higher education workforce need assistance in improving employee
    performance in such a rapidly shifting environment.
  - ○ The workforce and the student bodies of campuses are changing
    rapidly, yet many who are positioned to influence performance at
    various levels are stuck in a mid-20th century mind-set that some
    talent can be dismissed, while other talent should be valued.
  - ○ This mind-set serves neither employers nor students well, nor does
    it help build the interpersonal and performance competencies
    that *all* individual employees need and the capacities for agility
    that higher education institutions need to thrive in an increasingly
    complex world.
- The evolving position of higher education HR professionals to lead
  this work:
  - ○ This work is familiar to some and unfamiliar to many higher
    education HR professionals. It is familiar in that we have always
    provided talent development opportunities to our employees on
    compliance with Affirmative Action laws. However, a clear and
    unabashed focus on diversity, equity, and inclusion to advance
    institutional excellence may be unfamiliar to some. Leaders
    of CUPA-HR seek to instill a new mind-set in our employee
    communities. The new mind-set is one of commitment to our
    values and belief that by providing guidance every employee has
    the capacity to perform at high levels and not merely comply with
    nonexclusionary laws.
  - ○ We must also acknowledge the historical legacy of racial and ethnic
    discrimination and place a priority on addressing these legacies with
    new educational resources and practice tools such as this book.

Why now?

- We must do this work because it is needed now and because we can.
  - ○ Every employee has some connection and interaction with HR,
    which truly is the crossroads for all employees.

° The expertise and assistance that higher education HR professionals are best suited to provide differs at different levels in our institutions, so we must equip ourselves *now* to provide the best guidance possible to all employees to make certain our institutions achieve their excellence goals and remain vital well into the future.

I am very pleased to endorse *The New Talent Acquisition Frontier: Integrating HR and Diversity Strategy in the Private and Public Sectors and Higher Education* as an important resource for organization leaders to use in their effort to create an inclusive, high-performing organization.

Andy Brantley
President and Chief Executive Officer
CUPA-HR

Reference

Saulny, S. (2011, March 19). Black and White and married in the deep South: A shifting image. *The New York Times.* Retrieved from http://www.nytimes.com/2011/03/20/us/20race.html

FOREWORD 2

Benjamin D. Reese Jr.

I t was the Summer of 1971, and my employment application somehow stood out from the masses. I was asked to come in for an interview. This New York City hospital was one of the largest employers in the Bronx, so being called in for an interview was an accomplishment, or perhaps the luck of the draw. To this day, I'm not sure how the personnel department made its decisions. But after completing several official forms, I was introduced to the department as the new director of training. Colleagues were friendly enough, and patient, but it took me quite a while to figure out everything I was supposed to do. The general job expectation was to train people in improved race relations. I surmised that much of any tension in the workplace indeed related to insensitive racial comments, inequitable treatment of certain employees, and professional development opportunities that relied more on friendships and personal connections than highly honed skills and competencies. But so much was unclear and depended on whom you talked to. I was on my own. Individuals and departments did their own assigned tasks, with little collaboration or shared sense of mission. There was a dearth of organizational strategy with only a vague idea of values that were of significance to the hospital. Much has changed over the last 40 years, while some things seem to have simply been reworked or relabeled.

Edna Chun and Alvin Evans have avoided simply tweaking or rewording the usual organizational jargon. They have charted a new level of organizational collaboration and provided a thoughtful approach to melding the responsibilities of HR professionals and chief diversity officers (CDOs). They portray a synergistic relationship, based on research that in their words capitalizes on the organizational intelligence of HR professionals and diversity emotional intelligence. The resultant change is on a self and organizational performance level. The authors appropriately recognize that successful integration and collaboration of the two practices (HR and diversity) are clearly not the norm in most organizations. In fact, they go on to describe the obstacles or barriers that often, in an unintended way, work against productive integration of the functions. They are forthright and clear in this description. As a CDO and president of the National Association of Diversity Officers in Higher Education, I feel this is a particularly important section. Two of the prerequisites for CDO success are a direct reporting line to the president or chancellor and *full integration of the diversity work with the HR practice of the institution.* The latter is often lacking.

Much of this text is devoted to that synergy or integration. For example, HR and diversity professionals in higher education, corporate, or nonprofit environments will want to measure their programs and strategies against the authors' "Ten Predominant Themes in HR/Diversity Transformation Across All Sectors" (see Chapter 1, p. 14). This diagnostic tool can serve to point out strengths and opportunities for any organization. Although some judge higher education as generally slightly behind its corporate partners in the implementation of strategic HR/diversity practices, the authors provide examples of outstanding models for integration in particular higher education institutions. These examples and detailed case studies appear throughout the book. It seems that whenever the reader wonders how some particular practice might look on the ground, Chun and Evans provide an engaging case study.

Unlike my experiences in the 1970s, most organization administrators are not content with passive systems of staffing but are focused on strategically attracting and retaining outstanding talent. National and international competitive pressures make it imperative that organizations develop cultures that promote respect, encourage using the full potential of every contributor, and appropriately respond to workplace concerns and conflicts. Certainly the CDO role not only provides leadership in organizational transformation but is usually deeply engaged in this process of recruitment and retention of talent. This role cannot effectively occur in isolation but must exist, as the authors point out, as a long-term process of talent sustainability, a partnership with the institution's HR practice. Their discussion of the global nature of talent acquisition is not only relevant to multinational corporations but is increasingly applicable to colleges and universities building highly diverse workforces of international employees as well as institutions establishing programs and campuses abroad. Collaboration between CDOs, whose experience is often focused on domestic issues, and HR professionals, who have had a similar domestic focus, is vital to building a fully integrated global talent strategy.

Collaboration and integration is more than a mantra in this text; the authors provide a research basis, clear and user-friendly strategies, and a road map for the deep integration of HR and diversity practices that is critical to the present and future success of our colleges and universities. I trust my CDO colleagues will agree.

Benjamin D. Reese Jr.
President, National Association of Diversity Officers in Higher Education
Vice President for Institutional Equity, Duke University/
Duke University Health System

ACKNOWLEDGMENTS

Wedicate this book to our children—Alexander David Chun, Shomari Evans, Jabari Evans, Kalil Evans, and Rashida VanLeer—who we are confident will realize the promise of the new talent acquisition frontier. We would like to express our gratitude to John von Knorring, president of Stylus, for his commitment to this project and his dedication to the attainment of diversity and inclusion in American institutions. We especially thank the diversity and human resource leaders who shared their valuable time, insights, and perspectives with us in the preparation of the case studies.

We would like to express our deep appreciation to Joe Feagin, Ella C. McFadden Professor of Sociology at Texas A&M University, for his encouragement and invaluable suggestions in the evolution of the manuscript. We especially thank Kimberly Thompson for her skilled and responsive research assistance throughout the course of the project.

Alvin Evans wishes to thank Lester Lefton, president of Kent State University, for his visionary leadership of diversity. President Lefton's actions have been an inspiration to Alvin while doing the research for this book. He would like to thank Charlene Reed, secretary to the board of trustees and chief of staff in the Office of the President at Kent State University, for her generous support. Alvin would also like to acknowledge Rev. Ronald Fowler, special assistant to the president at Kent State, for his great source of inspiration and his continued support.

Edna Chun thanks chancellor Linda Brady and vice-chancellor Reade Taylor of the University of North Carolina at Greensboro for their inspirational leadership in the development of strategic talent management practices and diversity. She also thanks Levi Williams and Georgette Sosa Douglass for their courageous and forward-looking leadership in support of diversity as trustees of Broward College for the last decade.

We would like to express special appreciation to our family and friends for their continuous support. Alvin Evans would like to thank Ethel and Horace Bush, Patricia and Leon Scott, Karen and Hassan Rogers, Patricia and Donald Marsh, Brian and Lisa Marshall, Victoria Thomas, and Lesley Green. Edna Chun would like to thank Jay Kyung Chun, Alexander D. Chun, David and Laura Tosi Chun, George and Eleanor Chun, Ronnie Rothschild, and Karen Williams.

Edna Chun and Alvin Evans

1

THE BUSINESS CASE FOR INTEGRATING HR AND DIVERSITY STRATEGY

Organizations can be considered as modes of attention: what is attended to routinely can be thought of as what is valued. . . . Diversity work involves the effort of putting diversity into the places that are already valued so that diversity can come into view. (Ahmed, 2012, p. 30)

Talent is the primary strategic asset necessary for organizational survival and success in a globally interconnected world. The new talent frontier demands the optimization of human capital resources derived through unprecedented synergy between HR and diversity programs. Without such synergy, organizations will fail to attain their full talent potential.

The practices of talent management involve the orchestration of HR and diversity programs that enhance organizational capability by unleashing, mobilizing, nurturing, and sustaining the contributions of a diverse and talented workforce. Similarly, talent sustainability requires a high degree of integration between HR and diversity in the continuous development of systems, structures, processes, and a culture that heighten employee commitment, engagement, and inclusion.

This book presents a systematic approach to the integration of HR and diversity practices that lead to an inclusive, high-performance workplace. We chart pathways to the attainment of this goal using the latest research as well as first-person interviews with diversity and HR thought leaders in global organizations. As HR professionals, our focus is on concrete strategies and practical tools that will help organizations in this journey. Since the integration of HR and diversity is an evolutionary process, the case study is an ideal medium for studying process (Kezar & Lester, 2011). We share case studies from the private, public, and higher education sectors and from the two leading HR professional associations, the Society for Human Resource Management (SHRM) and the College and University Professional Association for Human Resources (CUPA-HR), to illustrate the dynamic intersection between HR and diversity practices.

We set the stage in this chapter by describing the competitive global environment that demands a strengthened alliance between HR and diversity practices across all sectors and types of organizations. Then we address prevalent misconceptions about HR's diversity role, and we identify barriers to diversity transformation in the public, private, nonprofit, and higher education sectors based on the research conducted for this book. Our essential thesis is that broad commonalities exist across all types of organizations in their efforts to attain strategic talent management practices. Yet organizations differ markedly in their level of attainment of synergistic HR/diversity programs and their speed of adaptation to rapidly shifting global realities. At the close of the chapter we examine some of the reasons for these differences.

As complex adaptive systems, organizations must relinquish control as the ultimate goal, and embrace the creation of adaptive capability as a primary organizational competence (Edmondson, 2012). To be effective, the development of synergistic HR/diversity practices needs to be systematic rather than piecemeal, integrated rather than isolated, responsive to external realities rather than merely internally focused, and strategically planned rather than sporadically implemented. To conclude the chapter, we introduce 10 common themes that will facilitate the alignment of HR and diversity programs and accelerate the process of diversity transformation.

The Global Imperative

The proverbial handwriting on the wall is clear. Three surveys identify the critical role of HR in diversity transformation. In a Forbes Insights survey (Egan, 2011) of 321 executives in large global enterprises with annual revenues of more than $500 million, the majority of respondents recognized the crucial role of diversity as a driver of innovation and as a critical component of being successful on a global scale. And 65% of the respondents identified HR as responsible for implementing programs and policies related to diversity and inclusion (Egan, 2011). Similarly, a survey of 546 executives in 47 countries commissioned by the Society for Human Resource Management (SHRM, 2009) found that HR was ranked by 42% of respondents as the primary advocate for diversity and inclusion, second only to top management. In 59% of companies surveyed, the point person for diversity is the head of HR (SHRM). Furthermore, an SHRM survey of 674 HR professionals found that in 62% of the companies represented, HR was responsible for leading diversity efforts ("An Examination of Organizational Commitment to Diversity and Inclusion: Survey Findings," 2011).

Yet despite this growing level of recognition of the leadership role of HR in diversity practices, many organizations still have not responded to the global imperative to create a systematic talent management platform that melds HR and diversity strategy. For example, a survey of 243 HR and diversity professionals primarily in higher education conducted by the American Association for Affirmative Action found that half the respondents viewed HR as a processing function that is not contributing to diversity goals ("Collaborative Relationships Between EEO/AA, Human Resources and Diversity Professionals: Survey Report," 2012). Nonetheless, three quarters of the respondents did report effective collaborative efforts between HR and diversity. The survey concluded that the "apparent disjunction" in the structure of HR, diversity, and Affirmative Action offices presents a barrier to mutual understanding and effective diversity planning (p. 2). Ironically, a major study of the newly evolving role and responsibilities of the chief HR officer does not even include diversity as a topic (Wright et al., 2011).

By contrast, consider the perspective of Carolynn Brooks, chief diversity officer for OfficeMax, a corporation with 29,000 employees, who described the impact of a change in the chief executive officer (CEO) and top HR leadership on collaborative HR and diversity efforts:

> The advantage I have now . . . is that we all sit down together and talk about how we are going to meet the goals and they are aligned with HR rather than in conflict with HR. What I love about it is we are . . . collaborating on how we can be a more diverse workforce and not combatting one another, in terms of that's not my job, or why am I doing this kind of thing. So maybe we've evolved to a place where we all own this, and that means we have got to get all of our HR business partners comfortable and in situations that are very sensitive and knowing how to handle them.

Similarly, Deborah Dagit, chief diversity officer from 2001 to 2012 at Merck, a global corporation with 84,000 employees in 144 countries, notes that diversity professionals must articulate the business case for the integration of diversity in HR processes:

> I think that it is important to acknowledge that historically there has been friction between diversity and HR that has largely arisen from either the lack of a sufficiently compelling business case, the perception that diversity and inclusion are more about corporate responsibility than about the business, and /or the lack of investment being made in helping HR professionals develop their confidence and capability in diversity constructs and skills. You will often hear people responsible for diversity lament that they take a lot of friendly fire from their HR colleagues in their company. . . . If we don't articulate the ROI [return on investment] to the business of diversity in a way that's compelling, it can become a lesser priority. When you have a strong business case, given the desire of HR to most effectively support the business, that's when you see the best integration. . . . The HR function is being

held accountable and rewarded for how well they support the business, so therefore they are less likely to get involved in diversity and inclusion if the business case is not in evidence. You also have to invest in the confidence and capability of HR professionals in order for them to be willing to engage in the diversity and inclusion work.

Julie Oyegun, chief diversity officer at the World Bank from 2001 to 2012, notes the necessity of forging a tentative alliance between diversity and HR. She describes a conversation she had in this regard with her vice president:

> I was beginning to appreciate that there is an antagonistic contradiction between HR and diversity. . . . [T]hat antagonistic contradiction exists I think in most HR departments between HR and diversity. . . . The diversity professional is an almost permanent critique of what's not working in HR. So it's difficult to be collaborative and to work really well. . . . I think that we go through the motions very efficiently. The bank is a very sophisticated organization and there are certain things that inevitably you have to do together, for example, annual reporting.

Organizational changes at the World Bank will bring the chief diversity officer position more closely into the mainstream of the HR organization by making this position a deputy to the vice president for HR, responsible for strategy, HR operations, and diversity.

T. Hudson Jordan, former global director of diversity at Pitney Bowes, also cites the importance of shared accountability for diversity work as a systemic issue:

> Shared accountability for an initiative like diversity to work is critical. All too often companies succeed in adopting a business case for diversity, but fail to design accountability into their diversity and inclusion strategies. Historically it has been difficult to create accountability through organization to produce meaningful business results. The key is to get as many engaged as possible. If diversity and inclusion are thought of and designed as a nice-to-have HR initiative then HR remains responsible. It is unlikely that such an initiative will achieve meaningful business results because it was not designed or intended to do so.

Diversity, Demography, and HR Strategy

The demographic context calling for unified HR and diversity strategy is compelling. Witness the profound demographic shifts in the United States that herald a new era in which minority populations will become the majority by 2042. Racial and ethnic minorities account for 91.7% of the nation's growth since 2000 (Passel, Livingston, & Cohn, 2012). And minority groups will increase from about one third of the U.S. population to 54% by 2050 (U.S. Census Bureau, 2008). According to the U.S. Census Bureau, by 2050 nearly one in three people in the United States will be Hispanic (29%), and the Hispanic growth rate is now triple that of the general population (Campbell, 2009). In 2010, for the first time in American history, minority births including Hispanics, Blacks, Asians, and those of mixed race represented the majority, or 50.4% of all births (Tavernise, 2012).

On the world stage, globalization has hastened the advent of the new talent frontier by eroding traditional barriers of time and distance through technologies that provide speed and connectivity regardless of physical location. Metaphorically speaking, the world has shrunk in size, moving from the period of globalization 1.0 in which countries vied for resources, to globalization 2.0 in which companies were the agents of globalization, to globalization 3.0 in which small groups and individuals are the forces of globalization (Friedman, 2005). Clearly, a more diverse group of non-Western and non-White individuals is going to drive this third phase of change (Friedman, 2005).

Globalization has created four unprecedented movements: the movement of capital across borders, the movement of humans across borders, the movement of information through the medium of cyberspace, and the movement of popular culture (Gardner, 2007). Foreign competitors have appeared in domestic markets, causing managers of businesses to think beyond traditional boundaries and become world class even when simply trying to retain local customers (Kanter, 2003). As a result, an emerging class division could take place between cosmopolitan businesses that are globally connected versus local organizations that are isolated from their competition (Kanter, 2003).

A globalized workforce has become the norm rather than the exception for the 100 or so major corporations that dominate the economic scene and are headquartered mainly in the United States, Europe, and Japan. Outsourcing labor is a common business practice. The offshore revolution in call centers across many industries can result in cost savings of 10% to 15% in countries like Canada, 20% in the Caribbean, and 30% to 50% in other countries (Read, 2005). India tops the list of desirable offshore call centers because of the quantity and quality of the workforce with three million college graduates every year and a potential workforce of 30 million college graduates (Read, 2005).

Furthermore, the rapid increase in diverse consumers across all industries means that corporations and institutions must design new multicultural marketing strategies for their clientele. In fact, Hispanic or Black consumers make up nearly 30% of the U.S. population with nearly $2 trillion in estimated spending power and growth rates estimated at twice the rest of the U.S. population (Palacios, 2008).

To respond to these dramatic developments, organizations now need to expand their capacity for diversity through a strategic framework that aligns HR and diversity programs. HR leaders can no longer afford to operate in isolated silos: HR must adapt or it will not survive. Facing the disruption caused by "the most turbulent marketplace in history" (p. 3) the C-suite will be turning to HR for bold action, not small steps (Fitz-enz, 2009). In the words of Jac Fitz-enz, "There is no god-given right for HR to exist" (p. 3).

Despite these trends, why have organizations failed to harness the synergy between HR and diversity to create a high-performance workplace? The pivotal role of HR professionals as diversity leaders has remained below the organizational radar. Diversity leadership is often not viewed as an essential component of the HR leader's portfolio of responsibilities. Some would even argue that diversity is outside the HR domain, based on notions of the abstract worker as without gender, ethnicity, age, or nationality (see Benschop, 2001). And a relative lack of empirical research on the subject leaves HR professionals in the dark about how to overcome the predominant leadership silos that have divided HR and diversity efforts in organizational structures.

Perhaps some of the confusion derives from the fact that the diversity management literature has not been well organized or provided specific linkages to the types of guidance needed to implement integrated practices (Marquis, Lim, Scott, Harrell, & Kavanagh, 2008). The importance of an organizationally specific framework linking HR and diversity functions has not risen to the level of an organizational priority for many organizations. While the logic relating to the need to turn diverse human capital into an organizational resource is strong, the actual strategies seem less clear (Beer, 2010). This book is designed to close that gap by providing a concrete road map for organizations and professionals to attain a coordinated HR and diversity strategy.

Driving Change From the Outside In

The pressure for organizations to foster inclusive cultures is clearly coming from the outside in. Similarly, a successful HR transformation in support of diversity starts with a clear understanding of the business context and rationale for change (Ulrich, Allen, Brockbank, Younger, & Nyman, 2009). In support of this thesis, a global research study now in the sixth round of data gathering reveals that HR competencies are driven by three major themes facing businesses today: outside/in, which means HR must translate external business trends and stakeholder expectations into internal strategies; individual/collective, which means HR must address individual ability and organizational capabilities; and event/sustainability, which means HR is not about piecemeal or single function programs but about integrated, sustained solutions (Ulrich, Younger, Brockbank, & Ulrich, 2012).

Not only must HR and diversity leaders respond to rapid changes in the external environment, but their work must also link from the inside of the organization to the outside to create value for the stakeholders outside the organization (Brockbank, 2009). HR and diversity officers now function as chief integrative leaders, pulling all the pieces together between geographically distributed units within strategic alliances and bringing diverse groups of employees into alignment with diverse customer markets (Avolio, 2005). With the advent of deregulation and globalization, new market entries have created increased competition, and HR professionals need to be equipped to ensure their organizations or firms can compete in nontraditional markets (Quinn & Brockbank, 2006).

Traditional views of HR that focus only on internal processes and internal stakeholders represent anachronistic approaches that isolate HR from overall business strategy and relegate the department to a merely transactional destiny. Ironically, even the notion of HR management derives from the Anglo-Saxon economic view that technical rationality characterizes human participation in an organization and that the laws of physics and engineering govern how human cultures participate in the workplace (Hampden-Turner & Trompenaars, 1998). This mechanistic view fails to account for the complexities, nuances, and ambiguities of organizational culture in the contemporary workplace. For example, Jeff Perkins, chief people officer and vice president for HR at National Public Radio, explains the critical link provided by HR between the company's diverse employment brand and its clientele: "A lot of it is around improving our hiring, expanding our employment brand to attract diverse audiences, [and] developing an organization that is open and accepting of people from all walks of life and all levels and cultures in the company."

In fact, the practices of talent management and talent acquisition are emblematic of the paradigm shift from transactional HR to strategic HR. In recruitment and staffing, HR must position the organization as the employer of choice not only for internal customers but the "employer of choice of employees that customers would choose" (Ulrich, Brockbank, Johnson, Sandholtz, & Younger, 2008, p. 187). High-performing HR departments have changed from serving primarily internal stakeholders to a "more boundary-less world" in which customer expectations "translate into employee behaviors" (Ulrich et al., 2008, p. 186). As a result, selection processes need to identify potential candidates who can serve diverse clients and whose behaviors reflect an in-depth understanding of diversity. Talent selection today must focus on the alignment of individual capabilities with organizational goals to maximize limited resources and create a high-performing workforce. With the luxury of more abundant economies, organizations may have engaged in employment practices that were not closely calibrated with organizational strategy or goals. By contrast, strategic hiring processes connect customer base and workforce competencies with an overall competitive strategy.

Misconceptions About HR's Diversity Role

In our view, four primary reasons account for the lack of recognition of HR's integral role in diversity. First, organizations may not have developed a clear approach that connects HR's ability to instigate cultural change in the context of line cultures to the role of diversity leaders as principal staff owners of diversity efforts. From this perspective, HR leaders represent social engineers facilitating the cultural change needed to embed diversity in an organization's DNA. We explore this aspect of HR's role further in Chapter 4.

Second, HR leaders may not have embraced their role as co-owners with diversity leaders of a deliberate approach that fosters alignment of all elements in the system with changes in human inputs (Cox, 2001). From this perspective, what more powerful instruments do organizations possess than their talent management processes? When HR leaders are absent from the diversity table, an organization will lack the systemic ability to orchestrate the complex tapestry of organizational practices to support diversity strategy.

The third reason for the bifurcation between HR and diversity leadership is that HR professionals themselves have been hesitant to venture into the field of diversity. They have simply not viewed diversity as an integral part of their work responsibilities and have relied on other specialists in their organizations or firms for the attainment of diversity goals. Many organizations, in turn, have not appreciated the real value that HR leaders can bring to diversity work or assigned the necessary resources and staffing to support this emerging role.

The fourth reason that integrated HR and diversity programs represent the exception rather than the rule is the absence of a concrete business case supporting these practices. Over the last decade and a half, exploration of the relationship between diversity and HR management has begun to garner some research attention (e.g., see Kossek, Lobel, & Brown, 2006; Marquis et al., 2008; Mathews, 1998; Richard & Johnson, 1999; Scott, Heathcote, & Gruman, 2011; Shen, Chanda, D'Netto, & Monga, 2009). Researchers have theorized that the effective management of employees deriving from cohesive diversity-related HR strategies leads to improved bottom-line results (Scott et al., 2011). In this view, workforce diversity affects financial performance by increasing the skill and talent base of employees; improving retention; enhancing problem-solving capacity, creativity, and flexibility; and boosting market share by mirroring the consumer market (Cox, 2001; Hubbard, 2004; Marquis et al., 2008). And a considerable literature has sprung up regarding measurement of diversity ROI (e.g., see Hubbard, 1999, 2001, 2004).

Yet while the most commonly cited motivation for an organization to increase its diversity is to improve business performance (Marquis et al., 2008), empirical findings on the impact of HR-related diversity programs have often been conflicting (see Richard, Murthi, & Ismail, 2007). One of the most significant studies, a 5-year research effort conducted on four large-scale corporations, found little correlation between diversity and firm performance (Kochan et al., 2003). Researchers in this study concluded that context is crucial in determining diversity's impact, since highly competitive contexts exacerbated racial diversity's negative effects, while environments that emphasized integration and learning perspectives supported a more positive impact (Kochan et al., 2003).

The role of organizational context as a moderator between diversity and firm performance has been substantiated in the research literature. For example, a study using a sample of 79 banks found that the more HR diversity practices an organization has, the greater the impact on organizational productivity (Richard & Johnson, 1999). Another study of a cross-section of Fortune 500 firms rated highest on diversity found a stronger relation between racial diversity and long-term performance in munificent environments with more than adequate resources (Richard et al., 2007).

While much more work remains to be done to ascertain the impact of diversity at the organizational level, a solid body of empirical research demonstrates the relationship between strategic HR practices and organizational and financial performance using significant samples from the private sector (see Evans & Chun, 2012). As a result, HR leaders may now need to adopt a more analytical role to understand the consequences of diversity and determine the conditions in which work units that are diverse outperform more homogenous units (Kochan et al., 2003). HR professionals also need to explore the environmental and contextual conditions that enable diverse work groups to flourish. In Case Study 4 in Chapter 2 (see p. 57), for example, we share the collaborative efforts of the chief diversity officer and chief HR officer at Duke University to promote the efforts of diverse constituencies in a complex, decentralized organizational environment. Observations from this case study provide strategies for creating the contextual conditions that support the alignment of HR and diversity practices.

In this regard, a study of executives at 14 best companies for diversity in *Fortune* magazine further validates the importance of establishing environmental conditions for diversity to flourish. Interviews with these executives reveal that the companies focus on being the best place to work rather than on the direct business case for diversity (Marquis et al., 2008). Several of these best practice diversity firms leverage HR programs—recruiting, promotion, and retention—in support of diversity initiatives (Marquis et al., 2008).

We now examine several of the typical misconceptions that arise about HR and diversity's interaction:

Misconception 1: HR and diversity work are separate and different entities. *Response*: The traditional functional separation of HR and diversity work is no longer viable as organizations seek to respond to the changing demographics of the United States and the sweeping changes brought about through globalization in the 21st century. Organizational success in a competitive global economy depends upon realizing the potential of diverse human assets, tapping into diverse markets, and serving a diverse clientele.

Misconception 2: HR leaders should focus only on core HR functions without making diversity an explicit emphasis. *Response*: This misconception derives from a common view of diversity as an extraneous rather than an integral focus of organizations today. In their commitment to organizational viability and success, HR professionals can no longer afford to assume such an exclusive role. In Case Study 6 in Chapter 4 (see p. 110), we examine the efforts of the College and University Professional Association to strengthen the role of HR in the attainment of diversity and inclusion on college and university campuses.

Misconception 3: HR leaders do not need specific diversity leadership competencies but can rely on existing functional knowledge of traditional HR specialties. *Response*: As we discuss in Chapter 3, diversity competencies have become an indispensable component of today's HR professional's portfolio and skill set. The repertoire of diversity skills needed by HR leaders in fact is broadening, deepening, and integral to organizational success. Such skills are neither nebulous nor magical. They require a nuanced understanding of organizational culture and behavioral interactions as well as significant tactical agility to bring about change in complex environments. These competencies enable HR leaders to work collaboratively with diversity leaders to implement innovative change processes that shift the cultural paradigm and overcome prevailing norms and assumptions that hinder inclusion.

When these three common misconceptions govern an organization or firm's thinking, efforts to implement a concerted diversity strategy may result in piecemeal and segmented efforts. As a starting point, HR and diversity leaders need to ask themselves the following questions:

1. Has the role of HR in my organization been connected with overall diversity strategy as a business ally in responding to the external environment and increasing overall effectiveness and financial growth?
2. Is HR in my organization viewed as a partner in transformative diversity change?
3. Have organizational leaders identified concrete structural, organizational, and behavioral approaches that delineate HR's contribution to diversity?

The answers to these questions will help determine the starting point for addressing diversity in an organization's HR practices. Some organizations or firms do not perceive HR as a change agent, nor want it to be. Some may simply focus on transactional HR and expect HR to take a back seat with regard to shaping organizational strategies. Some firms or organizations are focused on preserving the status quo, and when HR professionals swerve from this course, such deviations are not perceived favorably. And some organizations may perceive diversity as separate from the mainstream of HR activity. If all these factors are present in an organization or firm, the business case for integration of HR and diversity strategy still needs to be made. Even when explicit recognition of the importance of integrated HR and diversity programs is absent, HR and diversity leaders can begin the process of building support for their synergistic contributions.

Barriers to Integrated HR/Diversity Practices

The implementation of integrated HR and diversity practices presents common barriers across the public, private, nonprofit, and higher education sectors. In many ways the private sector is leading the way in the development of strategic HR and diversity talent practices. In response to competitive economic trends, global corporations have developed more comprehensive, systematic strategies for talent reviews, succession planning, and the acquisition and retention of diverse talent. Attention to the value added of strategic HR and diversity practices in the private sector may derive from the broader scope of HR operations, the for-profit focus, and reliance on performance-based, financial measures of success such as return on equity and return on assets (Evans & Chun, 2012). As we see in the case studies in Chapter 1 and Chapter 6, federal and state governments have also introduced forward-looking and inclusive strategies for diversifying the workforce based on the need to be responsive to changing demographics.

By contrast, higher education has been relatively slow to recognize the value of strategic HR/diversity talent practices. Academic and staff personnel responsibilities are typically bifurcated in terms of organizational reporting and scope of responsibility. Most HR offices provide the full range of HR services for staff, with services to faculty often limited to benefits and retirement. In many institutions of higher education, HR is still struggling to attain recognition as a true strategic partner and to participate in strategic planning (see Evans & Chun, 2012). As a result, academic research on strategic HR practices has been centered on the private sector. Research studies on higher education have been frequently approached in terms of distinct HR-related practices such as faculty compensation, an area that does not typically fall within the purview of the HR office.

Viewed holistically, the following five barriers represent the most significant challenges to the attainment of synergistic HR and diversity practices:

1. *Failure to integrate diversity into the mainstream structure and purposes of the organization.* A fundamental barrier to the attainment of integrated talent practices is the tendency to view diversity as extraneous to the mission and purposes of the organization. This barrier results from the failure to build the business case for diversity and can result in siloed diversity functions.

As an outgrowth of the silo conception of diversity, diversity operations frequently lack staffing and resources to accomplish their mission. As a rule, staffing sizes of the diversity office, even in global corporations, are small and dwarfed by the size of the HR operation. To some degree, this differentiation reflects the staff rather than the line focus of diversity in comparison with HR. Diversity offices frequently must rely on the HR organization for professional development resources and programs to advance diversity.

Budget and resources for the diversity function remain a continuing challenge. T. Hudson Jordan, former global director of Pitney Bowes, explains the tendency to view diversity as a luxury rather than a necessity:

> If it is seen as a nice-to-do, something extra, then when you have to buckle down, you cut out the extra stuff, right? But if this is critical to your livelihood, you figure out how you maintain those things and make room for them. So it's almost like an analogy to maintaining a home. . . . [C]able in my opinion is a nice-to-do, but not a necessity, right? But my food and my lights are. . . . So you might get rid of the extra stuff when you have to buckle down. And if there's no real clear value then that value needs to

be shown to the practitioner as well as to the organization. . . . Because if it's not valuable then you do get rid of it. Because then you trim the waste, trim the fat.

As we highlight further in Chapter 4, an indicator of silo diversity functions is the frequency with which diversity officers themselves are subject to the revolving door, This phenomenon alone suggests that diversity has still not attained a mission-critical status and may function in some settings as window dressing designed to improve the organization's image and its brand.

2. *Difficulty in bridging internal bureaucratic divides and hierarchies.* The divide that exists among the executive, managerial, administrative, and operational tiers represents a powerful challenge in developing integrated HR and diversity programs. In higher education, this divide has been exacerbated by the fact that most HR offices have a limited role in relation to the faculty, who represent the most significant organizational constituency. As a result, HR typically reports through the chief financial officer with a primary focus on functions that support administrators and staff, with the exception of benefits (see Evans & Chun, 2012).

In private industry, however, the prominence of HR as a strategic partner has elevated the profile of HR programs, helping HR to leverage influence and build collaboration with line managers. Interestingly, in public and private sector organizations, the diversity function reports through the chief HR officer with a dotted line to the CEO, such as the World Bank, the U.S. government, OfficeMax, Walmart, Ingersoll Rand, and Whirlpool, among others. This consolidation may also be driven by efforts to reduce expenditures in the latest economic downturn.

3. *Lack of integrated planning of HR and diversity programs.* Regardless of organizational structure and the reporting relationship, HR and diversity sometimes coexist in an uneasy alliance, as seen from the examples earlier in the chapter. Because of the lack of a clearly articulated business case for their interrelationship, these strategic functions often navigate in what could be described as parallel universes, without establishing coordinated and collaborative planning. Such planning would help capitalize on scarce resources, eliminate duplication, and enhance the organizational impact and effectiveness of both functions. In the words of Nancy Kichak, associate director of HR policy at the Office of Personnel Management in the federal government, "a willful effort" is needed to ensure that the HR office and the diversity and inclusion office "stay integrated and on the same mission."

4. *Cultural resistance and behavioral barriers that preclude the inclusion of diverse talent.* In many environments, HR and diversity face the daunting task of changing organizational culture to be receptive to diversity. Resistance may be strong, ongoing, and subtly expressed. And critical to overcoming

cultural barriers in large, decentralized organizations are the skill sets, behaviors, and actions of line managers as the purveyors of organizational norms.

Consider the perspective of the chief diversity officer at Ingersoll Rand, who emphasizes in Case Study 3 in Chapter 2 that time is needed to "embed soft skills into day-to-day behaviors and the everyday work environment" (p. 54) and to create an organizational climate that welcomes differences and values the innovative contributions of a diverse workforce. Leading-edge companies excel in the soft stuff. The hard stuff is made up of what finance and operations people value, such as cost, speed, supply chain, and analytics, and can be copied (Karlgaard, 2012). By contrast, the soft stuff is a differentiator and consists of a company's story, its narrative, and its culture (Karlgaard, 2012).

5. The tendency to view diversity as someone else's job and not a collective responsibility. Ingrid Jacobs, director of diversity at the Whirlpool Corporation, a global company with over 68,000 employees, notes the tendency for HR and business leaders to assume that diversity is the sole province of the diversity office. She said she sees barriers "when there is not a strong understanding of how all members of the organization need to be conscientious and intentional in ways to do business." This tendency surfaces, she said, when "HR and business believe diversity's role is to do all of it, rather than understanding that they have a significant role." In essence, all stakeholders in an organization are responsible for diversity, but they will only embrace diversity when the relation of diversity to an organization's core mission and business strategy has been made evident.

With these five barriers in mind, in the next section we identify 10 predominant themes that can lead to successful diversity transformation based on our research across the public, private, and higher education sectors.

Ten Predominant Themes in HR/Diversity Transformation Across All Sectors

Organizations that are making strides in the implementation of strategic HR/diversity programs have important characteristics in common. The 10 themes presented here can serve as diagnostic indicators for leaders to assess the extent to which a comprehensive HR/diversity talent management strategy has been undertaken and operationalized. These themes transcend specific organizational settings and clearly delineate the progress an organization has made in building a sustainable edifice of HR/diversity talent programs.

1. A clearly defined vision and business case for diversity. Throughout our interviews and case studies, a clearly articulated vision and business case for diversity surfaces as the sine qua non for building effective HR/diversity programs. Intangibles such as engagement, innovation, creativity, shared mind-set, and diversity are factors that are not measured through traditional accounting methods but lead to enhanced organizational capabilities (e.g., see Ulrich & Smallwood, 2003, 2004). Organizational capabilities represent the organization's ability to maximize intangible assets and deploy human capital to fulfill organizational mission and goals. As such, building diversity capability is an essential aspect of mobilizing human capital to meet the demands of globalization (Chun & Evans, 2009). Diversity is a differentiating intangible that is integral to excellence and quality. The emergence of the concept of inclusive excellence in higher education recognizes that the alloy of diversity and quality is stronger and more durable than its constituent parts (Clayton-Pedersen & Musil, 2005).

Articulation of the business case for diversity enables employees to understand diversity as an indispensable facet of business strategy that is responsive to the global business context. A well-defined business case for diversity links successful human capital practices to organizational effectiveness and outcomes. It extends beyond talent practices to include the systems, values, and culture of the organization. Consider how Jeff Perkins, chief people officer at National Public Radio, describes the business case for diversity:

> Diversity here focuses not just on diversity in our workplace but also in the content we produce. So it's not just about the hallways, it's also about what's on the air. We have a goal of reflecting America as we report, and that means reflecting a very diverse America. . . . [W]e are always looking for those benefits and opportunities that appeal to our broader population. We are all about inclusion and including all audiences as we put together our benefits for the organization.

2. Actionable leadership commitment to strategic HR/diversity programs. One of the primary difficulties HR and diversity leaders face is obtaining actionable leadership support for systematic diversity transformation. While often the chief diversity officer reports to the CEO or president or at least has a dotted-line reporting relationship to the chief executive, the willingness of the CEO/president to take action in support of diversity may vary substantially. Because of internal resistance, multiple constituencies, governance issues, and other seemingly more pressing priorities, the CEO/president may be reluctant to take risks by undertaking change initiatives that substantially alter the status quo.

3. A power structure that supports the attainment of strategic HR/diversity objectives. Since most organizations operate within a hierarchical framework, those in power define reality in terms of what is perceived as correct and normal (see Chun & Evans, 2012). The dominant group in power allows things to happen through ownership of the status quo and the ownership of organizational language (Rangasamy, 2004). Beneath a seemingly egalitarian veneer, organizational culture can reflect stereotypical ideas and even biased attitudes through the complex interplay of systems, principles, and practices (Rangasamy, 2004). The executive leadership team can wield substantial influence over the direction and strategy adopted by an organization and the ROI for its specific division or constituency. In addition, the board of trustees represents an important force that can neutralize, overturn, or affirm specific objectives and initiatives.

Take the experience of Rohini Anand, senior vice president and global chief diversity officer for Sodexo, when she first presented her vision for diversity as well as a diversity scorecard and metric to the executive team. As described in Case Study 4 in Chapter 2, she was literally chased out of the room. Yet Michel Landel, CEO of Sodexo North America who was later promoted to CEO of Sodexo, actively supported her and sought assurance that she was okay. Through a process of transformative change, Anand now feels that she no longer needs to be in the room to advance the cause of diversity. Line managers at Sodexo view diversity as a resource contributing to business success, and the company now has many other individuals who will help carry the work forward.

4. *Cultural change that builds trust-based relationships and eliminates a fear-based work environment.* Because of the power of organizational hierarchy, fear often governs the workplace. The belief that fear increases control has led society to become tolerant or even indifferent to a fear-based work environment (Edmondson, 2012). Fear limits interpersonal risks such as the willingness to speak up, as individuals engage in self-censorship for fear of being seen as ignorant, incompetent, negative, or disruptive (Edmondson, 2012). In Chapter 3, we discuss further the role of HR leaders in creating psychological safety that allows diverse individuals to have a voice and contribute their talents to the organization without fear of reprisal.

Organizational trust is a rare and fragile commodity. It can be undermined significantly by wild variations in compensation between leadership and rank-and-file workers, as well as by the commodification of employees as disposable entities. Trust is a key component of leader-subordinate relationships and can be a significant competitive advantage (Schoorman, Mayer, & Davis, 2007). The presence of trust can lead to risk taking in a relationship, since trust allows a willingness to be vulnerable to another party (Schoorman et al., 2007). And trust can enable organizations to recruit and retain highly motivated and diverse employees who are more likely to be engaged, innovate, and display organizational citizenship behavior such as helping coworkers (see Starnes, Truhon, & McCarthy, 2010).

The extension of trust-based relationships also is critical in terms of community outreach and establishing credibility with diverse consumers. As shared in the case study at the end of this chapter, Cheryl Burrell, administrator of the HR Outreach and Diversity Office of the State of Rhode Island, needed to establish the credibility of her office in terms of workforce diversity by rebuilding trust with community leaders. These leaders felt that the state had not given due consideration to diversifying the workforce. As a result, relationship building was an essential focus of Burrell's efforts to expand diversity outreach efforts.

5. *Recognition of diverse talent as an accelerator of innovation and the ability to leverage such talent to create new products and expand services.* Organizations that draw upon the rich diversity of talent available to them increase their innovative capacity. They recognize talent as the driver of innovation, regardless of race, ethnicity, sexual orientation, disability, or other differentiating characteristics. They do not squander the valuable resources of knowledge and creativity that can differentiate their performance. And they consciously design talent acquisition and retention programs that support a climate of participatory inclusion and empowerment. In contrast, when diverse individuals are marginalized, institutions and organizations will suffer and eventually deteriorate and decline (Feagin, 2010).

As noted in Case Study 6 in Chapter 4, Veronica Villalobos, director of the Office of Diversity and Inclusion in the U.S. Office of Personnel Management, views building innovation in the federal workforce as a central focus of diversity planning under the rubric of "diversify, include, and sustain" (112). Her use of the office's innovation labs for governmental agencies to develop their diversity and inclusion plans illustrates the close tie between diversity and innovation.

6. *Translating HR/diversity vision into a systematic, phase-based approach.* One of the most telling characteristics of HR/diversity progress is the ability to map an evolutionary pathway that identifies distinct phases and goals. Such a blueprint requires the sequential and sometimes complementary development of systematic practices, rather than stand-alone initiatives that create a momentary ripple in the organization's cultural waters. In emphasizing that change is not a quick fix, Kilmann (1984) recommends the creation of tracks that can be deployed sequentially or simultaneously, depending on organizational readiness. He identifies a culture track that creates mutual respect and trust, a management skills track that ensures management understands the complex issues and assumptions involved, a team-building track that allows teams to collaborate in solving the most difficult problems, a strategy-structure track that aligns resources and structures with strategic direction, and a rewards track that ties recognition to performance and represents the most significant track for overall success (Kilmann, 1984; also see Evans & Chun, 2007).

One of the most salient examples of a successful phase-based approach is the organizational diversity maturity model developed at Sodexo and described in Case Study 5 in Chapter 3. Rohini Anand advises of the importance of "chunking out" the lofty vision of being the diversity benchmark for the industry into "very digestible bites" that would allow the organization to "get their arms around it" to implement it (p. 85). Presenting 50 different things to managers did not work, because line managers wanted to know what the three things were they needed to do. Anand also emphasizes the importance of gauging organizational readiness for the next phase of diversity development through the medium of emotional intelligence.

7. Metrics that track diversity progress with accountability for results. A common denominator for successful HR/diversity talent practices is the development of solid metrics that establishes accountability for results and ties this accountability to compensation and evaluation practices. Prominent examples emerge from private industry in this regard. Walmart has established core metrics for workforce, workplace, and marketplace diversity and links these results to compensation recognition through the Diversity Goals Program. In this program 15% of bonus components for managers can be withheld if diversity goals are not fulfilled. Sodexo's Diversity Scorecard includes metrics on recruiting, retention, and promotion of women and minorities as well as measures of qualitative behavioral change. The scorecard is linked to 10% to 15% of the bonuses for managers and 25% of executive management bonuses.

8. Ability to implement core HR/diversity principles across decentralized unit/lines of business and in globally dispersed locations with differing cultural norms. In addition to the need to bridge internal hierarchies, organizations seeking to implement an enterprise-wide HR/diversity strategy face the considerable challenge of implementing talent management practices across geographically dispersed units often in international settings. Private corporations are not alone in this challenge, as universities are developing overseas campuses and operations that involve HR policies consistent with the home campus. Cultural differences require a sensitive and nuanced implication of the meaning of diversity and inclusion, especially in countries where, for example, the term *minority* may have a different meaning.

In Case Study 5 in Chapter 3, Rohini Anand describes the difficulty of obtaining common definitions of *diversity* in an international environment. She observes that gender is the common metric globally. Furthermore, the process of getting a handle on workforce demographics can be complex in global corporations and institutions. In Case Study 3 in Chapter 2, the chief diversity officer of Ingersoll Rand, for example, describes the necessity for a global HR information system to capture consistent data across the international spectrum.

9. Diverse team cultures that have an impact on organizational performance. Innovative organizations rely on diverse work teams to generate new insights, ideas, and inventions. The notion of *teaming* directly contracts with a transactional view of talent—that is, that talent is comparable across organizations, fungible, and acquired rather than developed (Beer, 2012). Instead, Amy Edmondson (2012) points out that teaming is the new engine of organizational learning, bringing people together to generate new insights and solve problems (see Edmondson). Edmundson uses teaming as a verb, a dynamic activity, unlike the established and static notion of team as a noun, a fixed group of people pursuing a common goal. As she observes, "At its best, teaming clarifies and magnifies human capacity" (p. 285).

Examples from innovative companies illustrate the creativity that arises from self-directed, empowered team-based interactions that promote participation, process redesign, and redistribution of responsibility to the workers themselves. Take the example of Intuit, the software company located in Mountain View, California, labeled by *Forbes* magazine as one of the world's most innovative companies. Intuit produces the QuickBooks accounting software used by 50 million small businesses. Founder Scott Cook meets monthly with 14 or 15 teams to conduct brainstorming sessions, with dozens of team projects and experiments taking place across the company simultaneously (Upbin, 2012). For one such project, small boxes are drawn on a large piece of oak tag containing questions such as, "What's your vision? What's your leap-of-faith assumption? What's your hypothesis?" (p. 72). In essence, Intuit is a science lab, testing new ideas daily through team-based innovation, experimentation, and entrepreneurship (Upbin, 2012). Diverse work teams focused on a common goal can serve as a catalyst for broader organizational inclusion by diminishing levels of intergroup bias (Gaertner & Dovidio, 2000). Direct contact among diverse team members reduces bias as shown in a large-scale research study based upon 515 individual studies (Pettigrew & Tropp, 2006). As a result, the process of diversity transformation benefits from collaborative interaction at all levels of the organization and can begin through the agency of diverse teams assigned to address mission-critical problems.

10. Systematic organizational learning programs that exemplify the principle of execution as learning. Organizational learning refers to the process by which an organization learns and changes. It means that a critical mass of individuals act in new ways, leading to the formation of new habits and assumptions (Argyris et al., 1994). The concept of execution as learning involves constant, small-scale learning that occurs in the course of day-to-day work

(Edmondson, 2012). Unlike execution as efficiency, execution as learning promotes sustainable success, changing the focus from getting things done more efficiently to learning faster (Edmondson, 2008). Since implementing concerted HR/diversity programs is still relatively new, and the literature in this area is relatively undeveloped, even organizations with considerable diversity capability are still learning from their successes. Innovation requires experimentation and generation of new possibilities, and execution as learning for diversity means developing groundbreaking solutions in the process of execution (Edmondson, 2012).

Unifying Bureaucracy to Create Synergistic Talent Approaches

Despite the existence of certain commonalities across all organizations, we have noted the slower rate of implementation of strategic HR/diversity practices in higher education as compared to private industry. As Kezar and Eckel (2002) point out, transformational change is unfamiliar to most institutions of higher education, since such change alters the culture and its underlying norms; it is intentional, deep, and pervasive; and it is sustained over time. Institutional leaders and policy makers lack the experience and meaningful empirical research on the process of change in academic settings to base such efforts on (Kezar & Eckel, 2002). And the politics of higher education often causes resistance to change because of the presence of different interest groups of faculty, staff, administrators, and students functioning in separate subcultures with different norms and constraints (see Kezar, 2008). The predominant modes of influence and persuasion in the academic environment rather than direct control also can limit the ability of leaders to mandate change (Kezar, 2008).

There are, however, notable exceptions that provide insights into how to overcome these obstacles. Consider the Initiative for Faculty Race and Diversity undertaken by the Massachusetts Institute of Technology (MIT) following a two-and-a-half-year period of preparation (Massachusetts Institute of Technology, 2010). This initiative began with a unanimous resolution in 2004 by the MIT faculty to double the number of underrepresented minority (URM) faculty and triple the number of URM graduate students within 10 years. The specific focus of this effort was on increasing the representation of African American, Hispanic, and Native American faculty.

The faculty-led effort was promoted by provost Rafael Reif, a distinguished electrical engineer and son of Eastern European émigrés who had settled in Venezuela, Ecuador, and Colombia. Reif spoke little English when he arrived at Stanford University to do his graduate work in electrical engineering. Hired in 1980 as assistant professor at MIT, Reif is an internationally recognized microelectronics researcher and was an early champion of micro- and nanotechnologies (Bradt, 2012). At his inauguration as president of MIT, Reif (2012) noted that universities today stand "at the crossroads of risk and opportunity" and noted MIT's global mission:

> We must realize our full potential as a university with global impact. The humanity we serve stretches across the planet. And it is clear that we must prepare our students to succeed in a global economic environment. So it is extremely important that we continue our active engagement with the rest of the world. (para. 27)

In his view, "the research university is not an ornament or a luxury that society can choose to go without," but instead is the great economic and social equalizer and the richest source of ideas, leaders, and economic growth ever known by the world (Reif, 2012, para. 12). Reif reinforced his commitment to the area of diversity and inclusion as one of his key priorities:

> I will lead MIT to continue to make significant contributions in the area of race and diversity, equity and inclusion. From the findings of the Initiative on Faculty Race and Diversity, and the reports of the Institute Diversity Summit, we have many compelling suggestions for practical change. These include better ways to search for and mentor new talent, and to improve the orientation process for new members of our community. I am asking every member of the administration to work closely with me to make sure that our best practices become the norm across MIT. (para. 28)

The faculty diversity model implemented at MIT illustrates the necessity of involvement of key constituents in transformational change efforts. Specific steps that overcame internal bureaucratic hurdles and strengthened faculty engagement in the process included

- a quality of life survey administered to the entire faculty,
- a cohort analysis of all faculty coming to MIT between 1991 and 2009,
- in-depth qualitative interviews of all URM faculty,
- junior and senior minority faculty forums,
- a full research team convened from within and outside MIT including a team of faculty from MIT's five schools,
- formation of committees of stakeholders to address faculty recruitment and retention, and

- involvement of governance structures such as the Academic Council and school councils in the discussion of recommendations.

The findings of the study are frank and even startling. The study identified the fact that there was more dissatisfaction among tenured URM faculty then their White counterparts, with Asian faculty in the middle. In addition, the study revealed that non-URM faculty viewed diversity as less critical to MIT's core value of excellence and pointed out the existence of tension on the concept of inclusion versus excellence.

The MIT model reflects the predominant themes identified as integral to HR/diversity talent transformation including a clearly defined vision for diversity linked to institutional mission; actionable leadership commitment; a power structure that supports the attainment of HR/diversity objectives; the tie between diverse talent and innovation; a systematic, phase-based approach with defined metrics; and the establishment of trust-based interactions through involvement of the faculty in the change process.

In summary, factors that impede the pace of change in higher education in comparison with private industry include bifurcated HR structures, the late emergence of HR as strategic partner, resistance that arises from multiple constituencies with conflicting viewpoints and priorities, limited academic research on the impact of HR/diversity programs, and the lesser ability to mandate change in subcultures that require influence, persuasion, and collaboration. Yet we see successful examples of overcoming these barriers in the case studies of Duke University in Chapter 2 and Kent State University in Chapter 6.

Strategic and Tactical Questions for Further Discussion

We conclude our overview of the business case for integrated HR and diversity strategy with several thought questions that may be useful in evaluating the strategic relationship between HR and diversity in your organization as well as the synergy needed for future development of this relationship. Two case studies drawn from state government and the Society for Human Resource Management highlight innovative approaches to the systematic integration of HR and diversity programs and initiatives.

1. What is the reporting relationship of HR and that of diversity? Are they given prominence in the organizational structure? Why or why not?
2. Do goals and action plans for HR work include diversity outcomes and vice versa?

3. What specific areas are most promising for an organizational and programmatic alliance between HR and diversity?
4. What formal and informal relationships between the HR and diversity functions will enhance the opportunity for collaboration and cooperation?
5. Through what specific programs or practices can the synergy between HR and diversity contribute to heightened employee engagement in your organization?

Case Study 1: Formation of the HR Outreach and Diversity Office in the State of Rhode Island

In 2001 Cheryl Burrell was hired as deputy administrator and program services officer of the newly established Human Resources Outreach and Diversity (HROD) office in the state of Rhode Island, reporting to administrator Beverly Dwyer. Burrell explained the forces that led to the creation of the new office (C. Burrell, personal communication, July 27, 2012):

> It was clear that we needed to focus our efforts on doing a better job in terms of outreach and recruitment which clearly fell under the authority of Human Resources. So we felt that by presenting the initiative as a partner and an enhancement to current efforts, we would be better positioned to achieve our goals.

Background

In 1999 Lincoln Almond, then governor of Rhode Island and a Republican, brought together a team of individuals from around state government to discuss ways their personnel process could be reformed to improve workforce representation of the state's diverse population in its government. These discussions followed an outcry by the minority community leadership that felt there should have been greater representation in government and outreach to the community to make them aware of opportunities in state government.

Demographic shifts in the state of Rhode Island that included increases in minority populations compelled the leadership of state government to work toward improving recruitment processes to take advantage of that change. The demographics of the state in 1990 compared to 2000 reveal growth in minority populations as shown in Table 1.1. These gains were reflected in incremental gains in the percentage of minorities and women in the state government workforce between 1995 and 2000 for classified, unclassified, and nonclassified employees.

TABLE 1.1
State of Rhode Island: Population, Labor Force, and State Government Workforce Demographic Data for Select Years Between 1990 and 2012

Year	Rhode Island Population per U.S. Census				Rhode Island Labor Force per U.S. Census			Rhode Island State Government Workforce			
	Total Population	% Minority	% Majority	% Women	% Minority	% Majority	% Women	Total Workforce	% Minority	% Majority	% Women
1990	1,003,464	10.7	89.3	52.0	9.2	90.8	47.2				
1995								14,846	8.5	91.5	51.5
2000	1,048,319	18.1	81.9	52.0	14.5	85.5	48.4	14,712	9.5	90.5	51.9
2005								12,846	11.7	88.3	52.5
2010	1,052,567	23.6	76.4	51.7	20.4	79.6	50.0	11,039	14.4	85.6	51.8
2012								10,940	15.0	85.0	52.0

Note: State government workforce data includes classified, unclassified, and nonclassified employees. Excluded classes of employees include seasonal, patient help, contract employees, summer help, legislative, emergency employees, and those on unpaid leave.

Data are from *Population of Rhode Island: Census 2010 and 2000 Interactive Map, Demographics, Statistics, Quick Facts*, by Rhode Island Division of Information Technology, 2012, http://censusviewer.com/state/RI

In April 2000 Governor Almond issued Executive Order 00-04, which established the HROD office in an effort to enhance the work of the Department of Administration's Office of Recruitment and Placement (Almond, 2000). The executive order also pointed out

- the compelling need for diversity in state government based on the shifting demographics in Rhode Island,
- the opportunity for diversity based on the expectation of losing one third of the state workforce over the next several years because of attrition and retirements, and
- the infrastructure for diversity administration in the HR organization.

In 2000–2001, the HROD office was created using existing staffing and resources by merging the recruitment office into the diversity office. The office reported to the deputy director of personnel and then through the director of personnel to the Department of Administration, which has regulatory authority over every other department in the executive branch. At the time HROD was formed, state agencies were responsible for their own HR operations in a decentralized structure. The newly formed HROD office was a separate entity under the existing HR department, as was the equal opportunity office, which had a more regulatory focus.

The Problem: Overcoming Barriers to Workforce Diversity

By the end of 2001 Dwyer, Burrell, and the HROD staff immediately set to work in relationship building and community partnerships to expand outreach efforts. Burrell recalled,

> I have always believed that all change begins with a conversation. So that really became the first initiative that we took on which was to meet with all of the stakeholders and to have a conversation about what they saw as the barriers, and recommendations and suggestions they had to help us overcome those barriers.

With her colleagues, she visited every state department and agency, including the education and court systems, and visited with elected officers, union officials, and equal opportunity and Affirmative Action officers.

Two primary barriers identified by stakeholders were union contracts that gave preferences for existing union employees by seniority, limiting opportunities for hiring and promotion of diverse talent, and the difficulty in finding qualified minority talent. After validating these concerns, HROD's first efforts were directed toward entry-level positions in the various hierarchies in government and nonunion positions, and partnerships with community-based organizations.

One of Dwyer and Burrell's first priorities was expansion of recruitment and outreach through the development of methods and guidelines to reach a wider and more diverse applicant pool. A database of contacts was formed with over 300 names including community-based organizations, minority-owned businesses, minority leaders, legislatures, and churches. Meetings were arranged with community leaders, and frank conversations were held about the concerns they perceived and how the new office could address them. As Burrell explained:

> And clearly what we found at that time was there was a lack of trust, lack of commitment and these were attitudes that had been in place for many years. They just didn't feel that we were giving due consideration to the interest of diversifying our workforce. And so, we were able to overcome many of those barriers just by virtue of building relationships and of course those relationships were built on trust. So that we were not going to promote jobs where there really was not an opportunity so as to create false hope. We assured them that our efforts would be focused on those jobs where we felt there were real opportunities.

These efforts went a long way toward establishing trust with the community. Burrell believes this strategy was successful, noting, "And I can tell you that across the board wherever we have partnered with the community-based organizations and the leadership with recruitments, they have always been successful."

The HROD office also turned its attention to civil service examinations and the process of merit selection in which applicants are ranked on an eligibility list based on their test scores. Historically, the state had not focused on community outreach in this area, so HROD developed recruitment and selection guidelines and the implementation of specific processes when a manifest imbalance of minorities and women in a job category exists.

In Burrell's view, "Every process begins with the need for a more diverse applicant pool. We found that to be one of the barriers." As a result, she created a process to collect demographic data from civil service exam applicants with safeguards to ensure that this data was separated from the HR process. Her office analyzed this information, and over time, the voluntary applicant response rate increased to between 50% and 80%. This data was helpful in measuring the effectiveness of outreach and the increase in the diversity of applicant pools to civil service list positions.

Changes on the Political Horizon

In 2005 Burrell assumed the position of administrator of HROD. When Almond left office, his successor, Donald Carcieri, a Republican, issued

Executive Order 05-02 in 2005, which affirmed the establishment of the HROD office and set forth its responsibilities, including the development of recruitment guidelines, partnerships with community-based organizations to support recruitment and outreach, diversity awareness training, annual benchmark reporting, policy review, the creation of a diversity advisory council, and development of a work environment of respect, responsibility, and accountability by valuing diversity ("Legal Framework," 2005). The executive order provided a more deliberate focus in identifying specific responsibilities of the HROD Office. The diversity advisory council, however, was not established, perhaps because of a number of other priorities at the state level.

Because of fiscal constraints in the state and a shifting focus on governmental functions, in 2009 the HR function became centralized in Rhode Island state government, and all the HR offices of the state agencies in the executive branch reported through the Department of Administration. This change made it easier for HROD to implement more consistent HR processes. However, agency administrators have indicated they would like to return to a more decentralized system. Burrell supports a decentralized system with centralized administrative oversight by building partnerships with state agencies and serving as a resource. At the same time, HROD was merged with the equal opportunity office, reporting through the equal employment opportunity administrator.

The State of Rhode Island has made significant strides in contributing toward the diversification of the workforce through efforts such as the explicit focus on HR recruitment and outreach in the HROD initiative. These structural changes have accelerated attainment of greater workforce diversity. State population figures shown in the table reflect continuing gains in minority populations that have been accompanied by a substantive increase in minority representation in the state government workforce.

The Current Outlook

When Lincoln Chaffee, an independent, became governor in 2011, he was faced with significant fiscal issues and the need for extensive pension reform that occupied a great deal of his time in his first 18 months. State government also faced significant attrition through workforce reductions with many positions left unfilled. Because of budget cuts, the equal employment office now has only one staff person compared to four previous staff members. Similarly, the HROD office has been cut to two staff members—Cheryl Burrell and Victor Mendoza. Burrell is continuing to work on the challenges of gathering applicant demographic data, especially in relation to civil service list positions, and expanding outreach efforts to build applicant pools.

Nonetheless, with reduced staffing, this once robust initiative is faced with limited resources to effect and accelerate change.

In looking toward the future, Burrell notes that while laudable progress has been made in reaching HROD office's diversity goals, the state government workforce remains significantly underrepresented by the largest minority group in Rhode Island, Hispanics. According to the U.S. Census, Hispanics made up 8.7% of the Rhode Island population in 2000. By 2010 their percentage increased to 12.4%, representing a 43.9% increase over this 10-year period ("Population of Rhode Island," 2012). However, Hispanics make up only 4.4% of the state government workforce. In addition, service-oriented departments in state government must meet the needs of their increasingly diverse client population in their clients' primary language.

This problem presents an additional challenge for the office since clearly targeted outreach strategies are needed as well as the development of specific cultural competency training programs to improve the work environment and support minority retention goals. Based on these factors, the critical question the HROD office now faces is how to address Hispanic underrepresentation in the state government workforce while protecting the interests of all groups. Burrell summarizes these challenges and the intersection of her office's responsibilities with the purposes of democratic governance:

> As a public governmental entity, we must balance the interest of all the people we serve, so that the goals of our democratic society are achieved. To this end, we recognize that it is critically important that we incorporate diversity at all levels of our organization, especially in policy making and leadership positions.

Note. State government workforce data includes classified, unclassified, and nonclassified employees. Excluded classes of employees include seasonal, patient help, contract employees, summer help, legislative, emergency employees, and those on unpaid leave.

Rhode Island Division of Information Technology (C. Burrell, personal communication, July 27, 2012).

Case Study 2: Leading a Global HR/Diversity Initiative at the Society for Human Resource Management

The Society for Human Resource Management (SHRM) is the world's largest professional HR association, with over 260,000 members in 140 countries, and has been in existence since 1947. In 2005 board chair Johnny C. Taylor Jr. realized that SHRM had an opportunity to take a leadership role in driving diversity and inclusion as a business imperative. If SHRM was to continue to remain relevant and respond to the demands of a changing workforce and global marketplace, a diversity leadership position at SHRM was needed to spearhead diversity efforts inside and outside the association. Taylor pushed the board to consider the need for a senior diversity leader. Soon afterward, the board voted and approved hiring SHRM's first diversity officer, Shirley Davis.

Testing the Cultural Waters

In 2006 Shirley Davis joined SHRM from corporate America, having worked in leadership positions at Bank of America, Circuit City, Capital One, and Constellation Energy. Her first task was to learn about the culture of the association, and she began by meeting with the chief HR officer whom she observed to be a smart, thoughtful, and strategically oriented professional. She learned that as a mission-driven organization, SHRM wanted to change the HR field to be a strategic partner in business, government, academia, and the nonprofit sector.

Davis soon realized that while the culture at SHRM was family-oriented with a strong sense of community, the organization also had a strong sense of legacy resulting from tenured CEOs at the helm and long-standing patterns of serving members of the association in certain ways. By talking to employees and reviewing engagement survey results and written comments, she found that SHRM generally focused on projects that were tried, true, and tested. Davis said, "They also love to try new things, but they really need it to be something that has already been done before, or that must be supported by lots of data and discussion." Davis also learned that even though SHRM is a nonprofit association, SHRM officials were very concerned about it being profitable and about their fiscal responsibility in managing the organization.

The creation of a transformative diversity change effort did not fit the mold of tried and tested projects. In her first 90 days, Davis initiated meet and greet sessions with more than 30 leaders across the organization to find out more about the association's practices, goals, values, and expectations. Through her experience in the corporate sector, she realized that a major change initiative required engaging support early and building strategy collaboratively. In her view, a leader should possess the skill sets and expertise to build a strategy but should not come into the organization with the strategy already prepared. Instead, strategy should be developed in collaboration with organizational leaders so they feel a sense of ownership and are more likely to be part of execution and accountability. From her vantage point, she had to create synergy across the entire organization.

When I came in, I did not have a team. The only way I was going to be successful in executing my strategy was to integrate [diversity] strategy into all the goals and objectives across every division and to obviously start with HR and embed it in HR's mission and then get it before the board and make it a strategic imperative. And that's exactly what happened; it became a board initiative.

The Vision for SHRM's Role as a Global Diversity Leader

Prior to Shirley Davis's being hired, SHRM had already begun a request for proposals process for a consultant or consultants to conduct research on the current state of diversity management in the field. Her first decision was to finalize the proposals request that was in progress and select Roosevelt Thomas, a former SHRM board member and one of the pioneers in the diversity and inclusion field, as a consultant to work on a project plan with his staff at the American Institute for Managing Diversity. The resulting survey, "2007 State of Workplace Diversity Management: A Survey Report by the Society for Human Resource Management" (SHRM, 2008), was the largest and most comprehensive U.S. survey on diversity of its kind with 1,400 respondents. HR and diversity professionals expressed concerns in the survey that the diversity field is still evolving, is not well defined or understood, and focuses too much on compliance.

Over the first year and a half, Davis set out to formulate a 3- to 5-year strategy for SHRM's role in the area of diversity and inclusion and how it could help HR professionals drive diversity and inclusion in their organizations. Based on the research from the 2007 survey, she began to determine what SHRM members needed in terms of resources, knowledge, and professional development. She knew that HR professionals required support in having conversations about diversity with senior leaders and in the execution of diversity strategy. Davis described her vision of SHRM's role in diversity and inclusion at the time (S. Davis, personal communication, August 31, 2012):

> We were going to be a recognized leader in the field, and . . . we were going to be at the forefront of some of the most pressing workplace issues; we were going to position ourselves to be that go-to organization for diversity and inclusion through leadership, tools, and professional development.

Reviewing the research from the 2007 workplace diversity survey, she realized the field lacked professionalization, rigor, clarity, and a common nomenclature and language. "We needed to really be much more solid about our value proposition and we weren't doing that," she said.

As she began to expand the vision for SHRM's diversity leadership role, diversity consultants who mainly practiced in one- or two-person firms became worried about SHRM putting them out of business, given the association's substantial resources and global footprint. Davis needed to reassure the consultants that SHRM would not supplant their work: "We had to be very cautious, careful, and sensitive in helping them to understand that there is enough work out there for everybody and that we want to work with them to accomplish more."

Realizing the Vision of a Global Diversity Strategy

To launch SHRM's global diversity strategy, Davis recognized the importance of bringing together diversity leaders from across the globe to participate in strategy formulation and execution. She said, "If we are going to be the recognized global thought leader, we have to get the global leaders to be part of this, let them know we want them to be part of this."

Under Davis's leadership, SHRM convened a one-and-a-half-day Global Leadership Summit on Diversity and Inclusion in 2008. For this global thought leaders' summit, SHRM brought 100 leaders from around the world to Washington, DC, including representatives from Australia, South Africa, Asia, Canada, Switzerland, Germany, Japan, and the United Kingdom. The goal of the summit was to develop diversity strategy and identify needed services, resources, and tools for the future. In Davis's view, "This is not about competition. This is about *cooperatition*." Diversity consultants, chief diversity officers, researchers, professors, and authors were all important contributors at this meeting and became an important part of SHRM's long-term planning process.

The summit embodied SHRM's desire for collaboration and its efforts to professionalize the diversity field, much as SHRM had done with the development of professional HR certifications: professional in HR (PHR), senior professional in HR (SPHR), and global professional in HR (GPHR). In Davis's view, the summit was designed to "tear down the walls" between SHRM and diversity leaders by committing to a joint partnership that would professionalize the field and provide resources and services representative of the best thinking from experts around the world. At the summit, participants examined assumptions and opinions gathered from scholarship and commentaries on the diversity and inclusion field including the following:

- After 25 years of diversity efforts, many HR professionals encounter the same challenges and resistance. The field seems to be spinning its wheels.
- The diversity and inclusion brand is perceived to be tarnished, and skeptics question its value.

- Too few globally competent leaders are available to help organizations adapt to diversity challenges.
- Organizations differ in the location of the diversity and inclusion function; some incorporate it into HR, while others retain it as a separate function.

Davis viewed the summit as a game changer:

It built a community for us. That actually started us on another path where we didn't have to build it by ourselves. This isn't just the house that SHRM built. I really give credit to our global thought leaders who have been a part of this ultimate mission because I think what they begin to see is [that] they are all trying to get to the same destination, and that is to add value . . . to our communities and to our customers and to our employees.

Following the summit, Davis analyzed the 4,000 data points gathered at the conference with the help of a consultant. She began to use these data points as input for revitalizing the diversity strategy that she believed "could change the game in the diversity and inclusion space."

In 2008 Davis expanded the work of the workplace diversity survey to include an examination of global diversity practices. The global diversity and inclusion report commissioned by SHRM (2009) and conducted by the Economist Intelligence Unit, a subsidiary of the Economist Group, researched the perceptions, attitudes, and practices of multinational corporations from 47 different countries to create a global diversity readiness index. The Economist Unit had in-country managers around the world and was positioned to study trends in these countries using measurable data points such as social inclusion, workplace inclusion, government inclusion, and compliance laws. Following publication of the survey, Davis reassembled global thought leaders to talk about the global landscape for diversity and inclusion and how SHRM could play a significant role in, as she put it, "helping to move the needle."

Diversity Professional Development as a Key SHRM Focus

Based on these comprehensive research efforts on the state of the diversity field, Davis undertook the expansion and dissemination of SHRM's repertoire of professional development practices to provide SHRM members with state-of-the-art diversity tools and resources. She focused upon enhancing SHRM's annual diversity and inclusion conference to make it one of the best offered in the field. She initiated new diversity educational programs that include SHRM's Strategic Diversity and Inclusion Leadership Program for chief diversity officers and senior directors, a two-day research-based program using real-life best practices designed to address the development of specific action steps and strategies. She implemented additional programs for 21st-century diversity professionals new to the field, and a program on global cultural competence for business leaders.

Davis also introduced a broad array of online tools and resources on SHRM's Web page dedicated specifically to diversity, that include an introduction to the human resource discipline of diversity and specific, detailed guidance on every aspect of leading diversity and inclusion initiatives. These resources have put SHRM at the forefront as an authoritative resource for diversity professional development. Additionally, SHRM has been an influential voice in the U.S. Congress regarding diversity-related legislation and policies, published several diversity and inclusion books featuring global thought leaders, and now offer diversity and inclusion solutions to corporate clients.

Developing Diversity and Inclusion Standards for the Profession

Moving forward with the identified need to professionalize the diversity field, SHRM next initiated the rigorous process of obtaining authorization to become the first organization in the United States to offer approved diversity and inclusion and HR standards. SHRM undertook the rigorous process of obtaining approval to provide these standards through the American National Standards Institute and the International Standards Organization.

Over a period of 15 months, Davis worked with a volunteer task force of 200 HR professionals, researchers, authors, and consultants to write the first diversity standards. The initial standards developed were focused on three areas: (a) the qualifications and expertise of a top diversity professional and the knowledge, competency, and skills needed for this role; (b) the strategy, goals, and tactics of an effective program; and (c) the minimum metrics for tracking and reporting diversity efforts. Following the draft of the standards, SHRM planned to share them for comment for a 60-day period (as required by American National Standards Institute procedures). After the close of this period, the task force was to respond to every comment and draft a final document. The development of these standards represents a major step forward in legitimizing and professionalizing the diversity field, an accomplishment that Davis views as one of her greatest contributions.

The View Ahead

As Davis looks ahead, she foresees a shift in how organizations manage talent in response to the complex needs of a global workforce in a changing political, social, technological, and demographic landscape. She noted that "the only way that organizations can be competitive and differentiate themselves from the competition is their talent." She emphasized the connection between talent management and innovation:

> We can't continue to do today what [we did] 20 years ago and we certainly won't be able to do in 2050 what we are doing here in 2012. So we're going to continue to have to innovate; we are going to have to shift and change our policies around the way that we manage our talent; we have to get away from our 8-to-5 and 9-to-5 and 60-hour workweek mind-set where . . . visibility equals value. . . . and we have to play a significant role in growing and developing great talent for the skill needs of the future and allow them to be productive when and where is best for them. Work is not where you work, it's when and how you work that matters and how you perform. We need to manage to results and not to schedules if we are to be competitive in the new global workforce.

Davis notes the complexity of managing a global workforce in different time zones and of a workforce with different generational values and needs. Organizations that do not have workers outside the United States may need to recruit from global talent or market their products to those abroad. These changing conditions require adaptive leaders: "It can't be a one-size-fits-all, they have got to be much more of a transformational, situational leader," Davis said. In her view, the business case for HR and diversity professionals is ongoing and here to stay.

> I think that it really comes down to helping people understand *why* change is necessary. The business case behind the change that we are trying to implement in HR and diversity and inclusion professionals is not going to go away and not to focus on it is a going-out-of-business strategy.

References

Ahmed, S. (2012). *On being included: Racism and diversity in institutional life*. Durham, NC: Duke University Press.

Almond, L. (2000). *Promotion of a diverse state government workforce*. Retrieved from http://www.uri.edu/library/special_collections/almond/execord/00-04.html

An examination of organizational commitment to diversity and inclusion: Survey findings. (2011). Retrieved from http://www.shrm.org/Research/SurveyFindings/Articles/Pages/AnExaminationofDiversity.aspx

Argyris, C., Bellman, G. M., Blanchard, K., Block, P., Bridges, W., Deane, B., et al. (1994). The future of workplace learning and performance. *Training and Development, 48*(5), 36–47.

Avolio, B. J. (2005). The chief integrative leader: Moving to the next economy's HR leader. In M. Losey, D. Ulrich, & S. Meisinger (Eds.), *The future of human resource management: 64 thought leaders explore the critical HR issues of today and tomorrow* (pp. 95–102). Hoboken, NJ: Wiley.

Beer, J. M. (2010). Diversity management's paradoxical negation of diversity. *International Journal of Diversity in Organizations, Communities and Nations, 10*(4), 1–14.

Beer, M. (2012). Counterpoint. In A. Tavis, R. Vosburgh, & E. Gubman (Eds.), *Point counterpoint: New perspectives on people & strategy* (p. 8). Chicago, IL: Society for Human Resource Management.

Benschop, Y. (2001). Pride, prejudice and performance: Relations between HRM, diversity, and performance. *International Journal of Human Resource Management, 12*(7), 1166–1181.

Bradt, S. (2012). L. Rafael Reif selected as MIT's 17th president. Retrieved from http://web.mit.edu/newsoffice/2012/rafael-reif-elected-president-0516.html

Brockbank, W. (2009). Tool 2.5 external environment. Retrieved from http://www.transformHR.com

Campbell, M. (2009, October 19). When the fastest-growing segment of the U.S. population is Hispanic. *Hispanic Outlook in Higher Education Magazine, 20*, 12–14.

Chun, E., & Evans, A. (2009). *Bridging the diversity divide: Globalization and reciprocal empowerment in higher education* (ASHE-ERIC Higher Education Reports, Vol. 35, No. 1). San Francisco, CA: Jossey-Bass.

Chun, E., & Evans, A. (2012). *Diverse administrators in peril: The new indentured class in higher education.* Boulder, CO: Paradigm.

Clayton-Pedersen, A., & Musil, C. M. (2005). *Introduction to the series.* In D. A. Williams, J. B. Berger, & S. A. McClendon, *Toward a model of inclusive excellence and change in postsecondary institutions* (pp. iii–ix). Retrieved from http://www.aacu.org/inclusive_excellence/documents/williams_et_al.pdf

Collaborative relationships between EEO/AA, human resources and diversity professionals: Survey report. (2012). American Association for Affirmative Action. Retrieved September 8, 2012, from http://www.affirmativeaction.org/aaaa-releases-survey-report-on-collaboration.html

Cox, T., Jr. (2001). *Creating the multicultural organization: A strategy for capturing the power of diversity.* San Francisco, CA: Jossey-Bass.

Edmondson, A. C. (2008). The competitive imperative of learning. *Harvard Business Review, 86*(7/8), 60–67.

Edmondson, A. C. (2012). *Teaming: How organizations learn, innovate, and compete in the knowledge economy.* San Francisco, CA: Jossey-Bass.

Egan, M. E. (2011). *Global diversity and inclusion: Fostering innovation through a diverse workforce.* Retrieved from http://images.forbes.com/forbesinsights/StudyPDFs/Innovation_Through_Diversity.pdf

Evans, A., & Chun, E. B. (2007). Building and sustaining an institution-wide diversity strategy. *CUPA-HR Journal, 58*(1), 3–10.

Evans, A., & Chun, E. B. (2012). *Creating a tipping point: Strategic human resources in higher education.* San Francisco, CA: Jossey-Bass.

Feagin, J. R. (2010). *The White racial frame: Centuries of racial framing and counter-framing.* New York, NY: Routledge.

Fitz-enz, J. (2009). Disruptive technology for human resources. *Employment Relations Today, 35*(4), 1–10.

Friedman, T. L. (2005, April 3). It's a flat world, after all. *New York Times Magazine,* 32–37.

Gaertner, S. L., & Dovidio, J. F. (2000). *Reducing intergroup bias: The common ingroup identity model.* Philadelphia, PA: Psychology Press.

Gardner, H. (2007). *Five minds for the future* (1st ed.). Boston, MA: Harvard Business School Press.

Hampden-Turner, C., & Trompenaars, F. (1998). *Riding the waves of culture: Understanding diversity in global business* (2nd ed.). New York, NY: McGraw-Hill.

Hubbard, E. E. (1999). *How to calculate diversity return on investment.* Petaluma, CA: Global Insights.

Hubbard, E. E. (2001). *Measuring diversity results* (Vol. 1). Petaluma, CA: Global Insights.

Hubbard, E. E. (2004). *Implementing diversity measurement and management.* Petaluma, CA: Global Insights.

Kanter, R. M. (2003). Thriving locally in the global economy. *Harvard Business Review, 81*(8), 119–127.

Karlgaard, R. (2012, October 22). The hard and soft stuff of business: Winners excel in both. *Forbes,* 42.

Kezar, A. J. (2008). Understanding leadership strategies for addressing the politics of diversity. *Journal of Higher Education, 79*(4), 406–441.

Kezar, A., & Eckel, P. (2002). Examining the institutional transformation process: The importance of sensemaking, interrelated strategies, and balance. *Research in Higher Education, 43*(3), 295–328.

Kezar, A. J., & Lester, J. (2011). *Enhancing campus capacity for leadership: An examination of grassroots leaders in higher education.* Stanford, CA: Stanford University Press.

Kilmann, R. H. (1984). *Beyond the quick fix: Managing five tracks to organizational success.* San Francisco, CA: Jossey-Bass.

Kochan, T., Bezrukova, K., Ely, R., Jackson, S., Joshi, A., Jehn, K., et al. (2003). The effects of diversity on business performance: Report of the diversity research network. *Human Resource Management, 42*(1), 3–21.

Kossek, E. E., Lobel, S. A., & Brown, J. (2006). Human resource strategies to manage workforce diversity: Examining "the business case." In A. M. Konrad, P. Prasad, & J. K. Pringle (Eds.), *Handbook of workplace diversity* (pp. 53–74). Thousand Oaks, CA: Sage.

Legal framework. (2005). Retrieved from http://www.diversity.ri.gov/eeo/eoopage7.htm

Marquis, J. P., Lim, N., Scott, L. M., Harrell, M. C., & Kavanagh, J. (2008). *Managing diversity in corporate America: An exploratory analysis.* Retrieved from RAND Labor and Population website: http://www.rand.org/pubs/occasional_papers/2007/RAND_OP206.pdf

Massachusetts Institute of Technology, Initiative on Faculty Race and Diversity. (2010). *Report on the Initiative for Faculty Race and Diversity*. Retrieved from http://web.mit.edu/provost/raceinitiative/report.pdf

Mathews, A. (1998). Diversity: A principle of human resource management. *Public Personnel Management, 27*(2), 175–185.

Palacios, S. (2008). *Aligning diversity, CSR and multicultural marketing*. Retrieved from http://www.added-value.com/source/.../Cheskin_HBR-Diversity_June2008.pdf

Passel, J., Livingston, G., & Cohn, D. (2012). *Explaining why minority births now outnumber White births*. Retrieved from http://www.pewsocialtrends.org/2012/05/17/explaining-why-minority-births-now-outnumber-white-births/

Pettigrew, T. F., & Tropp, L. R. (2006). A meta-analytic test of intergroup contact theory. *Journal of Personality and Social Psychology, 90*(5), 751–783.

Population of Rhode Island: Census 2010 and 2000 interactive map, demographics, statistics, quick facts. (2012). Retrieved from http://censusviewer.com/state/RI

Quinn, R. W., & Brockbank, W. (2006). The development of strategic human resource professionals at BAE Systems. *Human Resource Management, 45*(3), 477–494.

Rangasamy, J. (2004). Understanding institutional racism: Reflections from linguistic anthropology. In I. Law, D. Phillips, & L. Turney (Eds.), *Institutional racism in higher education* (pp. 27–34). Sterling, VA: Trentham Books.

Read, B. B. (2005). *Designing the best call center for your business* (2nd ed.). San Francisco, CA: CMP Books.

Reif, R. (2012). *Inaugural address*. Retrieved from http://president.mit.edu/speeches-writing/inaugural-address

Richard, O. C., & Johnson, N. B. (1999). Making the connection between formal human resource diversity practices and organizational effectiveness: Behind management fashion. *Performance Improvement Quarterly, 12*(1), 77–96.

Richard, O. C., Murthi, B. P. S., & Ismail, K. (2007). The impact of racial diversity on intermediate and long-term performance: The moderating role of environmental context. *Strategic Management Journal, 28*(12), 1213–1233.

Schoorman, F. D., Mayer, R. C., & Davis, J. H. (2007). An integrative model of organizational trust: Past, present, and future. *Academy of Management Review, 32*(2), 344–354.

Scott, K. A., Heathcote, J. M., & Gruman, J. A. (2011). The diverse organization: Finding gold at the end of the rainbow. *Human Resource Management, 50*(6), 735–755.

Shen, J., Chanda, A., D'Netto, B., & Monga, M. (2009). Managing diversity through human resource management: An international perspective and conceptual framework. *International Journal of Human Resource Management, 20*(2), 235–251.

Society for Human Resource Management. (2008). *2007 state of workplace diversity management: A survey report by the Society for Human Resource Management*. Retrieved from http://www.shrm.org/research/surveyfindings/articles/documents/the%20state%20of%20diversity%20managment%20surevey%20report.pdf

Society for Human Resource Management. (2009). *Global diversity and inclusion: Perceptions, practices, and attitudes survey report*. Retrieved from http://www

.shrm.org/research/surveyfindings/articles/documents/diversity_and_inclusion _report.pdf

Starnes, B. J., Truhon, S. A., & McCarthy, V. (2010). *A primer on organizational trust*. Retrieved from http://rube.asq.org/hdl/2010/06/a-primer-on-organizational -trust.pdf

Tavernise, S. (2012). Whites account for under half of births in U.S. *New York Times*. Retrieved from http://www.nytimes.com/2012/05/17/us/whites-account -for-under-half-of-births-in-us.html?_r=1&ref=sabrinatavernise

Ulrich, D., Allen, J., Brockbank, W., Younger, J., & Nyman, M. (2009). *HR transformation: Building human resources from the outside in*. New York, NY: McGraw-Hill.

Ulrich, D., Brockbank, W., Johnson, D., Sandholtz, K., & Younger, J. (2008). *HR competencies: Mastery at the intersection of people and business*. Alexandria, VA: Society for Human Resource Management.

Ulrich, D., & Smallwood, N. (2003). *Why the bottom line isn't!: How to build value through people and organization*. San Francisco, CA: Wiley.

Ulrich, D., & Smallwood, N. (2004). Capitalizing on capabilities. *Harvard Business Review, 82*(6), 119–127.

Ulrich, D., Younger, J., Brockbank, W., & Ulrich, M. (2012). Evolving expertise. *Human Resource Executive Online*. Retrieved from http://www.hronline.com/ HRE/story.jsp?storyId=533344456

Upbin, B. (2012, September 24). The 30-year-old startup. *Forbes*, 72–78.

U.S. Census Bureau. (2008, August 14). An older and more diverse nation by midcentury [Press release]. Retrieved from http://www.census.gov/newsroom/ releases/archives/population/cb08-123.html

Wright, P. M., Boudreau, J., Pace, D., Sartain, L., McKinnon, P., & Antoine, R. (2011). *The chief HR officer: Defining the new role of human resource leaders*. San Francisco, CA: Jossey-Bass.

2

RECIPROCAL EMPOWERMENT

The Foundation of Inclusive Talent Practices

The foundation for radical innovation must be a company's core competencies (what it knows) and its strategic assets (what it owns). (Hamel, 2002, p. 14)

We now explore the creation of a guiding philosophical framework that will support the development of inclusive talent practices. Why is such a philosophy necessary? As we stand on the threshold of an age of revolution, change itself has changed and is no longer additive and incremental but discontinuous, abrupt, and even seditious (Hamel, 2002). In this context, diversity is central to effective modern management and essential for what Gary Hamel terms "radical innovation" (p. 13). HR practices provide the medium for establishing a culture and climate that nurtures diversity and innovation.

To compete in the knowledge economy, organizations must move from routine to innovative operations, from high-volume repetitive work to pioneering research and discovery (Edmondson, 2012). Systems of mass production that consist of small repetitive tasks that are easily monitored are now superseded by innovative operations that require new ways of leading (Edmondson, 2012). Rather than the flavor of the month, revitalized management practices that draw upon the power of a diverse workforce will lead to enhanced employee contributions and the creation of a high-performance workplace. In this chapter, we propose a reconceptualized leadership philosophy congruent with innovative talent practices. Following examination of the varied meanings of diversity and inclusion, we explore the role of diversity as a core intangible asset that will drive innovation and success. We then share a model of HR's diversity evolution that will require the redesign of HR practices for diversity.

Reciprocal Empowerment as Organizational Commitment

We propose the concept of reciprocal empowerment as a grounding principle for management approaches that enable all employees to attain their full talent potential and to contribute to a high-performance workplace. *Reciprocal empowerment* by definition is based on *mutuality*: It implies the interdependence and interrelationship of management and employees, supervisors and subordinates, and peer-to-peer in teams. Empowerment knits together the contextual organizational features necessary for the success of diversity change initiatives (Kezar, Glenn, Lester, & Nakamoto, 2008). It is a moral framework that links organizational values, culture, and workplace practices to the world outside (Chun & Evans, 2009). As such, it is aligned with the most cherished ideals of democracy in the United States (Prasad, 2001).

As a guiding philosophy, reciprocal empowerment reestablishes how organizations are managed and involves what Lawler and Worley (2011) call a *management reset*. These theorists describe the historical evolution of management structures in three phases: command and control organizations that evolved from the marriage of mass production with bureaucracy, high-involvement organizations that emphasized talent as a source of competitive advantage, and sustainable management organizations (SMOs) with the capability of supporting rapid change, social well-being, and a concern for the environment while simultaneously generating profit. SMOs are distinguished by the way value is created, work is organized, people are treated, and behavior is guided (Lawler & Worley, 2011). SMOs have elevated the importance of HR to the level of a strategic player that not only is at the table but sets the table (Lawler & Worley, 2011).

Reciprocal empowerment represents a new behavioral paradigm for a management reset. Through reciprocal empowerment, leading and managing are transformed into processes of engagement, motivation, and inclusion. In essence, reciprocal empowerment involves three powers: the power of self-determination (the power to define one's own identity), the power of distributive justice (the power to give oneself and others adequate resources), and the power of democratic participation (the power to give oneself and others a voice; Prilleltensky & Gonick, 1994). Self-determination is a cumulative process rooted in the sense of self-awareness and how individual identity is determined intrapersonally and in relation to others (Ortiz & Patton, 2012). Distributive justice refers to the equitable distribution of resources and power. Research has identified disparities in the relationship between rank and power based on gender and race, for example, showing that the positional power of minorities can be more vulnerable to attack and less stable than that of majority group members (e.g., see Ragins, 1997; Smith, 2002). And the power of democratic participation includes the ability to have voice, not only to be at the table but to speak and be heard. Speaking up requires psychological safety, a critical feature of organizations where workers need to collaborate and knowledge is changing (Edmondson, 2012).

The frame of reciprocal empowerment will assist organizations in the work of sense making as a superordinate strategy, that is, helping employees change how they perceive their skills, mind-sets, and roles as a central component of diversity transformation (Kezar & Eckel, 2002). Through this lens, we operationalize the concepts of intangibles and organizational capabilities based on the extensive HR research literature developed by Dave Ulrich (Ulrich, Brockbank, Johnson, Sandholtz, & Younger, 2008; Ulrich & Smallwood, 2004) and others (Huselid, Becker, & Beatty, 2005).

Since many organizations struggle to reach a common definition of *diversity and inclusion*, we begin by untangling the often contested meanings of diversity and inclusion. We then delve further into the nature of intangible assets, leading to a reformulation of HR's diversity role and its strategic design. These preliminary steps allow us to move to the broader platform of reciprocal empowerment and its role in the evolution of a transformational HR/diversity strategy.

Defining the Discourse of Diversity and Inclusion

To clarify the conceptual basis for integrated HR and diversity strategy, we first need to clarify the intertwined meanings of diversity and inclusion that have accompanied diversity discussions. The *discourse of diversity* refers to the complex web of ways we speak about, represent, and actualize diversity in organizational settings. It represents a complex array of "enunciatory, representational, and institutional practices" that shape "the multiple (and often contradictory) constructions and enactments of difference" (Prasad, 2001, p. 55). From this perspective, the discourse of diversity includes not only a range of characteristics that differentiate individuals but also how these differences are described and shaped in organizational contexts.

A useful way of articulating the multiple aspects of diversity is to distinguish primary dimensions of diversity or attributes we are born with such as race, ethnicity, physical ability, sexual orientation, and gender; secondary dimensions that are acquired such as geographic location, marital status, parental status, and educational background; and third-level organizational dimensions such as management status, union affiliation, and so on (Sainte-Rose, 2005). Another similar approach is to contrast core diversity

Figure 2.1 Dimensions of Diversity

Note: From *Diversity and the Bottom Line: Prospering in the Global Economy*, p. 184, by P. K. Henry, 2003, Austin, TX: TurnKey Press. Copyright 2003 by P. Henry. Reproduced with permission.

dimensions that are generally more visible or observable with the variable unobservable secondary dimensions that contain an element of control or choice (Hubbard, 2004; Roberson, 2006).

Figure 2.1 reveals that the lens of diversity is broad, touching upon the multiplicity of characteristics that represent social and individual identity. Unlike the discourse of discrimination, which focuses on injustice, the discourse of diversity broadens the conversation to include all categories of difference (Prasad, 2001).

The discourse of diversity cannot ignore historical legacies of exclusion or the fact that categories such as gender, class, and race have a social reality that create real effects for the actors involved (Bonilla-Silva, 2006). In essence, the discourse of diversity can help individuals in the ongoing process of unraveling the complex identity strands of their experiences in a society where important life dimensions are shaped by the simultaneous interplay of domination and subordination (Tatum, 1997).

Why is a discourse of diversity necessary? A discussion in which everyone is equal in their diversity masks the importance of power differentials in organizations (Beer, 2010). Terms such as *historically disadvantaged* or *systematically excluded* reflect the infusion of power and privilege that are embedded in group relations (Prasad, Pringle, & Konrad, 2006). As a result, organizations must be attentive to the need to deliver actual benefits to diverse individuals who have been the recipients of past discrimination through concrete programs such as Affirmative Action and equal opportunity (Beer, 2010).

To guide the thought process about diversity, Hubbard's (2004) conceptualization of the four dimensions of diversity important for organizations today provides a useful conceptual frame of reference. These dimensions include (a) workforce diversity, or the group and situational identities of employees (race, ethnicity, economic background and status, etc.); (b) behavioral diversity, or work styles, communication styles, beliefs, and value systems of employees; (c) structural diversity, which addresses the relationships among organizational levels and resulting stratification; and (d) business diversity, or the relation to external markets, clients, and consumers. In Chapter 6, we examine ways to operationalize these four dimensions in the development of a strategic HR/diversity plan.

As a cautionary note, the mere presence of diversity in any of the four organizational dimensions of workforce, structural, behavioral, and business diversity is merely a precursor to the attainment of inclusion. Diversity can exist without inclusion, but inclusion only has meaning when it involves diversity. Inclusion transcends organizational demography by focusing on the removal of barriers to individual participation and contribution of employees (Roberson, 2006). For example, a research study involving three separate samples of mainly HR and diversity practitioners found that diversity is interpreted to refer to the spectrum of human differences and similarities, while inclusion refers to how an organization configures structures and systems to leverage employee potential and limit the disadvantages of differences (Roberson, 2006). Indicators of inclusion are the degree of influence individuals exercise in decision making, their access to information, and their job security (see Roberson, 2006). And an inclusive organization is one in which the leadership "is committed to optimizing the potential and contributions of all its employees through trust, respect and empowerment" (Henry, 2003, p. 184).

From this perspective, diversity and inclusion is about "the differences that differences make" (Owen, 2008, p. 187). Diversity is not about magical thinking, which assumes that mere numerical representation of differences will create environments conducive to realizing diversity's benefits (Chang & Ledesma, 2011). Rather, diversity and inclusion requires active commitment, planning, and intervention (Chang & Ledesma, 2011).

Given the clarification provided by these definitions, we now turn to a discussion of diversity capability and HR's role in developing this capability. We then identify the concrete practice areas in which strategic/HR practices lead to the attainment of inclusion.

Diversity Capability as a Core Intangible Asset

HR departments represent the dynamic nexus or intersection between an organization's strategy and its talent. This locus of responsibility is of strategic importance, since intellectual or creative capital is the organization's only appreciable asset (Florida & Goodnight, 2005; Ulrich, 1998). Other physical assets such as plant, machinery, and equipment deteriorate as soon as they are acquired (Ulrich, 1998). As a result, organizations that recognize the importance of human capital are human-capital-centric, or HC-centric organizations, since they create the infrastructure and conditions that allow talented and diverse individuals to work together effectively (Lawler, 2008).

At the heart of the business case for diversity is its role as an intangible asset, a defining factor that distinguishes organizational performance. While not captured in traditional accounting measures, intangible assets have been shown to affect financial results and organizational effectiveness (Ulrich, 1998; Ulrich, Allen, Brockbank, Younger, & Nyman, 2009; Ulrich et al., 2008; Ulrich & Smallwood, 2003).

Table 2.1 depicts 15 organizational capabilities that characterize well-managed organizations (see Evans & Chun, 2012). We added diversity to this list as a strategic organizational capability that differentiates organizational performance. Such capabilities are inherent in well-managed organizations and have specific implications for what HR professionals should do to promote them (Ulrich et al., 2008).

Over the past two decades, intangible intellectual assets have experienced a "meteoric rise" as they relate to an organization's structure, scope, and value (Lev, 2001, p. 2). In fact, intangible assets have driven wealth and growth in today's economy, while physical and financial assets generally only yield an average return on investment (ROI; Lev, 2001). As a result, the 21st-century organization is now, more than ever, dependent on its organizational capital or human resources that are major inputs into its innovation or creativity processes (Lev, 2001).

As an intangible asset, diversity is a distinct organizational capability defining the identity and personality of the organization by the way it permeates the organizational culture (Huselid et al., 2005; Ulrich et al., 2008; Ulrich & Smallwood, 2004). Unlike individual competencies that refer to the knowledge, skills, and behaviors individuals use to get

TABLE 2.1 Organizational Capabilities	
Capability	*Description*
Talent	Attracting, motivating, and retaining competent people
Speed	Making important changes happen fast
Shared mind-set	Common framework of understanding communicated to internal and external stakeholders
Accountability	Ensuring responsibility and quality results
Collaboration	Working across boundaries to ensure efficiency and leverage
Learning	Generating and generalizing ideas with impact
Leadership	Embedding leaders throughout the organization
Client connectivity	Building enduring relationships of trust with clients and stakeholders
Strategic unity	Articulating and sharing an intellectual, behavioral, and procedural agenda for strategy
Innovation	Creating new ideas and deliverables
Efficiency	Reducing costs by managing process, people, and projects
Simplicity	Keeping strategies, processes, and deliverables simple
Social responsibility	Contributing to communities and broader public good
Managing and anticipating risk	Managing disruption in a volatile economy
Diversity	Building a culture of inclusive excellence

Note: From *Creating a Tipping Point: Strategic Human Resources in Higher Education*, p. 38, by A. Evans & E. B. Chun, 2012, San Francisco, CA: Jossey-Bass. Reprinted with permission.

their work done, capabilities represent the organization's ability to deploy its resources to accomplish goals (Ulrich et al., 2008). And more than any other function, HR is responsible for developing and maintaining capabilities and making intangibles tangible (Ulrich & Brockbank, 2005; Ulrich et al., 2008).

Building the organizational capability for diversity needs to be a central and not a peripheral HR focus. Because the human resource is the most expensive and least poorly managed resource, organizations now must replace the notion of a "war *for* talent" with a "war *with* talent" (Becker, Huselid, & Beatty, 2009, p. 5; italics in original). Most important, a war with diverse talent is the way to win the war with talent in a global economy. Take the example of Aramark, a food services and facilities corporation with 200,000 employees. In 2002 Aramark adopted the concept of the kaleidoscope of diversity as a core business strategy, forming a diversity leadership council to achieve global objectives by retaining and developing a diverse, high-performing workforce (Sainte-Rose, 2005). This approach represents a proactive response to global realities designed to build the talent base needed to realize diversity capability.

In an era of shrinking resources, no organization can afford to overlook the talent it possesses. As budgets contract, organizations may be tempted to feel that diversity represents an extraneous expenditure and is not a necessary focus—something nice to have but not essential. Yet major corporations have recognized for some time the importance of diversity because they cannot effectively do business in a global economy without it (Elmuti, 1993).

Organizations or firms will fail to realize their own potential when they consciously or unconsciously ignore the potential for diverse talent to contribute to strategic outcomes. Oddly enough, individuals with the most intellectual capital are frequently the least appreciated (Ulrich, 1998). When an organization overlooks or devalues its diverse human capital assets, it seals itself off from immense sources of innovation and creativity. And in this knowledge-based economy, the loss of talent resources ultimately has an impact on survival in an intensely competitive marketplace.

In seeking to maximize diversity capability, organizations need to evaluate how the presence (or absence) of HR-related diversity practices influences individual and organizational outcomes. For example, a study of 51 large, publicly traded organizations found that inclusion factors were a critical component of broader human resource initiatives such as conflict resolution processes and collaborative work arrangements designed to foster greater involvement of employees in decision-making processes (Roberson, 2006). As a second example, the demography of the supervisor-subordinate relationship and similarity-attraction paradigm is a significant factor in job success, since substantive research supports the proposition that those in power prefer similar others (see Evans & Chun, 2012). Through awareness of the impact of workplace demography, HR leaders can help level the playing field for diverse employees by ensuring equity in organizational processes.

The difference that HR makes in building an inclusive culture affects how the organization responds to its clients, how individuals work together within the organization, and the ways employees can contribute their creative talents and discretionary effort to goals and outcomes. Since firms and organizations essentially represent hothouses for talent, inclusive human resource practices provide a channel or medium that facilitates the expression of individual innovation and creativity. Research has confirmed that talent tends to flourish in geographic regions where diversity and tolerance are greater (Florida, 2002). In such regions, the outcome of enhanced creativity and diversity is increased entrepreneurial activity with a greater impact than tax rate, human or venture capital, or entrepreneurial zone (Lee, Florida, & Acs, 2004).

HR's Diversity Evolution

HR's diversity progress parallels what the research literature has described as an evolution from operational executor to strategic partner (Brockbank, 1999). Four stages characterize this continuum: operationally reactive in addressing day-to-day business demands, operationally proactive in the design and delivery of HR fundamentals, strategically reactive in supporting existing business strategies, and strategically proactive in focusing on the creation of future strategic alternatives (Brockbank, 1999).

Similarly, in the early stages of diversity efforts, HR's role may be operationally reactive and ancillary to the implementation of preexisting initiatives. In the next phase of diversity evolution, HR leaders become operationally proactive in designing responses to existing initiatives such as by expanding applicant pools, designing creative advertising plans, and implementing aggressive diversity recruitment and hiring practices. In the third phase of this evolution, HR leaders expand their diversity portfolio and competency base to strategically respond to large-scale diversity initiatives. And in the final phase of this evolution, they not only respond to company or organizational strategy but initiate integrated HR diversity strategy and operate in a transformational capacity with respect to changing the culture.

In essence, the stages of HR's diversity evolution enable HR professionals to enter the realm of organizational *value creation*, which provides the bridge between what the organization or firm says about diversity and what it actually does. By engaging in value creation, HR can represent the organizational glue that promotes the connection between theory and practice in the area of diversity. The continuum of diversity value creation is threefold and consists first of value creation, then value preservation, and finally value realization (Eccles, Herz, Keegan, & Phillips, 2001). The value of diversity must be preserved and then actualized in the culture of the organization. Strategically proactive HR leaders are engaged in value realization by translating diversity into the organization's culture, policies, and day-to-day practices.

HR Redesign for Diversity

Contemporary HR transformation must focus on business context and business strategy, leading to fundamental HR redesign (Ulrich et al., 2009). As a result, fundamental redesign of HR services calls for an explicit architecture for diversity embedded in core HR functions. We know that HR practices have become increasingly integrated, innovative, and aligned, operating more like a business within a business with explicit strategy and channels of dissemination (Ulrich, Brockbank, Johnson, & Younger, 2007). As a result, the design of HR practices and services needs to reflect a systematic, integrated approach to diversity.

What then are the specific HR domains that require integration? Table 2.2 contains a list of practice areas that necessitate a redesign for diversity. These eleven areas constitute a baseline for strengthening HR's design and practices in relation to diversity.

Another way of conceptualizing HR's redesign for diversity subdivides the strategic, tactical, and operational levels of HR practices (Shen, Chanda, D'Netto, & Monga, 2009). Strategic-level practices involve organizational diversity culture, vision, mission, and formalized policies; tactical-level practices include compensation, performance evaluation, and professional development; and operational-level practices support communication, workplace flexibility and work/life balance (Shen et al., 2009). However, this conceptualization overlooks the strategic contributions of all the HR practices identified, as compared to more transactional functions within HR's purview such as keeping payroll records.

TABLE 2.2 HR Practice Areas With Diversity Impact	
HR Practice Area	*Redesign Considerations*
Recruiting, retaining, and sustaining a diverse workforce	Talent acquisition and talent management as core HR functions with link to Affirmative Action office to support attainment of representational diversity
Implementing integrated conflict management systems	Integrated employee and labor relations, complaint resolution, mediation, and employee assistance programs
Monitoring employment outcomes and supervisory/employee demography	HR analytics linked with employee relations
Facilitating teamwork, group collaboration, and interaction across differences	Leadership and professional development programs that implement experiential, team-based models for enhanced dialogue across differences

TABLE 2.2 (Continued)

HR Practice Area	Redesign Considerations
Fostering a positive work climate that supports inclusion	Partnership with diversity function to conduct climate studies and cultural audits
Creating policies that support diversity and equity in organizational outcomes	Explicit HR/diversity focus on policy development and implementation
Maximizing the strategic organizational capability of diversity	Strategic HR/diversity planning
Reshaping organizational culture to be receptive to diversity through organizational learning	Systematic HR/diversity organizational learning programs and interventions
Designing an organizational architecture that facilitates the attainment of diversity and inclusion	Strategic staffing analysis and organizational consulting
Building a high-performance workplace that capitalizes on diversity	Total rewards strategy including performance evaluation, professional development, reward and recognition, and compensation programs
Enhancing the commitment, competence, and engagement of a diverse workforce	Total rewards strategy including work/life, performance evaluation, professional development, reward and recognition, and compensation programs

The Pathway to Inclusion: Why Reciprocal Empowerment Matters

In light of the structural requirements for HR's contribution to diversity, we return to examine the role of reciprocal empowerment in the creation of inclusive talent management practices. High-performance organizations thrive because they create conditions that foster discretionary employee contributions. Although HR leaders are responsible for concrete organizational processes, they should also focus on addressing how organizations develop a behavioral and interactional climate of empowerment and democratic participation.

What is meant by reciprocal empowerment in this context? The broad view of empowerment recognizes the conditions of powerlessness that exist in the totality of an organization and addresses the need to remove the structural, institutional, cultural, and psychological conditions that may lead to powerlessness (Prasad, 2001). Conditions of powerlessness have arisen in the context of sociohistorical formation resulting in the systemic reproduction of White social power and privilege in organizational settings (Feagin, 2006; Prasad, 2001).

The focus on reciprocity in empowerment reflects the enrichment that comes to those who are able and willing to share power. Leaders who foster reciprocal empowerment facilitate innovation, offer opportunities rather than constraints on individual mind-sets, and allow the transmission of extensive resources, power, and information throughout the organization (Spreitzer, 1996; Spreitzer, de Janasz, & Quinn, 1999). Empowerment must be pervasive in an organization to counteract abusive environments and overcome the negative forces of poor communication, weak leadership, lack of teamwork, and an excessive bottom-line orientation (Davenport, Schwartz, & Elliott, 1999).

Researchers indicate that empowerment has four important dimensions in relation to individual work roles: meaning, or the value of the work and its congruence with personal values; competence, or the individual's belief in his or her ability to perform; self-determination, or the ability to have choice in initiating actions; and impact, or the ability to influence strategic, operational, or administrative outcomes at work (Spreitzer, 1995; Thomas & Velthouse, 1990). Structural characteristics in the workplace that facilitate empowerment include (a) low ambiguity of role, (b) sociopolitical support, (c) access to information, (d) access to resources, (e) a participative climate, and (f) a wide span of control of the employee's supervisor that allows subordinates to make decisions within their realm of responsibility (Spreitzer, 1996).

Talent theories stress the importance of getting the "right people on the bus" (Collins, 2001, p. 63), implying that the main task is having the right people. Yet having the right people in and of itself will not get the bus moving in the right direction. Talent is only the precursor of organizational success: An empowering workplace is a necessary condition for talent to flourish. In this regard, organizations must create a growth mind-set environment that conveys an emphasis on learning and perseverance rather than on ready-made talent (Dweck, 2006).

Transformational leadership, unlike transactional leadership, develops employees by empowering and mentoring them beyond their day-to-day responsibilities (Jogulu & Wood, 2007). Human-capital-centric organizations create the infrastructure and conditions that allow talented individuals to work together effectively (Lawler, 2008). Norms of reciprocity enhance workplace satisfaction by improving the internal social structure and enhancing communication and cooperation (see Combs, Liu, Hall, & Ketchen, 2006).

Empowering environments facilitate engagement, the psychic and behavioral energy that emanates from individuals into their behaviors and commitments (Macey, Schneider, Barbera, & Young, 2009; Rogelberg, 2009). High-performance workplaces create the conditions for engagement since employees are motivated to engage, have the capacity to do so, possess the freedom needed, and know how to engage (Macey et al., 2009). Engagement means that employees are involved in their work and motivated to contribute through their discretionary efforts. Since the intellectual capital of an organization is a product of competence multiplied by commitment, commitment and engagement are multipliers that will exponentially increase the contributions of competent employees (Ulrich, 1998).

Yet chief executive officers (CEOs) may undermine empowerment and engagement in subtle ways, opting in practice for a command-and-control model (Argyris, 1998). Like the fable of the emperor's new clothes, this model creates internal contradictions and sends mixed messages in organizational change programs (Argyris, 1998). Organizations may revert to external employee commitment or the contractual compliance that occurs when employees have little control over their destinies, as opposed to building individuals' internal commitment to programs through their own volition or internal motivation by involving employees in defining work objectives and ways to achieve them (Argyris, 1998).

Why then does reciprocal empowerment matter? It reinforces a culture of dignity that allows employees to determine their own identities, ensures distributive justice in the allocation of resources, and fosters democratic participation and collaboration. It represents the antithesis of oppression and asymmetric power relations (see Chun & Evans, 2009). As the chief diversity officer (CDO) at Ingersoll Rand notes in Case Study 3 in this chapter, the goal of the company's diversity council is "to make sure that when people came into the company that they felt like they could be themselves in the company" and that the organization would welcome differences "so that new ideas could flourish and grow" (see p. 55).

As a central focus of responsibility, HR and diversity leaders must be concerned with whether the organization is drawing on the talents of all its members through empowering and engaging practices that unleash discretionary contributions in an environment of psychological safety. To build a climate of reciprocal empowerment, engaged HR and diversity leaders forge connections across traditional organizational boundaries and build an integrated practice that embeds inclusion and diversity in organizational processes. They activate the human resource potential of the workforce and ensure that diverse creative capital, as a precious organizational resource, is empowered to contribute to the attainment of strategic objectives.

Consider the example of empowering leadership modeled through a partnership between HR and diversity functions in the Baptist Health System in Southeast Florida. Ricardo Forbes, CDO of the Baptist Health System of seven hospitals with 15,251 employees in Dade, Broward, and

Monroe counties in Southeast Florida, emphasized that HR and diversity must be true partners in three domains: the workplace, the workforce, and the marketplace. In his view, this synergy must become part of the culture, part of the routine. Reinforcing this perspective from a communications standpoint, Forbes stresses that this partnership needs to be described not as something new, but as something that is already being done.

Corey Heller, corporate vice president for human resources in the Baptist Health System, oversees an HR organization of 265 staff and describes the partnership with the diversity office as a "healthy codependency" of collaboration and cooperation. He sees HR as facilitators, champions, and catalysts for change, working to optimize the richness of a diverse population in talent acquisition, engagement, retention, and succession planning. In his words, "Everything we do, we look at from a talent management perspective." Heller said that he tries to help his customers and internal colleagues see integrated HR/diversity strategy as a business imperative that enables Baptist Health to distinguish itself from the competition in employee and patient experiences and clinical outcomes.

Given our discussion of reciprocal empowerment as the foundation for revitalized talent practices, in Chapter 3 we examine the specific competencies that contribute to the HR leader's diversity skill set and discuss how these competencies lead to successful diversity outcomes for the organization as a whole.

Strategic and Tactical Questions for Further Discussion

The following questions provide the opportunity for reflecting on the shared meaning of diversity and inclusion in the organization as well as the specific practices that model reciprocal empowerment in the workplace:

1. Has your organization developed shared definitions for diversity and inclusion? If so, what was the process used to determine these definitions?
2. What organizational capabilities are identified in your organization's strategic plan? How do these capabilities link to the outside world?
3. What specific models of reciprocal empowerment can you locate in current HR/diversity practices?
4. In what concrete ways can line managers model reciprocal empowerment?
5. What are the indicators of a lack of reciprocal empowerment in the workplace?

To conclude the chapter, we present two case studies that address the creation of diversity capability in large, complex organizations: the first in a global manufacturing corporation and the second in an elite, private research university.

Case Study 3: Building Diversity Capability at Ingersoll Rand

In the fall of 2010 Ingersoll Rand, a global manufacturing company with 40,000 employees in 58 companies, was going through a transformative process with relation to diversity and inclusion. Ingersoll Rand is a 140-year-old company based in Davidson, North Carolina, that manufactures 476 products for four business sectors: security technology including home and commercial security systems, air-conditioning or HVAC systems, club cars for golf courses or other transportation needs, and tools such as air pressure tools and drills. The company has engineering and design centers in China, India, and the Czech Republic and foresees half of its future revenue growth coming from outside North America and Western Europe, that is, China, India, Brazil, and Eastern Europe (Minter, 2010). Centers in these areas will support product development tailored to emerging local and regional markets (Minter, 2010).

Ingersoll Rand had never had a CDO. The new CEO appointed in 2010, who also served as chairman of the board, had considerable global experience that gave him insight into how inclusion and diversity could affect the soft skills needed to manage differences in the workplace and differentiate the operations of the organization. While efforts had made to jump-start diversity efforts a number of years earlier, they had not taken root or resulted in any ground-level programs.

The CEO had already determined three key focus areas for Ingersoll Rand: inclusion and diversity as a way to increase employee engagement at every level, growth and innovation to generate new ideas and rethink how the company does business in terms of new market opportunities and products, and operational excellence and standardizing processes to improve efficiency and meet customer needs.

Members of a newly formed Diversity and Inclusion Council, made up of vice presidents, directors, and sector presidents as well as functional area representatives from talent acquisition, compensation, finance, and procurement, realized the company needed to hire a head of diversity to operationalize the business case for diversity. A goal of the diversity position was to promote the development of the company's minority leaders whose ideas would help enhance growth in foreign markets (Kwoh, 2012). Based on these objectives, the council recommended the creation of a CDO position under the senior vice president for HR with a dotted-line reporting relationship to the CEO.

Diversity and Cultural Change

When the first CDO came on board in 2011, she learned that unlike many Fortune 500 corporations the company had identified diversity as a core part of its business strategy.

> [The company] had already positioned inclusion and diversity as part of the overarching business strategy of the company, not just a stand-alone effort or program under the HR function, but had really made it part of the enterprise goals and objectives. So, a lot of the Fortune 500 companies that do have diversity programs, don't have diversity at the heart of the enterprise strategy. And that's what made this organization a unique organization.

Yet she faced the daunting challenge of implementing diversity in a globally dispersed culture that was built around efficiency, productivity, and delivery of quality results. The slow work needed for deep cultural change contrasted with the expectations for immediate results that characterize an engineering-based manufacturing company. The CDO observed:

> The manufacturing side of the corporate culture is very process-driven, because there are a lot of engineers, and very focused on generating results, by looking at what is the ROI [return on investment]. But in general the people in the organization are very down-to-earth. . . . It is a culture based upon [the notion that] we brought you in because we feel that you have the talents and the capabilities to make a difference and now we want you to get to work and generate the results.

The CDO knew that expectations for immediate results do not easily translate to diversity efforts that require time to embed soft skills into day-to-day behaviors and the everyday work environment because of the differences people bring to the workplace. In her view,

> Every individual, regardless of who they are or regardless of what profession they are in, everyone, has certain lenses, certain ways of doing things; expectations; or assumptions that they have learned or make about other individuals that they work with. And so, in a corporate environment, when you're trying to change behaviors, it doesn't happen overnight.

The CDO's immediate goal was to help the organization pace itself in its diversity journey and embark on a process of cultural change in response to the expectations of the diversity council, whose members had already concluded that they wanted the organization to be much more aggressive in attracting diverse talent; their expectations went beyond the hiring process to the kind of working environment they wished to nurture. As she described it:

> They wanted to make sure that when people came into the company that they felt like they could be themselves in the company; and not have to curtail their behavior or their knowledge or experience and who they are in their primary being to adapt to the organization. But rather really wanted the organization to welcome those differences, in thought and communication styles and ability to think out of the box so that new ideas could flourish and grow—the value of the skills, and talents of differences that others would bring to the table.

With what tools could the CDO begin leadership of the diversity journey?

Melding Workforce Analytics and Diversity Strategy

The CDO determined that the key to the development of a cohesive diversity strategy was to obtain a cultural read on the organization. She needed demographic information to develop diversity metrics: turnover rates analyzed by ascriptive characteristics, employee engagement data by race and ethnicity, information on how promotions occurred and who had been promoted, and succession planning data. Such data would help her evaluate areas of challenge and areas of success for different demographic groups.

While HR had begun to track potential diverse hires, diversity was not embedded in the HR processes of promotion, talent development, and succession planning. Furthermore, the company was developing a global Human Resource Information System (HRIS) to capture consistent data across the international spectrum and ensure commonality in the operations in multiple countries. This system was not due to be complete until the close of 2012. And the company had not yet hired a director of workforce analytics. These factors were initial decision blockers for the CDO.

To accomplish these goals, the CDO began work with the HR business partners to help embed diversity in HR processes and to ask key questions about those processes. Her questions were specific to how diversity is incorporated in the talent management continuum such as the selection process and how individuals are selected for promotion. Furthermore, she believed it was critical to create an internal brand for diversity to strengthen external partnerships and set in motion a diverse talent pipeline for the future. As she explained, "And so part of the business challenge is helping the organization begin to rethink about where they look for talent and what other avenues could be used to help bring that talent, and once you have the talent, help them understand how to work toward keeping that talent."

She knew she had to address the symptomatic issues that serve as road-blocks to the advancement of talent.

The CDO also believed the collaboration with HR was critical in deter-mining how diversity could affect the ability of departments to generate new business ideas or rethink approaches from different angles. From her perspective, diversity could add a "different level of value that was not in the room before," helping Ingersoll Rand identify new market niches or products responsive to a diverse clientele. And in her view, integrating HR and diversity strategy required a fundamental understanding of HR systems in order to effect organizational change:

> If you don't have that HR background that allows you to connect with [the] recruiting system, and HRIS system, or employee relations or with the compliance in the company, you may tend as a Chief Diversity Officer or a director of diversity or manager of diversity to only focus on the brand-ing piece and get really comfortable with that, not realizing that you have to tackle learning and development issues, soft skill issues, that managers and other leaders in the company need to learn to cope with in order to really have an impact in changing the culture of the organization.

A director of workforce analytics was hired in 2012. An immediate challenge for the new director was to standardize and integrate data from several existing systems into a single global HRIS platform. Data privacy and protection laws vary in different countries, complicating the process of obtaining a global view of the data. The director began to focus on predictive analytics: advising the organization on the workforce needed to put in place the company's business strategy.

For example, when penetrating a new market, the director of workforce analytics realized that the salespeople must be available to sustain new growth. Hiring too early or hiring too late in the cycle places the company in a dis-advantageous position. Her role in workforce planning involves looking at Ingersoll Rand's 3- to 5-year growth strategies and the critical roles and com-petencies needed for these strategies. To do this, she must understand work-force availability; gauge potential turnover; review talent pools, succession planning, and training; and forecast the staffing resources needed.

Future Perspectives

Marrying workforce analytics with diversity strategy appears to be a win-ning combination for building diversity capability internally and market share externally for Ingersoll Rand. As the CDO contemplates the future, she notes that domestic economic growth is slowing down to an average of 3.5%, while international growth is averaging 8% to 10%. Given these statistics, the CDO asks herself two primary questions: What does Ingersoll Rand need to do to position itself for global growth? How do you leverage inclusion and diversity to increase overall market share and get an edge on the market?

Case Study 4: Strategic HR and Diversity Collaboration at Duke University

Duke University, a private doctoral research university located on 8,700 acres in Durham, North Carolina, has 35,000 employees including its health system of three major hospitals, cancer institute, a large outpatient system, and affiliated medical practices. Duke consistently has ranked among the top 10 universities in the United States for undergraduate programs over the past 20 years ("Duke Places Eighth in U.S. News Ranking," 2006; "National University Rankings," 2013) and has a student population of 13,000 undergraduates and graduate students.

In December 2009 Kyle Cavanaugh joined Duke University as vice president for administration with oversight of HR and a core staff of 120 people. Reporting to the executive vice president of finance and administration, Cavanaugh's responsibilities quickly expanded to include Duke Police, Emergency Management, Disability Management for students and employees, and Parking and Transportation Services. The HR officer for the health system has a dotted line to Cavanaugh's position. As is the case at many universities, HR's administrative responsibilities for faculty are focused in the areas of benefits and workers' compensation, with faculty recruitment and compensation delegated to the dean and departmental levels. A major focus of Cavanaugh's position is the administration of Duke's self-insured benefits plan, which covers 62,000 lives, and its own retirement system.

Cavanaugh quickly formed a close working relationship with Benjamin Reese Jr., vice president of the Office of Institutional Equity and CDO for Duke University and the Duke University Health System. Reese, a clinical psychologist, reports to the president and joined the university 17 years ago. He is the only CDO nationally who has full responsibility for diversity in the research university and its health system, although a few CDOs are involved in both sides. When the CDO position was created a quarter century earlier, the role encompassed the campus and Duke's hospital, and then a decade ago, the Duke University Health System was formed. Reese now oversees a staff of nine people, three of whom are directors responsible for diversity, inclusion, affirmative action, and complaint resolution and harassment/discrimination prevention.

In addition to his responsibilities as Duke's CDO, Reese is president of the National Association of Diversity Officers in Higher Education and has made an active commitment to make sure his office is involved in national policy leadership and discussions.

Trust, Transparency, and Strategic Alignment

Prior to Cavanaugh's arrival, Reese describes the relationship between HR and diversity as more ad hoc and less structured. Many issues were discussed only when they reached a certain level of severity. The partnership between HR and diversity that has developed between Cavanaugh and Reese now reflects strong collaboration in three areas: regular structured meetings, alignment of the philosophy on diversity and inclusion and the resultant strategy, and the development of trust and transparency between the two leaders themselves that results in synergistic outcomes. In addition to their regular standing meetings, Cavanaugh also holds an HR forum monthly in which Reese participates. Both leaders serve as staff to the board of trustees' HR committee.

Cavanaugh sees the convergence of HR and diversity efforts in several broad areas: proactive initiatives that begin at the point of recruitment and orientation and include managerial and leadership training programs with a diversity component; regulatory efforts like the Affirmative Action Plan and collection of applicant tracking data; and complaint resolution issues that may affect employment such as discipline or termination. The coordination needed in these areas requires interaction not only between Cavanaugh and Reese but also between their staffs. For example, in the applicant tracking area overseen by HR, the university averages 14,000 applicants per month, a volume that requires a high level of tracking and analysis. This data is the basis for Affirmative Action and equity reviews of hiring processes. Reese tracks the number of vacancies at senior levels and the number of women and minorities hired into these positions on a monthly basis and presents a progress report annually to the HR committee of the board of trustees.

Despite differences in Cavanaugh's and Reese's reporting relationship, Reese said that the organizational structure "is really secondary to the alignment of philosophy and the relationship of transparency and trust. It doesn't mean that we agree on every single issue but we are aligned in terms of philosophy." Cavanaugh similarly notes that "every organization is structured slightly differently," adding, "my personal opinion is that the organizational structure is somewhat irrelevant. I think what becomes most important is do you have that trust, transparency and collaboration that we have talked about?"

The two leaders view alignment of their offices' mission with the university's mission as the primary focus of their strategic planning processes. When undertaking new initiatives, Reese asks himself if the step he is about to take is grounded in inclusion and if it includes departments that should have significant engagement in the strategy. He also wants to ensure that the strategy fosters diversity in its broadest sense, involving different perspectives, viewpoints, and cultures.

Reese produces an annual report on diversity progress but has not created a separate diversity strategic plan. He says his primary focus is on alignment with the overall institutional strategic plan. When the university's strategic plan was created, Reese helped ensure that the documents submitted by all the professional schools contained a diversity and inclusion component, but more important, related to the university's overall direction. In his view, "that kind of approach is more productive than a diversity plan that is not connected to where the institution is going." As a result, Duke's strategic plan identifies diversity as one of five enduring themes that define and continue to define Duke. The plan, titled "Making a Difference: The Strategic Plan for Duke University (2006)," describes diversity as an ongoing commitment:

> Duke is committed to the value of diversity in all its forms as part of the celebration of human life and as a fundamental foundation for effective teaching, learning, inquiry, and collaboration. This commitment is never perfectly realized; it has deep roots, but requires constant nurturing. (p. 2)

Kyle Cavanaugh engages in an annual strategic planning process in which each functional area establishes goals, objectives, and metrics that cascade downward into a performance plan and roll upward into institutional directions. This planning process involves a scan of the internal and external environment.

The process of integrated HR/diversity planning takes place in response to specific issues as well in the development of new initiatives and programs. For example, Reese oversees the task force on lesbian, gay, bisexual, and transgender issues for faculty and staff, and works with Cavanaugh to involve the committee in their activities and recommendations. The two leaders review employee processes and procedures in the area of diversity such as in approaches to health coverage for transgender issues. When Cavanaugh established a new year-long leadership program, he tapped Reese for the steering committee, since one of the goals of the leadership program is to identify minorities and women with potential for leadership roles to facilitate a diverse pipeline for succession planning.

The Challenge of Organizational Culture

The culture of higher education poses distinct challenges for collaborative HR and diversity practices because of the environmental characteristics of size, complexity, and decentralization. For example, Reese met with a cross-section of people to discuss the possibility of forming a health disparities working group. The stakeholders in the meeting recognized there were probably two or three or four other conversations going on at the same time somewhere across the institution. As Reese pointed out, "That is sort of the nature of these kinds of organizations and presents some challenges in putting together a focused strategy, having knowledge of what implementation approaches work, and what area is doing what."

Cavanaugh described the challenge of size, complexity, and decentralization as a "difference" and also a "reality" that may exact an implementation tax in terms of time:

> If one works especially in the higher education area and less so in the health care environment and expects that you are going to change that culture, that's going to be a tough road to go every day. I think that one needs to recognize and embrace those differences. In the case of . . . diversity activities, it's understanding that it may take a long period of time to get initiatives going, because you must engage many constituents. The actual outcome can actually be much broader and deeper because you have so many people involved. I see it as a difference, but actually there are as many advantages as there are disadvantages.

To build synergy across the large, complex health system, Reese has implemented a three-level structure for engaging hospital leadership in diversity. Beginning in 2001, he created diversity leadership groups at each of the three hospitals that include the hospital president and 18 to 25 key stakeholders. Once a quarter, a systemwide diversity leadership group composed of the presidents of hospital units and senior leaders from the health system meet to align strategies and develop new approaches. At the highest level, an executive diversity leadership group for the entire health system meets to create overall direction for diversity and implement three areas of focus: human capital (increasing the number of women and underrepresented minorities at the senior level), cultural competence, and health disparities.

Diversity at Senior Leadership Levels

In crafting a comprehensive diversity strategy for the university, Reese continues to brainstorm with Cavanaugh about helping the institution strengthen diversity at senior levels of the institution. In former years, Reese made presentations at the first meeting of the search committees for deans or senior officials. He soon recognized that hundreds of critical interactions and conversations would take place during the search process and that search committee members could quickly forget about the initial meeting.

On the recommendation from a group of faculty members to the president, Reese became an active ad hoc member of every senior-level search. This change coincided with a shift in the way the provost interacted with search committees. As a result of this new strategy, the first minority dean of a professional school (the graduate school) was hired in 2012, followed by the hiring of a second minority dean for the Duke chapel.

In the continuing discussion between the president and Reese about ways to engage senior leaders in diversity strategy in their areas of responsibility, Reese worked with the president to implement a plan in 2012 that requires each of the university's top 35 leaders to develop three strategies/initiatives that affect diversity and submit them to the president. In April 2013 these strategies were compiled in a report for the president and ultimately the HR committee of the board of trustees. The 35 university leaders each sent two people to a half-day workshop to discuss the definition of *diversity and inclusion* and its alignment with the university mission. The development of key strategies by each area has involved people more actively than previously, a process that Reese described as a "healthy stretch" (B. Reese, personal communication, February 1, 2013). He is currently developing a template of what a submission should look like to ensure greater clarity and impact.

Future Challenges

What challenges remain that will require further collaboration? The area of internationalization and global engagement offers new opportunities for continued synergy between the two areas. The university's strategic plan states that "Duke has long recognized that we cannot be a great university without being an international university" ("Making a Difference: The Strategic Plan for Duke University," 2006). Duke is building a full campus in Kunshan, China, which has involved Kyle Cavanaugh extensively in the entire workforce planning process.

Ben Reese also foresees changes in his role as the schools at Duke become more proficient in leading their own diversity initiatives:

> I suspect in the years to come if I am successful in getting units to really focus on diversity strategy that aligns with their work, they will need a different kind of help from him, as they become more skilled at doing their own diversity work. I imagine my own responsibilities will shift. (B. Reese, personal communication, February 1, 2013)

The School of Medicine has hired its own CDO because of the need for a more exclusive focus on medicine, and hired Reese's director of diversity and inclusion as its first CDO.

Looking toward the future, Cavanaugh and Reese envision a continued partnership that will further embed diversity in organizational culture and take them beyond the bounds of the university's geographic location to fulfill Duke's mission as an international research university.

References

Argyris, C. (1998). Empowerment: The emperor's new clothes. *Harvard Business Review, 76*(3), 98–105.

Becker, B. E., Huselid, M. A., & Beatty, R. W. (2009). *The differentiated workforce: Transforming talent into strategic impact.* Boston, MA: Harvard Business School Press.

Beer, J. M. (2010). Diversity management's paradoxical negation of diversity. *International Journal of Diversity in Organizations, Communities and Nations, 10*(4), 1–14.

Bonilla-Silva, E. (2006). *Racism without racists: Color-blind racism and the persistence of racial inequality in the United States* (2nd ed.). Lanham, MD: Rowman & Littlefield.

Brockbank, W. (1999). If HR were really strategically proactive: Present and future directions in HR's contribution to competitive advantage. *Human Resource Management, 38*(4), 337–352.

Chang, M. J., & Ledesma, M. C. (2011). The diversity rationale: Its limitations for educational practice. In L. M. Stulberg & S. L. Weinberg (Eds.), *Diversity in higher education: Toward a more comprehensive approach* (pp. 74–85). New York, NY: Routledge.

Chun, E., & Evans, A. (2009). *Bridging the diversity divide: Globalization and reciprocal empowerment in higher education* (ASHE-ERIC Higher Education Reports, Vol. 35, No. 1). San Francisco, CA: Jossey-Bass.

Collins, J. (2001). *Good to great: Why some companies make the leap . . . and others don't.* New York, NY: HarperCollins.

Combs, J., Liu, Y., Hall, A., & Ketchen, D. (2006). How much do high-performance work practices matter? A meta-analysis of their effects on organizational performance. *Personnel Psychology, 59*(3), 501–528.

Davenport, N., Schwartz, R. D., & Elliott, G. P. (1999). *Mobbing: Emotional abuse in the American workplace.* Ames, IA: Civil Society Publishing.

Duke places eighth in U.S. news ranking: Duke also listed in "great bargain" list. (2006). Retrieved from http://today.duke.edu/2006/08/usnews.html

Dweck, C. (2006). *Mindset: The new psychology of success.* New York, NY: Random House.

Eccles, R. G., Herz, R. H., Keegan, E. M., & Phillips, D. M. H. (2001). *The value-reporting revolution: Moving beyond the earnings game.* New York, NY: Pricewater-houseCoopers.

Edmondson, A. C. (2012). *Teaming: How organizations learn, innovate, and compete in the knowledge economy.* San Francisco, CA: Jossey-Bass.

Elmuti, D. (1993). Managing diversity in the workplace: An immense challenge for both managers and workers. *Industrial Management, 35*(4), 19–22.

Evans, A., & Chun, E. B. (2012). *Creating a tipping point: Strategic human resources in higher education.* San Francisco, CA: Jossey-Bass.

Feagin, J. R. (2006). *Systemic racism: A theory of oppression.* New York, NY: Routledge.

Florida, R. (2002). The economic geography of talent. *Annals of the Association of American Geographers, 92*(4), 743–755.

Florida, R., & Goodnight, J. (2005). Managing for creativity. *Harvard Business Review, 83*(7/8), 124–131.

Hamel, G. (2002). *Leading the revolution: How to thrive in turbulent times by making innovation a way of life.* Boston, MA: Harvard Business School.

Henry, P. K. (2003). *Diversity and the bottom line: Prospering in the global economy* (1st ed.). Austin, TX: TurnKey Press.

Hubbard, E. E. (2004). *The manager's pocket guide to diversity management.* Amherst, MA: HRD Press.

Huselid, M. A., Becker, B. E., & Beatty, R. W. (2005). *The workforce scorecard: Managing human capital to execute strategy.* Boston, MA: Harvard Business School.

Jogulu, U., & Wood, G. (2007). Leadership empowerment: Power struggle. *Engineering Management Journal, 17*(3), 36–37.

Kezar, A., & Eckel, P. (2002). Examining the institutional transformation process: The importance of sensemaking, interrelated strategies, and balance. *Research in Higher Education, 43*(3), 295–328.

Kezar, A. J., Glenn, W. J., Lester, J., & Nakamoto, J. (2008). Examining organizational contextual features that affect implementation of equity initiatives. *Journal of Higher Education, 79*(2), 125–159.

Kwoh, L. (2012). Firms hail new chiefs (of diversity): "CDOs" join senior ranks to include more women, minorities; some report directly to CEO. *Wall Street Journal.* Retrieved from http://online.wsj.com/article/SB100014240529702038 99504577129261732884578.html

Lawler, E. E., III. (2008). *Talent: Making people your competitive advantage.* San Francisco, CA: Jossey-Bass.

Lawler, E. E., III., & Worley, C. G. (with Creelman, D.). (2011). *Management reset: Organizing for sustainable effectiveness.* San Francisco, CA: Jossey-Bass.

Lee, S. Y., Florida, R., & Acs, Z. J. (2004). Creativity and entrepreneurship: A regional analysis of new firm formation. *Regional Studies, 38*(8), 879–891.

Lev, B. (2001). *Intangibles: Management, measurement, and reporting.* Washington, DC: Brookings Institution Press.

Macey, W. H., Schneider, B., Barbera, K. M., & Young, S. A. (2009). *Employee engagement: Tools for analysis, practice, and competitive advantage.* San Francisco, CA: Wiley.

Making a difference: The strategic plan for Duke University. (2006). Retrieved from http://stratplan.duke.edu/pdf/plan.pdf

Minter, S. (2010, December 20). IR's Mike Lamach: Building on a strong hand. *IndustryWeek.* Retrieved from http://www.industryweek.com/global-economy/irs-mike-lamach-building-strong-hand

National university rankings. (2013). *U.S. News and World Report*. Retrieved March 9, 2013, from http://colleges.usnews.rankingsandreviews.com/best-colleges/rankings/national-universities

Ortiz, A. M., & Patton, L. D. (2012). Awareness of self. In J. Arminio, V. Torres, & R. L. Pope (Eds.), *Why aren't we there yet?: Taking personal responsibility for creating an inclusive campus* (pp. 9–32). Sterling, VA: Stylus.

Owen, D. S. (2008). Privileged social identities and diversity leadership in higher education. *Review of Higher Education, 32*(2), 185–207.

Prasad, A. (2001). Understanding workplace empowerment as inclusion: A historical investigation of the discourse of difference in the United States. *Journal of Applied Behavioral Science, 37*(1), 51–69.

Prasad, P., Pringle, J. K., & Konrad, A. M. (2006). Examining the contours of workplace diversity: Concepts, contexts and challenges. In A. M. Konrad, P. Prasad, & J. K. Pringle (Eds.), *Handbook of workplace diversity* (pp. 1–22). Thousand Oaks, CA: Sage.

Prilleltensky, I., & Gonick, L. S. (1994). The discourse of oppression in the social sciences: Past, present, and future. In E. J. Trickett, R. J. Watts, & D. Birman (Eds.), *Human diversity: Perspectives on people in context* (pp. 145–177). San Francisco, CA: Jossey-Bass.

Ragins, B. R. (1997). Diversified mentoring relationships in organizations: A power perspective. *Academy of Management Review, 22*(2), 482–521.

Roberson, Q. M. (2006). Disentangling the meanings of diversity and inclusion in organizations. *Group & Organization Management, 31*(2), 212–236.

Rogelberg, S. G. (2009). Series editor's preface. In W. H. Macey, B. Schneider, K. M. Barbera, & S. A. Young, *Employee engagement: Tools for analysis, practice, and competitive advantage* (pp. xiii–xiv). West Sussex, UK: Wiley-Blackwell.

Sainte-Rose, S. (2005). *Dimensions of diversity: Stevens Sainte-Rose, lecture*. Retrieved from http://www.eclips.cornell.edu/search?collection=11&title=Minority%20Entrepreneurs%20and%20Experts&isCUWA=&type=&id=11&clipID=8513&tab=TabCasesPage

Shen, J., Chanda, A., D'Netto, B., & Monga, M. (2009). Managing diversity through human resource management: An international perspective and conceptual framework. *International Journal of Human Resource Management, 20*(2), 235–251.

Smith, R. A. (2002). Race, gender, and authority in the workplace: Theory and research. *Annual Review of Sociology, 28*, 509–542.

Spreitzer, G. M. (1995). Psychological, empowerment in the workplace: Dimensions, measurement and validation. *Academy of Management Journal, 38*(5), 1442–1465.

Spreitzer, G. M. (1996). Social structural characteristics of psychological empowerment. *Academy of Management Journal, 39*(2), 483–504.

Spreitzer, G. M., de Janasz, S. C., & Quinn, R. E. (1999). Empowered to lead: The role of psychological empowerment in leadership. *Journal of Organizational Behavior, 20*(4), 511–526.

Tatum, B. D. (1997). *"Why are all the Black kids sitting together in the cafeteria?"*: A *psychologist explains the development of racial identity.* New York, NY: Basic Books.

Thomas, K. W., & Velthouse, B. A. (1990). Cognitive elements of empowerment: An "interpretive" model of intrinsic task motivation. *Academy of Management Review, 15*(4), 666–681.

Ulrich, D. (1998). Intellectual capital = competence x commitment. *Sloan Management Review, 39*(2), 15–26.

Ulrich, D., Allen, J., Brockbank, W., Younger, J., & Nyman, M. (2009). *HR transformation: Building human resources from the outside in.* New York, NY: McGraw-Hill.

Ulrich, D., & Brockbank, W. (2005). *The HR value proposition.* Boston, MA: Harvard Business School Press.

Ulrich, D., Brockbank, W., Johnson, D., Sandholtz, K., & Younger, J. (2008). *HR competencies: Mastery at the intersection of people and business.* Alexandria, VA: Society for Human Resource Management.

Ulrich, D., Brockbank, W., Johnson, D., & Younger, J. (2007). Human resource competencies: Responding to increased expectations. *Employment Relations Today, 34*(3), 1–12.

Ulrich, D., & Smallwood, N. (2003). *Why the bottom line isn't! How to build value through people and organization.* San Francisco, CA: Wiley.

Ulrich, D., & Smallwood, N. (2004). Capitalizing on capabilities. *Harvard Business Review, 82*(6), 119–127.

3

DIVERSITY COMPETENCIES OF THE HR LEADER

Innovative ideas flourish at the intersection of diverse experience, whether it be others' or our own. . . . Put simply, innovators intentionally maneuver themselves into the intersection, where diverse experiences flourish and foster the discovery of new insights. (Dyer, Gregersen, & Christensen, 2011, pp. 45–46)

If diversity is a driver of innovation and linked to global success, what are the competencies linked to such success? A study that interviewed over 100 inventors concluded that the ability to generate innovative ideas is not simply a function of the mind but a function of behaviors as well (Dyer, Gregersen, & Christensen, 2011). And such behaviors include the ability to make connections, to associate, and to bring together diverse cultures, ideas, and experiences.

Given rapid, nonincremental innovation as the centerpiece of a new age of revolution (Hamel, 2002), we argue that HR leaders must not only be change agents and innovation experts but must have the necessary attributes that will enable them to meld diversity teaming and innovation within the crucible of organizational culture. HR leaders themselves need to bring to the table a comprehensive and well-honed set of diversity competencies that will allow them to expand an organization's diversity capability on a large scale. They must not only understand differences, but engage and leverage difference in support of identified strategy (Davidson, 2011).

Diversity competencies can play a catalytic role by enabling HR practitioners to elevate the organization's diversity awareness and understanding in support of innovation and expansion of organizational capacity. Core competencies play a catalytic role in the "production function" of strategic assets, that is, assets that are nontradable and difficult to imitate (Markides & Williamson, 1994, p. 157). As a result, HR leaders themselves must possess focused diversity competencies that will enable them to leverage diversity capability at the organizational level.

Consider how Carolynn Brooks, chief diversity officer for OfficeMax, describes the value of a structured and nuanced HR approach to diversity:

> In the past, we did not have a very structured HR approach, which was probably my greatest frustration. . . . And now with our new leadership we are looking at what do we do to get them prepared. . . . and it's really about the sensitivity, the understanding of privilege and how it operates in a male-dominated environment. Our HR organization can understand how you help them address it . . . because again it goes back to what are your biases, but it's helping HR peel theirs back as well and understand how they need to approach it. . . . If you can't figure out how to be included and inclusive in HR then you really can't figure out how to be inclusive in the whole corporation.

Over the past two decades, researchers have begun to explore the meaning and attributes of diversity competency. Two notable models include the competency framework developed by Cox and Beale (1997), which identifies the developmental phases of awareness, understanding, and action steps in relation to individual and organizational effectiveness, and Hubbard's (2008) comprehensive taxonomy of 46 diversity competencies organized into six clusters. The clusters Hubbard identifies are diversity knowledge and skills, technical competencies, business competencies, interpersonal competencies, intellectual competencies, and personal competencies (Hubbard, 2008). With these models in mind, we propose a framework specifically focused on the integration of HR and diversity strategy that extends the well-researched literature pertaining to HR competencies. Since diversity leaders may already have considerable expertise by virtue of their existing role, we focus specifically on the repertoire of competencies needed by HR leaders.

The Six Competency Domains for Diversity

The substantial empirically based literature on HR competencies represents a critical starting point for HR leaders seeking to advance and gain credence in a diversity leadership role. The research of Ulrich and others (Ulrich, Brockbank, Johnson, Sandholtz, & Younger, 2008; Ulrich, Brockbank, Johnson, & Younger, 2007) drawn from five waves of data gathering provides an in-depth perspective on the HR competencies that add value to an organization. This research was based on 40,000 questionnaires from 417 discrete companies in six global regions and was updated with a sixth wave of results using a sample of 20,000 responses from 650 organizations (Ulrich, Younger, Brockbank, & Ulrich, 2012). Through a 360-degree evaluation based on the responses of HR professionals and their colleagues, the following six competency domains for HR professionals were identified: strategic positioner, credible activist, capability builder, change champion, HR innovator and integrator, and technology proponent (Ulrich et al., 2012).

The sixth wave of data collection on HR competencies involves a clear shift in emphasis with the emergence of two new competencies: capability builder and technology proponent. These new attributes have replaced the former competencies that identified HR as business ally and operational executor in the earlier samples. This shift suggests a greater emphasis on HR's central role as the architect of organizational capabilities and the co-owner with line managers of these capabilities (see Figure 3.1).

The six competency domains form the groundwork for the strategic qualities and tactical know-how necessary for the HR/diversity leadership role. As change champion in the realm of diversity work, the HR leader

Figure 3.1 2012 HR Competencies

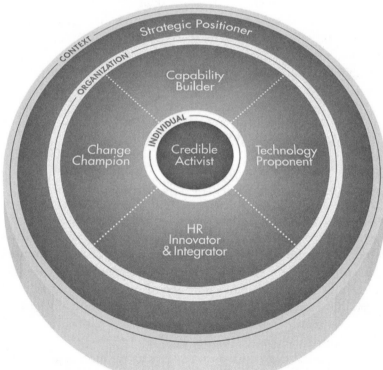

Note: From *Global HR Competencies: Mastering Competitive Value from the Outside In*, p. 24, by D. Ulrich, W. Brockbank, J. Younger, & M. Ulrich, 2013. Copyright 2013 by McGraw-Hill. Reproduced with permission.

must help overcome historic, systemic forms of discrimination by addressing underlying cultural norms and assumptions related to diversity. As innovator and integrator, he or she must instigate systematic organizational design and devise innovative diversity strategies that align with overall organizational goals.

Furthermore, the HR leader must leverage his or her individual diversity competency to build the organizational capability for diversity through integration of strategic, tactical, and operational approaches. The competency of credible activist is particularly important, since it leads all other competencies and accounts for 93% of an HR professional's individual performance (Ulrich et al., 2008). In this capacity, activist HR leaders create a vision for diversity that is grounded in credibility, offering an activist view of diversity change or what some would call "HR with an attitude" (Ulrich et al., 2007, p. 6).

In the multiple roles of activist, designer, executor, manager, and steward, HR leaders are engaged in actions that deliver results. As initiators rather than bystanders, HR leaders must understand the concrete behaviors that achieve intended consequences, possess the skills and concepts to attain necessary outcomes, and master the situational context that will facilitate goal attainment (Argyris, 2000). They must avoid generating blame against individuals and the system and overcome defensive routines (Argyris, 2000). As realists, they do not bypass controversial problems or expect them to be fixed in minutes (Argyris, 2000).

In Table 3.1, we extrapolate from the HR competency framework established by Ulrich and others to derive a set of HR/diversity competencies and their associated outcomes and deliverables.

Intercultural Sensitivity and Engagement

Another key dimension for consideration in the development of diversity competency is intercultural sensitivity. Since experience depends on how one construes events, greater perceptual and conceptual capacity can enhance the richness of experience (Hammer, Bennett, & Wiseman, 2003). Empirical evidence from the expatriate literature indicates that the content domain of intercultural competence involves the three dimensions of cognitive perception: management, relationship management, and self-management (see Bird, Mendenhall, Stevens, & Oddou, 2010).

Monocultural socialization only provides access to one's own cultural worldview and can inhibit distinctions between one's own perception and withhold humanity from those who are culturally different (Hammer et al., 2003). By contrast, the developmental model of intercultural sensitivity developed by Bennett and others (see Hammer, Bennett, & Wiseman,

TABLE 3.1
HR Diversity Competencies, Outcomes, and Deliverables

Diversity Competency	Diversity Outcomes	Diversity Deliverables
Credible activist: Translating the business case for diversity into action	Create a collaborative diversity action plan to ensure tangible outcomes	Establish accountability through formal diversity policies Conduct an organizational diversity audit and assessment
Change champion: Fostering organization-wide change through research-based principles	Transform the culture to be receptive to diversity	Build a research-based change model Design systemic organizational learning initiatives
HR innovator and integrator: Designing initiatives that maximize human capital potential	Ensure that the organization attracts and retains talented and diverse employees	Build diversity leadership models and alliances Design innovative, integrated HR/diversity strategies Foster an inclusive, high performance workplace
Strategic positioner: Developing visionary diversity strategies for the global millennium	Develop a diversity strategic plan and assessment strategy with accountability structure	Form partnerships with stakeholders to develop diversity strategic plan Establish steering committees for specific groups and issues Contribute to marketing plans and branding to convey diversity commitment to stakeholders
Technology proponent: Developing systems and metrics for diversity progress	Develop organizational metrics for diversity return on investment	Develop diversity scorecard, measurements, and dashboard Strengthen diversity accountability through concrete metrics related to organizational effectiveness

Note: First column from *Global HR Competencies: Mastering Competitive Value from the Outside In*, by D. Ulrich, J. Younger, W. Brockbank, & M. Ulrich, 2013, New York, NY: McGraw-Hill.

2003) identifies a conceptual continuum in the attainment of intercultural sensitivity that ranges from ethnocentrism to ethnorelativism.

Ethnocentrism includes

- denial—the individual's own culture is experienced as the only real one.
- defense—the individual is more openly threatened by cultural difference and views such difference as an attack on his or her values.
- minimization—the individual neutralizes the threat of cultural difference by subsuming these differences into more familiar categories while preserving the dominance of his or her own worldview.

Ethnorelativism includes

- acceptance—the individual is adept at identifying the role of cultural differences in human interactions.
- adaptation—the individual's worldview is enlarged to include constructs from other worldviews.
- integration—the individual's experience of self involves movement in and out of differing cultural world views.

Intercultural sensitivity can also be understood in terms of identity inclusivity that results in intercultural behavior (Kim, 2009). Identity inclusivity reflects greater cognitive refinement in relations with culturally dissimilar others, fostering "communicative synchrony" (Kim, 2009, p. 57). In a new era of connectivity HR professionals are called upon to be interculturally skilled leaders—*edgewalkers*—who must respond to differing expectations and needs that include the continuous restructuring of organizations, partnerships, and alliances (Pusch, 2009). Behavioral and cognitive flexibility, cross-cultural empathy, and tolerance for ambiguity are attributes that enhance intercultural interaction (see Pusch, 2009). Such skills contribute to boundary-spanning leadership that transcends social identity boundaries and creates links among groups (Ernst & Yip, 2009).

In our exploration of diversity competency, we now consider the expansion of traditional concepts of intelligence to include new forms of global and diversity intelligence that enrich intercultural sensitivity and engagement.

The New Frontiers of Intelligence

Competencies that expand diversity intelligence represent a new avenue for exploration in the realm of organizational behavior. HR and diversity leaders can draw on the emerging research related to these new forms of social intelligence to inform the process of organizational change.

The importance of these ways of knowing for HR practitioners resides in their value as forms of *organizational intelligence*, which in essence represents the ability to diffuse knowledge and institutionalize it through organizational systems, promoting adaptation to the environment (Glynn, 1996). And the translation of organizational intelligence into specific diversity competencies provides the capacity to influence behavior, interactions, culture, climate, strategy, and outcomes. Since adaptation to the environment is critical for organizational survival, expansion of diversity intelligence and competencies could have significant effects upon a range of HR practices including organizational learning and talent management. Three domains of organizational intelligence have particular relevance to this discussion: global intelligence, diversity emotional intelligence (DEI), and innovative intelligence.

Global Intelligence

Psychologist Howard Gardner (1999) offers the theory of *multiple intelligences*, which he defined as potentials or a core set of operations that solve problems or create products that are valued within one or more cultural settings. Gardner proposed that seven intelligences exist: linguistic, logical-mathematical, musical, bodily-kinesthetic, spatial, interpersonal, and intrapersonal. He also suggested the possibility of additional intelligences such as naturalist, spiritual, and existential (Gardner, 1999).

The concept of global intelligence could form a new multidisciplinary type of intelligence based on interconnectedness: (a) the ability to respect, value, and bridge difference; (b) the synthetic and creative capacity to bring together diverse individuals, information, and ideas through a cross-cultural lens; and (c) the ability to take positive and responsive action based on global understanding. Note the relevance of the three parts of this definition to creation of a climate of inclusion.

In his in-depth study of the meaning of global intelligence, Spariosu (2004) defines *global intelligence* as "the ability to understand, respond to, and work toward what is in the best interests of and will benefit all human beings and all other life on the planet" (p. 6). He emphasizes that global intelligence represents interactive and responsive understanding that "can never be separated from the willingness to undertake positive, responsive action, the causally reciprocal effects of which will then propagate by amplifying feedback loops or resonance through the entire social system" (p. 65). Global intelligence is built upon intercultural dialogue, research, and mutual cooperation and is an emergent phenomenon requiring lifelong learning (Spariosu, 2004).

Diversity Emotional Intelligence

The emergence of an extensive literature on emotional intelligence suggests that this concept has significant value for the field of diversity. The term *emotional quotient* was first used by Reuven Bar-On (1988) as a counterpart of *intelligence quotient* and defines an array of social and emotional knowledge and abilities that affect the ability to cope with environmental demands (see Goleman, 2001b). Emotional intelligence refers to interpersonal and intrapersonal competencies that enhance self-awareness, the capacity for recognizing our own feelings and those of others, and the capacity for self-management of emotions (Goleman, 1998). Emotional competence is a learned capability that leads to enhanced job performance through the dimensions of self-awareness, self-management, social awareness, and relationship management (Goleman, 2001a). Figure 3.2 illustrates the framework of emotional competencies that affect work performance.

Preliminary findings have reported a relationship between emotional intelligence and work performance, including supervisory ratings of interpersonal facilitation, stress tolerance, integrity, productivity, and leadership (see Abe, 2011; Brackett, Rivers, & Salovey, 2011). One model of emotional intelligence and organizational effectiveness emphasizes the interrelationship among three elements: leadership, HR functions, and organizational climate and culture (see Figure 3.3). These three components, in turn, affect

Figure 3.2 A Framework of Emotional Competencies

	Self (Personal Competence)	**Other** (Social Competence)
Recognition	**Self-Awareness** • *Emotional self-awareness* • *Accurate self-assessment* • *Self-confidence*	**Social Awareness** • *Empathy* • *Service orientation* • *Organizational awareness*
Regulation	**Self-Management** • *Emotional self-control* • *Trustworthiness* • *Conscientiousness* • *Achievement drive* • *Initiative*	**Relationship Management** • *Developing others* • *Influence* • *Communication* • *Conflict management* • *Visionary leadership* • *Catalyzing change* • *Building bonds* • *Teamwork and Collaboration*

Note: From "An EI-Based Theory of Performance," by D. Goleman, p. 28, in C. Cherniss & D. Goleman (Eds.), *The Emotionally Intelligent Workplace: How to Select For, Measure, and Improve Emotional Intelligence in Individuals, Groups, and Organizations* (2001a), San Francisco, CA: Jossey-Bass. Copyright 2001 by Jossey-Bass. Reprinted with permission.

Figure 3.3 A Model of Emotional Intelligence and Organizational Effectiveness

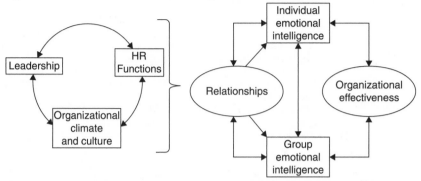

Note: From "Emotional Intelligence and Organizational Effectiveness," p. 8, by C. Cherniss, in C. Cherniss & D. Goleman (Eds.), *The Emotionally Intelligent Workplace: How to Select For, Measure, and Improve Emotional Intelligence in Individuals, Groups, and Organizations,* 2001, San Francisco, CA: Jossey-Bass. Copyright 2001 by Jossey-Bass. Reprinted with permission.

relationships among organizational members that are influenced by individual and group emotional intelligence. Of particular interest for our study is the reciprocal relationship between leadership and HR functions that influences HR's ability to enable organizational members to enhance their emotional intelligence (Cherniss, 2001). This systemic approach suggests that multiple components interact in the attainment of organizational emotional intelligence leading to organizational effectiveness. And efforts to improve the emotional intelligence of organizational members will fail unless these efforts address naturally occurring relationships among members (Cherniss, 2001).

Based on the model of emotional intelligence developed by Daniel Goleman that builds on the work of Peter Salovey and John Mayer (see Cherniss, 2001), we introduce our model of DEI, which expands the realm of emotional intelligence to interactions in a diverse, global society. While research is still in its early stages regarding diversity emotional intelligence, its potential to contribute to organizational effectiveness, cultural change, and business performance is significant.

By extension of the hypotheses of the emotional intelligence research, we propose that DEI also involves the four quadrants of self-awareness or self-identity and self-management on the level of personal competence and social awareness, and relationship management on the level of social competence (see Figure 3.4). Similarly, a model of emotional intelligence and diversity proposed by Gardenswartz, Cherbosque, and Rowe (2008, 2010) identifies the four quadrants of affirmative introspection (self-awareness), self-governance (self-management), intercultural literacy (social awareness),

Figure 3.4 A Model of DEI

	Self (Personal Competence)	Other (Social Competence)
Recognition	**Self-Awareness** • Celebration of individual uniqueness • The power to define one's own identity • Affirmation of a positive identity despite differences • Self-esteem and self-confidence	**Social Awareness** • Cultural sensitivity • Awareness of historic legacies of oppression and how these manifest themselves • Adaptation to cultural factors/expectations in communication • Creation of synergistic, superordinate goals
Regulation	**Self-Management** • Emotional self-control • Anticipation of challenges based upon ascriptive characteristics • Development of coping strategies	**Relationship Management** • Creating desired relationships across difference • Building diverse teams • Catalyzing change • Building bonds across difference • Resolving conflicts across difference

Note: From "An EI-Based Theory of Performance," by D. Goleman, p. 28, in C. Cherniss & D. Goleman (Eds.), *The Emotionally Intelligent Workplace: How to Select For, Measure, and Improve Emotional Intelligence in Individuals, Groups, and Organizations* (2001a), San Francisco, CA: Jossey-Bass. Copyright 2001 by Jossey Bass. Adapted with permission.

and social architecting (relationship management). We also find considerable overlap with the content domain of intercultural competence described earlier.

In our view, DEI reaffirms the concept of reciprocal empowerment that involves mutuality and reciprocity rather than power, subordination, and domination (see Prilleltensky & Gonick, 1994). In this light, we delineate characteristics of DEI that heighten the mutuality of understanding between majority groups and traditionally stigmatized individuals.

Self-awareness. The concept of self-identity is one of the pillars of reciprocal empowerment. In this regard, the power of the DEI model is twofold. For stigmatized groups such as women, minorities, people with disabilities, and lesbian/gay/bisexual/transgendered individuals, existing stereotypes can shape perceptions of their work performance and preclude their ability to develop and express their own identity. For majority groups, the ability to celebrate differences in identity among all organizational members is essential to the creation of a climate of inclusion. As a result, an affirmative emotional climate of acceptance and inclusion is critical for organizational effectiveness.

Self-management. The concept of self-management in this context refers to control of negative emotions relating to diversity that hinder effective communication. It is a process of self-governance that includes being in charge of self-talk and making ambiguity an ally (Gardenswartz et al., 2008). For diverse individuals, coping strategies that minimize the effects of perceived discrimination through regulation of emotions, cognitive restructuring, reframing events, and sharing difficult experiences can serve to desensitize negative feelings and thoughts arising from discriminatory experiences (see Chun & Evans, 2012). For members of all groups, replacement of negative emotions, attitudes, and feelings based on characteristics of difference with positive emotions of interest, inquiry, and openness will lead the way to effective organizational communication.

Social awareness. The quadrant of social awareness involves cultural sensitivity and includes understanding the dynamics of intercultural interactions. For example, nonverbal behaviors, silence, choice of vocabulary, speaking up in public, directness and indirectness, dealing with criticisms and disagreements, and communication of status and power vary in different cultural contexts (Brislin, 2008). Misinterpretation and miscommunication because of such factors in the workplace can give rise to stereotypes, wrong assumptions, and even conflicts. Social awareness also requires an understanding of the histories and legacies of oppression. For example, White men, as members of a dominant group, have not had the history of self-doubt that arises from a lifetime of rejection (Cross, 2000). As a result, they may have a sense that they deserve to be at the top or that they earned it and interpret the struggles of others in this meritocratic framework (Cross, 2000).

Relationship management. DEI affects relationship management by creating desired relationships across difference. Consider the following example of how to expand relationship management across difference. Intergroup dialogue is an innovative program of intergroup education, begun at the University of Michigan and implemented at over 40 college and university campuses, that encourages exchange regarding contentious issues such as social identity and the dynamics of privilege and oppression in society (Zuniga, Nagda, Chesler, & Cytron-Walker, 2007). It creates a safe and structured environment where people can listen and learn from diverse participants and build skills to maintain relationships across differences that enable them to take responsive action for equity and social justice (Zuniga et al., 2007). Its principles stress the importance of developing a language and capacity for dialogue through deep listening, suspending judgments, becoming aware of assumptions, reflecting, and inquiring. By reflecting on oneself and others as members of social groups in a social context characterized by inequality and privilege, individuals develop skills to work with differences and conflicts as opportunities for increased understanding ("Multi-University Intergroup Dialogue Research Project," n.d.).

Like emotional intelligence, DEI competency among organizational members should influence organizational effectiveness, provided that the functions of HR and leadership support competency attainment. Efforts to improve diversity understanding and intelligence will fail unless they address the relationships among organizational members.

Taking Control of the Emotional Elephant

The theory and practice of diversity emotional intelligence hinges on the fact that emotional impulses and affective responses permeate relationships in organizational life. Emotional responses have been shown to undergird and pervade reactions to difference and can also result in discriminatory events (Picca & Feagin, 2007). Put metaphorically, according to psychologist Jonathan Haidt (2006), our emotional side is an elephant and our rational side is its rider. The rider's control is precarious since the rider is so little compared with the elephant. Yet when contemplating change, the elephant gets things done and makes progress toward a goal with drive and energy (Heath & Heath, 2010).

Change involves getting people to behave in a new way that requires motivation and energy from the elephant and planning and direction from the rider (Heath & Heath, 2010). Yet the rider is an adviser or servant and not a king or president with a firm grip on the reins, while the elephant represents emotions, gut feelings, and visceral reactions (Haidt, 2006). This metaphor clarifies that diversity change will not occur without addressing the emotional substrate of employees' affective responses.

We submit that expanding the quotient for diversity emotional intelligence among an organization's members is necessary to begin to shift the emotional tide in support of diversity. Furthermore, diversity emotional intelligence can contribute to an organization's emotional capability, which increases creativity through an emotional connection to the work context, harmonizes emotional states to foster innovation and organizational functions, and enables managers to channel negative emotional states and support positive emotional states through appropriate solutions and problem solving (Akgün, Keskin, & Byrne, 2009).

Although little is known about how emotional capability is operationalized, a study of 174 Turkish firms by Akgün et al. (2009) found a relationship between emotional capability as reflected in management practices that foster enthusiasm, hope, and joy, and innovation through novel products and services. This relationship was strengthened through the ability of individuals in the firm to communicate their emotions with others, understand the feelings of other organizational members, and read subtle social cues to determine what emotions were expressed (Akgün, Keskin, & Byrne, 2009).

These findings provide evidence for the link between emotional intelligence and innovation. This correlation was strong when the environment was characterized by high uncertainty (Akgün, Keskin, & Byrne, 2009). What are the characteristics of relationships that bridge the dimensions of difference in the workplace through diversity emotional intelligence? Such relationships have four key characteristics:

1. They promote positive affect and rapport.
2. They promote mind-sets that encourage ongoing learning.
3. They have longevity and are resilient despite factors that might encourage separation.
4. They lead to effective work and developmental outcomes (Davidson & James, 2007).

HR leaders play a pivotal role in creating the conditions that can advance diversity intelligence in the workplace. Responsive action requires that HR leaders create psychological safety for diverse groups in organizational working environments to allow the development of responsive understanding. They must work to foster intercultural resonance, empathetic, interactive dialogue in which participants preserve each other's integrity and identity (Spariosu, 2004, p. 65). Earmarks of such dialogue include listening, feedback, and participatory action to improve participation and understanding.

And HR leaders need to institute systematic programs that specifically help individual organizational members expand their competency for global and diversity emotional intelligence. This expansion will create greater capacity for adaptive organizational intelligence. For example, diversity emotional intelligence among individuals and groups in the organization influence supervisory-subordinate relationships, peer relationships, and intergroup dynamics. As a result, having a few people with high DEI will not generate the conditions necessary to improve teamwork and group effectiveness (Cherniss, 2001). Norms and enduring processes are necessary to support awareness and regulation of diversity emotional intelligence among group members (Cherniss, 2001). By building on diversity emotional intelligence, organizations can overcome internal barriers, stereotypes, and emotional blockages that inhibit the acceptance of diversity.

Innovative Intelligence

The concept of innovative intelligence has importance in a world of discontinuous change in which radical innovation based on nonlinear ideas is required to generate new wealth (Hamel, 2002). Weiss and Legrand (2011) define *innovative intelligence* as the "capability of gaining insight into complex problems and discovering new and unforeseen implementable solutions" (p. 36). Despite the lack of research evidence offered in support of their theory, the notion of innovative intelligence as a separate intelligence domain is congruent with the importance of radical innovation as a pathway to organizational success.

As a final consideration in this chapter, we discuss specific ways that HR leaders can advance their own diversity competency and influence the organization's diversity competency, taking into account their institutional position and level of power or influence.

Creating Vanguard Organizations Through HR/Diversity Leadership

The model depicted in Figure 3.3 identifies the three factors of leadership, HR functions, and organizational climate and culture as influenced by and influential in the development of emotional intelligence. HR/diversity leaders are charged with the difficult task of infusing relationships with the diversity emotional intelligence needed to support the evolution of transformational, global enterprises.

Why should HR leaders focus on the intersection of leadership, climate, and HR practices that support the development of diversity emotional intelligence? Individuals with high diversity emotional intelligence foster creativity by encouraging organizational members to identify and act upon creative opportunities (Zhou & George, 2003). They stimulate creativity by using emotion to facilitate cognitive processes that undergird problem identification recognition and opportunity recognition. They enhance organizational learning leading to innovation as a primary driver of organizational performance (Yeung, Lai, & Yee, 2007). And they appraise and manage conflict and tension in groups by identifying common goals for groups' creative efforts (Zhou & George, 2003). In other words, HR/diversity leaders facilitate the creation of vanguard firms and organizations that are characterized by

- a culture that endures over the long term and encourages continual renewal and change,
- a guidance system of values and principles,
- an innovation process driven by strong social purposes and social connections,
- humanistic approaches that create positive and productive collaborations, and
- diversity that encourages common ground and the expression rather than the suppression of individual identity (Kanter, 2011).

From a practical perspective, how can HR leaders leverage diversity competency and diversity emotional intelligence in support of the creation of a vanguard corporation? What are the practical strategies that enable them to expand the organizational capacity for positive intergroup dynamics and heightened diversity intelligence? We share here two examples that illustrate the interrelationship of leadership, HR functions, and organizational climate and culture in relation to diversity in two major corporations.

Xerox has the characteristics of a vanguard corporation in terms of its culture, guidance system, innovation process, and diversity. It is one of only a few major American corporations with women in the top two leadership positions, one in five with women at a vice presidential level or higher, and 23% minority professionals. Xerox officials became aware of the need for change in the 1960s and early 1970s as a result of a number of galvanizing events, including passage of the Civil Rights Act of 1964; implementation of Executive Order 11246, which brought Affirmative Action for federal contractors into being; two sets of race riots in Rochester, New York; the rise of Black caucus groups that was at first met with resistance; and a class action suit brought against Xerox by African American employees (Sessa, 1992). Because of increased competition in the technology market, in the 1980s the corporate vice president of personnel convinced the president that HR should have an integral role in the development of the company's business plan (Sessa, 1992). This participation resulted in an emphasis on workforce diversity, structural diversity, and business diversity, three of the major components of Hubbard's (2004) diversity framework cited earlier.

Ursula Burns, named as chief executive officer of Xerox in 2009, became the first African American woman to lead a Fortune 500 company and a company of Xerox's size with 130,000 employees in 160 countries. Burns was named by her predecessor, Anne Mulcahy, as chief executive, representing the first time a female chief executive has replaced another female chief executive at a Fortune 500 company. Burns's promotion to this role signals that a minority woman can run a major corporation that is a leader in global technology. Burns views diversity as a key contributor to Xerox's success and teaming as the way firms and organizations work globally to solve problems (Bryant, 2010; Vance, 2009). Burns de-emphasized the notion of global competition with nations such as China and India in favor of the idea of teaming with other nations to solve global issues and problems.

As can be seen from this example, diversity became an integral part of HR strategy at Xerox, resulting in the ability to affect structural and business strategies in global markets. The early realization of the value of diversity in HR strategy in the 1980s culminated three decades later in the appointment of the first African American chief executive officer (CEO). The melding of

HR and diversity strategy represented a long-term and systematic approach that ultimately affected firm performance.

As a second example, consider the rise of Don Thompson in March 2012 from president and chief operating officer of McDonald's Corporation to become the first African American CEO of the iconic fast-food giant with 32,000 restaurants in 118 countries. Unlike the other 99% of Fortune 500 companies, Thompson joins three other African Americans, including Ursula Burns, who now head these global companies (Isidore, 2012). Nonetheless, Black executives at the next two top levels of the corporate ladder still represent only 2% of available positions (Isidore, 2012).

Thompson has been a strong spokesperson for the inclusivity of the entire McDonald's system in terms of diversity in franchisees, supply chain, and talent, indicating that diversity has been important in fostering innovation and creativity in products and the development of new ideas for efficiency and increasing shareholder value ("McDonald's Makes Historic Hire of First Black CEO," 2012). Reinforcing the link between diversity and talent management, Thompson believes that further development of McDonald's diverse talent pool will propel the company's growth in the decades ahead, particularly because more than 50% of McDonald's managers are women and minorities (Dingle, 2011). A systematic approach to diversity and talent management characterizes McDonald's business strategy.

Both examples demonstrate the responsibility of HR professionals to integrate diversity as a HR principle throughout the organization through the HR competency framework. The capacity of HR/diversity leaders to influence organizational results depends on their own diversity competency as well as their ability to instigate systematic change in support of an organization's overall diversity capability. By enhancing diversity competencies and diversity emotional intelligence, they function as behavioral science experts and agents of change (Mathews, 1998).

Building awareness of the organizational need for diversity competency and diversity emotional intelligence is a needed step in an organization's diversity evolution. Too often, diversity competencies have been viewed as an extraneous and even superfluous skill set. The focus of this chapter has been to bring the role of diversity competencies to the fore and to define components of that skill set using research-based HR principles. To the extent that organizations recognize the growing importance of diversity competency and diversity emotional intelligence, they will be positioned to channel the proverbial elephant of affective responses that shape behavior and attitudes, workplace climate, team functioning, and supervisory/subordinate relationships. Too little attention has been paid by HR theorists and professionals to the emotional components of diversity acceptance in organizations.

The development of cognitive and behavioral dimensions of diversity competence can strengthen organizational performance by overcoming internal conflicts, improving social interactions, and creating empowering conditions that foster creativity and innovation in a diverse workforce.

Strategic and Tactical Questions for Further Discussion

Consider the following questions in relation to the development of your organization's diversity competency and the level of its diversity emotional intelligence:

1. Do position descriptions for HR professionals include a requirement for diversity competence? If so, how is this competency specified?
2. How are diversity competencies for organizational leadership evaluated?
3. Does your organization offer training in emotional intelligence? In diversity competency?
4. Has your organization addressed the affective components of diversity in experiential learning programs?
5. Does the repertoire of skills of professionals in employee relations, mediation, or ombudsperson functions in your organization include diversity competency?

The case study that follows illustrates the calibration of diversity efforts in the culture of a global Fortune 500 corporation and the development of a systematic approach to organizational change.

Case Study 5: Visioning and Planning—Diversity and HR at Sodexo

Rohini Anand was hired as chief diversity officer for Sodexho, North America, in 2002. Sodexo is a leading food services and facilities management corporation that employs more than 413,000 people in 80 countries at 34,000 locations. Anand brought a strong HR and professional development focus to her work, having served as vice president of the National Multicultural Institute where she designed and developed organizational change initiatives for domestic and global clients. Her hiring followed a 2001 class-action lawsuit filed by 2,400 plaintiffs against Sodexho-Marriott Services who charged Sodexho with discrimination in promotion decisions beginning in 1998. Sodexho-Marriott was formed in 1998 by a merger of Marriott International's food service division with Sodexho's North America division. The company changed its name to Sodexho, Inc., in 2001 and later to Sodexo in 2008. (For consistency in this case study we use the current spelling, Sodexo.)

Organizational Structure for Integrating Diversity and HR Strategy

When she joined the organization in 2002, Anand was reporting to HR, but a year later she was promoted and began reporting to the CEO of Sodexo, North America, Michel Landel. Upon joining the executive team and becoming peers with the chief human resources officer, Anand found her colleague to be a strong supporter and ally in the diversity journey, even serving as executive sponsor of network groups. Anand explains the growth of their professional relationship:

> While she was always very committed, she did experience a series of epiphanies for her as well. One in particular was the work that we did around women of color. That was one that she had not quite internalized around the importance of really addressing issues around women of color. And I think that experience helped her to get even more committed. And then her involvement with the network groups, our affinity groups.

Anand and the head of HR sit on the Diversity Leadership Council chaired by the CEO, a body that makes many of the strategic decisions on the direction of diversity and inclusion. The next level down in the organizational structure is the HR Diversity and Legal Working Group, which addresses difficult issues, such as adverse impact analysis or strategic issues, which are then presented to the Diversity Leadership Council. Anand also has a representative on the HR leadership team and often invites representatives from HR to present to the diversity leadership team.

At Sodexo each of the company's eight market segments has a dedicated diversity vice president assigned to it who reports to the market president with a dotted line to Anand. These segments, which include corporate, education, health care, justice, sports, and leisure, are very tightly aligned to HR in the market, and the vice presidents sit on the HR market team as well. Some resistance arose when the market leads were assigned to the market presidents among those who felt that these positions should fall under HR.

Phases in the Diversity Journey

Since joining Sodexo, Anand has led a systematic process of organizational change through implementation of a phased diversity model. She described the early vision for the diversity:

> I had a very clear vision of what the endpoint was going to be and I knew that the most important component of achieving my mission was the fact that I had the unequivocal support of the CEO, Michel Landel. And he, too, had a vision . . . early on, when there were many naysayers in the company. He saw Sodexo as not only the benchmark in our industry, but the benchmark in corporate America.

Landel and Anand never wavered from this vision, despite the fact that it seemed like a long shot at the time. In a tactically focused food service company operating on a low margin, managers at that time were focused on getting the meal on the table.

Anand describes the industry then as "not glamorous, not the first industry of choice for people of color." The industry itself was a decade behind in progressive practices and policies for minorities and women. At that time, Sodexo was demographically homogenous, with White men predominantly in leadership positions and a lack of diverse role models. Company management did not have a clear understanding why a diversity strategy was needed and what its relation to the business was. As a result, when Anand presented her diversity vision to the executive team, she was literally chased out of the room. Landel was unwavering in his support of her and in his concern to ensure that she was okay despite this initial reception.

Faced with implementing a comprehensive diversity strategy in a large geographically dispersed organization, Anand quickly realized that a lofty conceptual orientation would not work. She knew she needed to roll the diversity initiative out in chunks or phases:

> So it's about taking the sort of lofty vision about being the benchmark and chunking it out in very digestible, small bite sizes so that the organization could get their head around it, get their arms around it, and then implement it. To talk about 50 different things and to talk about the lofty vision really didn't [work] because our managers want to know "the three things I need to do." What we did was to actually phase it in a very deliberate manner.

Anand began the first phase of the diversity evolution at Sodexo with compliance and infrastructure positioning. Recognizing that Affirmative Action was not a familiar concept for many managers, her initial efforts were devoted to education and developing the business case for diversity. She put in place the basic compliance and educational framework, using external speakers, clients, and other companies as part of this effort.

She also worked over the next few years with Landel to develop diversity metrics and a scorecard that includes metrics on recruiting, retention, and promotion of women and minorities as well as measures of qualitative behavioral changes. The implementation of the diversity scorecard triggered initial resistance to the metrics and their validity, particularly since the scorecard was linked to 10% to 15% of the bonuses for managers and 25% of executive management bonuses. Bonuses are paid by the company regardless of the rise and fall of earnings.

Anand then moved to the inclusion phase of the diversity effort focused on awareness and ways to engage a geographically dispersed organization. In the United States alone Sodexo has nearly 10,000 locations, and a highly organized effort was needed to get the word out. The method for this dispersion involved the development of employee resource groups and diversity councils as well as a robust training and learning strategy designed to involve everyone in the organization.

As a result of this initiative, Sodexo created partnerships vertically across the organization through seven employee network groups with over 6,000 members that infuse the diversity strategy throughout the organization. Furthermore, Sodexo's diversity and inclusion learning strategy is designed as a progressive series of 10 levels beginning with diversity awareness and competency and reaching the highest level of integrating and embedding diversity in the culture ("Global Diversity & Inclusion Report," 2009).

The next phase of the diversity journey involved creating community partnerships and reaching out externally "We were so internally focused that we did not focus on the external community. And when we got pressure externally, we started engaging with the community that we recruit from, the community that we do business in, et cetera," she said.

About four years into the journey, Anand feels the organization reached a tipping point in the realization of an integrated diversity and inclusion management strategy. Managers operating out of client sites began to recognize the value of diversity effort in client relations. As she said, managers started to see the benefits:

> I can talk to my client about what we are doing, I can sit on my client's diversity council, I can share resources, and this helps me to get access to more senior level decision makers, it helps me to kind of expand . . . my relationships and I can actually leverage this because the resources Sodexo spent on diversity is a differentiator, because none of my competitors are doing it, so I can leverage it to grow my business.

Managers started to view diversity as a resource facilitating business success. This development was particularly important because Sodexo does not own real estate, and client relationships had sometimes surfaced as a reason or even an excuse not to focus on diversity.

In 2005 Michel Landel was promoted to CEO of Sodexo, and he and Anand worked to embed strategic diversity and inclusion globally as the next phase of the diversity maturity model. In 2007 Anand was promoted to senior vice president and global chief diversity officer with a dual reporting relationship to Landel and to George Chavel, CEO of Sodexo, North America. The emphasis in this phase of the diversity journey was on reinforcing talent and business excellence by going deeper, wider, and becoming more sharply focused in terms of the company's diversity efforts. By 2010 the company had developed a strong focus on its global strategy with an emphasis on inclusion for business breakthroughs.

Staying the Course

Sodexo's diversity and inclusion strategy has four primary goals:

1. to sustain and enhance leadership engagement;
2. to increase recruitment, development, engagement, and retention of top talent;
3. to embed diversity and inclusion at all levels and foster a culture of inclusion; and
4. to leverage diversity and inclusion as a differentiator to retain and expand the business.

In working toward the attainment of these goals, Sodexo has a bifurcated global and domestic diversity strategy. The main challenges in the United States have been the lack of knowledge and understanding of diversity's value to the business. To counter potential resistance, Anand has concentrated on education and providing tools to managers to help them obtain the benefits of diversity.

From a global perspective, a principal barrier has been developing an understanding of the meaning of diversity and inclusion. The only common metric globally is gender, and the concept of minorities means different things in different countries. In relation to gender, Anand sees the need to implement diversity in a way so that men see the benefit of addressing gender issues. And she has had to overcome the resistance women sometimes have in relation to gender once they have reached the top and tend to distance themselves from this issue. In response to these issues, Michel Landel spearheaded the Sodexo Women's International Forum for Talent in 2009 to accelerate the attainment of gender balance through the leadership of high-level women. One of the company's goals is to increase the number of women among Sodexo's senior leaders by 25% by 2015.

Overall, Anand believes the following four areas contribute to Sodexo's long-term ability to sustain the diversity effort:

1. A unique structural organization for diversity
2. Clear metrics and accountability for all managers
3. Linking to the core business strategy to leverage and enhance business value
4. Cultural changes through a top-down, bottom-up, and middle-out strategy, which involves commitment from the top with grassroots involvement in a decentralized organization

Anand's systematic approach to diversity transformation is shown in Figure 3.5. She has focused on calibrating diversity efforts to the culture of the company and conducting analyses to understand where the gaps and bottlenecks are as well as developing strategies to overcome them. In her words, "It was not initiatives just for the sake of initiatives. It needs to be for really understanding why we are doing it, what are we trying to address through it."

Readiness and timing are important considerations in her approach to new initiatives. Anand believes that gauging organizational readiness requires

Figure 3.5 Sodexo Organizational Diversity Maturity Model

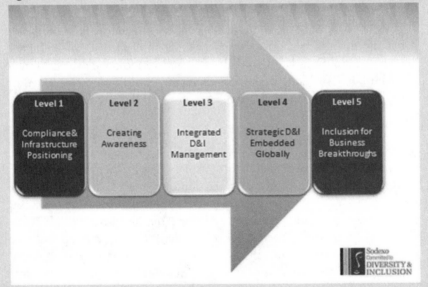

Note: From "An Overview of Sodexo's Diversity & Inclusion Strategy and Catalyst Award-Winning Initiative," by R. Anand, 2012, PowerPoint presentation at Catalyst Benchmarking Session, Gaithersburg, MD. Copyright 2012 by Sodexo. Used with permission.

emotional intelligence to know how to influence the organization and position initiatives strategically.

The formation of network groups is a case in point. Anand began the network groups with the African American group, followed by the network for women, and the Asian American and Latino groups. Early in the process, she was approached about forming a lesbian/gay/bisexual/transgender network group. Anand realized the organization was not ready and that the initiative would encounter significant resistance. She advised the individuals involved to first educate the organization and build the infrastructure before launching the initiative to ensure its success. Similarly when she received other requests for additional network groups, she waited until she felt the organization was ready before forming them.

Open Questions

In contemplating the future, Anand views the biggest issues Sodexo faces as the need for continued cultural change and avoidance of diversity fatigue. Dramatic change has occurred since she was chased out of the room when she presented the diversity scorecard and metrics to the executive team. Now she feels she doesn't even need to be in the room. The company has enough individuals who know that diversity is important to the organization's identity and will carry the work forward. This transformative change has freed Anand to do other things, including leading Sodexo's sustainability efforts. Yet as Anand ponders the future, she says, "I think as we look ahead the open issues really are around how do we embed diversity and inclusion deeper within the organization; how do we avoid diversity fatigue; with so many competing priorities, how do we stay the course?"

References

Abe, J. A. (2011). Positive emotions, emotional intelligence, and successful experiential learning. *Personality and Individual Differences, 51*(7), 817–822.

Akgün, A. E., Keskin, H., & Byrne, J. (2009). Organizational emotional capability, product and process innovation, and firm performance: An empirical analysis. *Journal of Engineering and Technology Management, 26*(3), 103–130.

Anand, R. (2012, August). *An overview of Sodexo's diversity & inclusion strategy and catalyst award-winning initiative.* PowerPoint presentation at the Catalyst Benchmarking session, Gaithersburg, MD.

Argyris, C. (2000). *Flawed advice and the management trap: How managers can know when they're getting good advice and when they're not.* New York, NY: Oxford University Press.

Bar-On, R. (1988). The development of an operational concept of psychological well-being (Unpublished doctoral dissertation). Rhodes University, Grahamstown, South Africa.

Bird, A., Mendenhall, M., Stevens, M. J., & Oddou, G. (2010). Defining the content domain of intercultural competence for global leaders. *Journal of Managerial Psychology, 25*(8), 810–828.

Brackett, M. A., Rivers, S. E., & Salovey, P. (2011). Emotional intelligence: Implications for personal, social, academic, and workplace success. *Social & Personality Psychology Compass, 5*(1), 88–103.

Brislin, R. (2008). *Working with cultural differences: Dealing effectively with diversity in the workplace.* Westport, CT: Praeger.

Bryant, A. (2010, February 20). Xerox's new chief tries to redefine its culture. *New York Times.* Retrieved from http://www.nytimes.com/2010/02/21/business/21xerox.html?pagewanted=all&_r=1

Cherniss, C. (2001). Emotional intelligence and organizational effectiveness. In C. Cherniss & D. Goleman (Eds.), *The emotionally intelligent workplace: How to select for, measure, and improve emotional intelligence in individuals, groups, and organizations* (pp. 3–12). San Francisco, CA: Jossey-Bass.

Chun, E., & Evans, A. (2012). *Diverse administrators in peril: The new indentured class in higher education.* Boulder, CO: Paradigm.

Cox, T., & Beale, R. L. (1997). *Developing competency to manage diversity: Readings, cases & activities.* San Francisco, CA: Berrett-Koehler.

Cross, E. Y. (2000). White men as champions. *Diversity Factor, 8*(3), 2–7.

Davidson, M. N. (2011). *The end of diversity as we know it: Why diversity efforts fail and how leveraging difference can succeed.* San Francisco, CA: Berrett-Koehler.

Davidson, M. N., & James, E. H. (2007). The engines of positive relationships across difference: Conflict and learning. In J. E. Dutton & B. R. Ragins (Eds.), *Exploring positive relationships at work: Building a theoretical and research foundation* (pp. 137–158). Mahwah, NJ: Erlbaum.

Dingle, D. T. (2011). Don Thompson's recipe for growth. *Black Enterprise, 41*(6), 58–60.

Dyer, J., Gregersen, H., & Christensen, C. M. (2011). *The innovator's DNA: Mastering the five skills of disruptive innovators.* Boston, MA: Harvard Business School Press.

Ernst, C., & Yip, J. (2009). Boundary-spanning leadership: Tactics to bridge social identity groups in organizations. In T. L. Pittinsky (Ed.), *Crossing the divide: Intergroup leadership in a world of difference* (pp. 87–100). Boston, MA: Harvard Business School Press.

Gardenswartz, L., Cherbosque, J., & Rowe, A. (2008). *Emotional intelligence for managing results in a diverse world: The hard truth about soft skills in the workplace.* Boston, MA: Nicholas Brealey.

Gardenswartz, L., Cherbosque, J., & Rowe, A. (2010). Emotional intelligence and diversity: A model for differences in the workplace. *Journal of Psychological Issues in Organizational Culture, 1*(1), 74–84.

Gardner, H. E. (1999). *Intelligence reframed: Multiple intelligences for the 21st century.* New York, NY: Basic Books.

Global diversity & inclusion report. (2009). Retrieved from http://pt.sodexo.com/ ptpt/Images/Sodexo_Diversity_Inclusion_Report_tcm241-284660.pdf

Glynn, M. A. (1996). Innovative genius: A framework for relating individual and organizational intelligences to innovation. *Academy of Management Review, 21*(4), 1081–1111.

Goleman, D. (1998). *Working with emotional intelligence.* New York, NY: Bantam Dell.

Goleman, D. (2001a). An EI-based theory of performance. In C. Cherniss & D. Goleman (Eds.), *The emotionally intelligent workplace: How to select for, measure, and improve emotional intelligence in individuals, groups, and organizations* (pp. 27–44). San Francisco, CA: Jossey-Bass.

Goleman, D. (2001b). Emotional intelligence: Issues in paradigm building. In C. Cherniss & D. Goleman (Eds.), *The emotionally intelligent workplace: How to select for, measure, and improve emotional intelligence in individuals, groups, and organizations* (pp. 13–26). San Francisco, CA: Jossey-Bass.

Haidt, J. (2006). *The happiness hypothesis: Finding modern truth in ancient wisdom.* New York: Basic Books.

Hamel, G. (2002). *Leading the revolution: How to thrive in turbulent times by making innovation a way of life.* Boston, MA: Harvard Business School Press.

Hammer, M. R., Bennett, M. J., & Wiseman, R. (2003). Measuring intercultural sensitivity: The intercultural development inventory. *International Journal of Intercultural Relations, 27*(4), 421–443.

Heath, C., & Heath, D. (2010). *Switch: How to change things when change is hard.* New York, NY: Broadway Books.

Hubbard, E. E. (2004). *The manager's pocket guide to diversity management.* Amherst, MA: HRD Press.

Hubbard, E. E. (2008). *The diversity discipline: Implementing diversity work with a strategy, structure and ROI measurement focus.* Petaluma, CA: Global Insights.

Isidore, C. (2012, March 22). *African-American CEOs still rare.* Retrieved from http://money.cnn.com/2012/03/22/news/companies/black-ceo/index.htm

Kanter, R. M. (2011). How great companies think differently. *Harvard Business Review, 89*(11), 66–78.

Kim, Y. Y. (2009). The identity factor in intercultural competence. In D. K. Deardorff (Ed.), *The Sage handbook of intercultural competence* (pp. 53–65). Thousand Oaks, CA: Sage.

McDonald's makes historic hire of first Black CEO. (2012). Retrieved from http://newsone.com/business/dlchandler/don-thompson-mcdonalds/

Markides, C. C., & Williamson, P. J. (1994). Related diversification, core competences and corporate performance. *Strategic Management Journal, 15*, 149–165.

Mathews, A. (1998). Diversity: A principle of human resource management. *Public Personnel Management, 27*(2), 175–185.

Multi-university intergroup dialogue research project: Guidebook. (n.d.). Retrieved from http://sitemaker.umich.edu/migr/files/ migr_guidebook.pdf

Picca, L. H., & Feagin, J. (2007). *Two-faced racism: Whites in the backstage and frontstage*. New York, NY: Routledge.

Prilleltensky, I., & Gonick, L. S. (1994). The discourse of oppression in the social sciences: Past, present, and future. In E. J. Trickett, R. J. Watts, & D. Birman (Eds.), *Human diversity: Perspectives on people in context* (pp. 145–177). San Francisco, CA: Jossey-Bass.

Pusch, M. D. (2009). The interculturally competent global leader. In D. K. Deardorff (Ed.), *The Sage handbook of intercultural competence* (pp. 66–84). Thousand Oaks, CA: Sage.

Sessa, V. J. (1992). Managing diversity at the Xerox corporation: Balanced workforce goals and caucus groups. In S. E. Jackson & Associates, *Diversity in the workplace: Human resources initiatives* (pp. 37–64). New York, NY: Guilford Press.

Spariosu, M. I. (2004). *Global intelligence and human development: Toward ecology of global learning*. Cambridge, MA: MIT Press.

Ulrich, D., Brockbank, W., Johnson, D., Sandholtz, K., & Younger, J. (2008). *HR competencies: Mastery at the intersection of people and business*. Alexandria, VA: Society for Human Resource Management.

Ulrich, D., Brockbank, W., Johnson, D., & Younger, J. (2007). Human resource competencies: Responding to increased expectations. *Employment Relations Today, 34*(3), 1–12.

Ulrich, D., Brockbank, W., Younger, J., & Ulrich, M. (2013). *Global HR competencies: Mastering competitive advantage from the outside in*. New York, NY: Mc-Graw-Hill.

Ulrich, D., Younger, J., Brockbank, W., & Ulrich, M. (2012). Evolving expertise. *Human Resource Executive Online*. Retrieved from http://www.hronline.com/HRE/story.jsp?storyId=533344456

Vance, A. (2009, May 21). At Xerox, a transition for the record books. *New York Times*. Retrieved from http://www.nytimes.com/2009/05/22/technology/companies/22xerox.html?ref=ursulamburns

Weiss, D. S., & Legrand, C. (2011). *Innovative intelligence: The art and practice of leading sustainable innovation in your organization*. Mississauga, Ontario, Canada: Wiley.

Yeung, A. C. L., Lai, K-h., & Yee, R. W. Y. (2007). Organizational learning, innovativeness, and organizational performance: A qualitative investigation. *International Journal of Production Research, 45*(11), 2459–2477.

Zhou, J., & George, J. M. (2003). Awakening employee creativity: The role of leader emotional intelligence. *Leadership Quarterly, 14*(4/5), 545–568.

Zuniga, X., Nagda, B. A., Chesler, M., & Cytron-Walker, A. (2007). *Intergroup dialogue in higher education: Meaningful learning about social justice*. San Francisco, CA: Jossey-Bass.

4

HR LEADERS AS ARCHITECTS OF DIVERSITY CHANGE

These dynamic processes of culture creation and management are the essence of leadership and make one realize that leadership and culture are two sides of the same coin. (Schein, 2004, p. 1)

In light of the nonlinear, discontinuous, and rapid nature of change, organizational leadership must not only accelerate the processes of cultural transformation but do so without missteps to maintain competitive advantage. Building change capacity requires extraordinary organizational agility. And in this context, the expertise of HR leaders as strategic positioners, change champions, talent managers/designers, and credible activists is called into play to foster new mind-sets; overcome inertia and counteract subterranean resistance; and reculture or establish new norms and values that replace the status quo.

If HR leaders are indeed the social engineers facilitating the cultural change needed to embed diversity in an organization's DNA, how do they prepare for this process? And how can they successfully work in partnership with diversity leaders to design, facilitate, and implement systemic processes that shift the cultural needle and create readiness for change? These are difficult and knotty questions without simple answers. Cultural change in organizations is arguably complex and long term. It brings into play behavioral factors, psychological reactions, and emotional responses. It requires examination of prevailing norms and assumptions that are often buried deep within an organization's cultural substrata.

As Edgar Schein (2004) said, since leadership and culture are "two sides of the same coin" (p. 1), the rigidity and inflexibility of cultures that have been permitted to prevail over long periods of time must be overcome. When an organization has not designated diversity explicitly as part of HR's role, HR leaders may feel uncomfortable in taking actions that could be viewed as outside their direct responsibilities or even as encroaching on the diversity officer's territory. Sometimes the power of culture may seem overwhelming, and the tides of resistance defy easy solutions. Nonetheless, in building the architecture for diversity, HR leaders must develop a systematic plan that enables them to align and create congruity among the principal building blocks of values, systems, and structures. They must draw upon research-based models and frameworks to assist them in this integrative process.

The fundamental reason for HR leaders' instrumental role in cultural change lies in HR's expertise in organization development (OD). The conceptual focus of OD is planned change through systemic, long-range efforts designed to increase organizational effectiveness and sustainability (see Evans & Chun, 2012). OD interventions focus on organizational learning and the modification of approaches that can produce new outcomes based on new insights, awareness, or knowledge (Edmondson, 2012). Such interventions can include interpersonal strategies involving work relationships among employees, structural strategies that address organizational design, and intrapersonal strategies such as team building and networking (Evans & Chun, 2012).

In unraveling the complex strands of the change process, this chapter focuses on the role of HR/diversity leaders as change agents and organizational designers of systemic change. In this chapter, we introduce tools that provide the opportunity for HR/diversity leaders to assess their own readiness to serve as diversity change agents as well as organizational readiness. We then identify approaches to organizational learning that will facilitate long-term cultural change. To guide the reflective process, we identify key principles from the research literature that can facilitate the change process as well as barriers to collaboration. The chapter concludes with a case study that provides insight into the planning for a systemic diversity and inclusion planning process led by the U.S. Office of Personnel Management.

HR Leader Self-Assessment

We focus first on the readiness of HR leaders to embark upon a process of cultural change in partnership with diversity leaders. Throughout the book, we have noted the relative reluctance of HR leaders to enter the domain of diversity and to see themselves as co-owners of diversity progress. The assessment in Exercise 4.1 can serve as a goal-setting agenda for HR leaders seeking to expand the scope and impact of their diversity work.

Integration of HR and Diversity Programs: Self-Assessment Profile for HR Leaders

Directions: This profile will assist you in assessing the extent and scope of your HR/diversity work. Please circle the response that most closely reflects your incorporation of diversity into your current role and responsibilities.

Section One

1. Communicates a vision of diversity as a key aspect of the HR leader's responsibility
   (1) Never   (2) Sometimes   (3) Often   (4) Almost always
2. Encourages line managers to incorporate diversity in key HR programs
   (1) Never   (2) Sometimes   (3) Often   (4) Almost always
3. Asks diversity leaders for their input into HR programs
   (1) Never   (2) Sometimes   (3) Often   (4) Almost always
4. Expects HR staff to include diversity in their program planning
   (1) Never   (2) Sometimes   (3) Often   (4) Almost always

Section Two

1. Communicates frequently and effectively with diverse individuals/groups
   (1) Never   (2) Sometimes   (3) Often   (4) Almost always
2. Creates diverse work teams to resolve issues with substantial impact
   (1) Never   (2) Sometimes   (3) Often   (4) Almost always
3. Encourages expression of individual social identity(ies) in the workplace
   (1) Never   (2) Sometimes   (3) Often   (4) Almost always
4. Consciously seeks to create psychological safety in the workplace for diverse individuals
   (1) Never   (2) Sometimes   (3) Often   (4) Almost always

Section Three

1. Actively works to embed diversity and inclusion in organizational culture
   (1) Never   (2) Sometimes   (3) Often   (4) Almost always
2. Develops creative approaches to overcoming diversity resistance
   (1) Never   (2) Sometimes   (3) Often   (4) Almost always

(Continues)

3. Works with diversity leaders at different organizational levels to develop a concerted diversity strategy
   (1) Never   (2) Sometimes   (3) Often   (4) Almost always
4. Provides a safety net for diverse individuals in the organization
   (1) Never   (2) Sometimes   (3) Often   (4) Almost always

Section Four

1. Collaborates with line managers to incorporate diversity into organizational processes
   (1) Never   (2) Sometimes   (3) Often   (4) Almost always
2. Develops systematic organizational learning programs to strengthen diversity awareness and competency
   (1) Never   (2) Sometimes   (3) Often   (4) Almost always
3. Recognizes and rewards diverse individuals/groups equitably
   (1) Never   (2) Sometimes   (3) Often   (4) Almost always .
4. Develops diverse pipelines through hiring, mentoring, and promotion
   (1) Never   (2) Sometimes   (3) Often   (4) Almost always

Section Five

1. Monitors organizational processes and outcomes for equity purposes
   (1) Never   (2) Sometimes   (3) Often   (4) Almost always
2. Evaluates impact of supervisor/subordinate demography on employment actions such as promotion, compensation, and termination
   (1) Never   (2) Sometimes   (3) Often   (4) Almost always
3. Examines why diverse individuals leave the organization
   (1) Never   (2) Sometimes   (3) Often   (4) Almost always
4. Resolves discrimination-related issues before formal actions are initiated
   (1) Never   (2) Sometimes   (3) Often   (4) Almost always

To score your survey, add up the number in front of each answer (1–4) for a total score by category:

Section One: Develops strategic diversity vision

Total score:

Section Two: Promotes inclusive climate

Total score:

EXERCISE 4.1 (Continued)

Section Three: Leads cultural change

      Total score:

Section Four: Ensures inclusiveness in organizational processes

      Total score:

Section Five: Promotes diversity outcomes

      Total score:

Now add the scores of each section for an overall score: _____

The interpretation of your self-assessment profile is as follows:

Excellent: 65–80

You have integrated diversity vision with action-oriented approaches to embed diversity in the organizational culture, review organizational structures and process, and promote diversity outcomes.

Very good: 50–64

You have laid the groundwork for future success by making inroads into the key dimensions of workplace diversity. Focus on areas in this survey that can help you advance in the implementation of an inclusive workplace climate.

Average: 35–49

While you have strengths in certain areas, seek opportunities to have greater impact on the areas that received the lowest scores in small but tangible ways. Identify your areas of strength and build further on these.

Poor: 20–34

Consider ways to expand your HR/diversity skills and competencies and structural avenues to strengthen your contribution in the areas of responsibility you have in your organization. Seek guidance from internal and external mentors that may have insight into ways to enhance your impact and contributions.

Note: Adapted from Hubbard, E. E. (2004). *The Manager's Pocket Guide to Diversity Management*, pp. 2–9, by E. E. Hubbard, 2004, Amherst, MA: HRD Press. Adapted with permission.

Assessing Organizational Readiness for HR/Diversity Strategy Integration

We now turn to an examination of organizational readiness for HR/diversity integration. To build organizational capability for diversity that involves the integration of HR/diversity systems, organizational culture provides the ceiling, or values, that link strategy and practices (Yeung, Ulrich, Nason, & Von Glinow, 1999). Beneath this cultural ceiling, four critical areas are the pillars supporting strategy attainment: competence, consequences, governance, and capacity for change through work systems and processes (Yeung et al., 1999):

1. competence—the knowledge skills and abilities of individuals or teams
2. consequences—reinforcement of congruent actions and outcomes through evaluation and awards
3. governance—how the organization is structured and decisions are made
4. capacity for change through work systems and processes—the ways work is accomplished and allocated and the structuring of work systems to reinforce the capacity for change

The next step is to take the organizational pulse to determine areas that may need focused attention and to develop an action plan based on this assessment. Given our extensive discussion of diversity competency in the previous chapter, we now provide a sample organizational assessment that builds on the dimensions of consequences, governance, and capacity for change that support the organizational culture and mind-set. This assessment (see Exercise 4.2) provides an overview of the factors present in the organization that support or inhibit diversity change and require the active engagement of HR and diversity leaders.

In reviewing the dimensions addressed in this organizational assessment, consider how the Kellogg Company's diversity and inclusion strategy builds organizational capability for diversity through the organizational culture and mind-set, consequences, governance, and capacity for change. The company's strategy focuses on consequences by building accountability for diversity and inclusion throughout the organization, capacity for change by recruiting diverse talent and promoting diversity education and awareness, and organizational culture by creating an environment for inclusion ("Kellogg Company's 2010 Corporate Report on Diversity and Inclusion," 2011, cited hereafter as "Kellogg Company"). Kellogg's talent strategy seeks to create a workforce that mirrors its customer base among its 17,000 U.S.

EXERCISE 4.2
Organizational Readiness for Systematic HR/Diversity Integration

Organizational Culture and Mind-Set	*Yes*	*No*	*Needs Development*
HR initiatives that focus on diversity are an accepted part of our culture.			
We have a business case for diversity that integrates HR's role.			
Diversity is articulated as a value in our strategic planning documents and linked to HR systems.			
We have a shared and articulated diversity vision and mission that includes HR systems and outcomes.			
We have implemented formal and informal programs that promote dialogue across difference.			
We expect all organizational members to participate in a shared mind-set of diversity.			
We have developed experiential organizational learning programs that address diversity awareness.			
We have taken concrete steps to evaluate our climate for inclusiveness and to address microclimates of inequity.			
Consequences			
HR leaders play a visible role in delineating the importance of diversity in organizational processes.			
Performance evaluations require evidence of diversity outcomes in organizational processes.			
Organizational processes in each department/ division are reviewed regularly to ensure equity and inclusion.			
Recognition is given to organizational leaders who create inclusive workplaces through integrated HR/ diversity processes.			
Governance			
The organization is inclusive in its governance and strategic planning processes.			
The organization builds diverse cross-functional task forces and teams.			

(Continues)

EXERCISE 4.2 (Continued)

Organizational Culture and Mind-Set	Yes	No	Needs Development
Decision-making authority is held by diverse individuals in the organization.			
The organization maintains a focus on distributive justice to ensure equitable distribution of resources.			
The organization encourages external benchmarking to attain more inclusive practices.			
Information regarding governance discussions is disseminated at all levels.			
Capacity for Change Through Work Systems and Processes			
The organization values and rewards innovation and creativity regardless of the source.			
Managers create psychological safety for employees that allows creativity and innovation.			
Diverse clients are involved in the design of products and solutions to provide feedback.			
Inclusive stretch goals are set for creation of an inclusive organization.			
The organization creates engagement on issues of diversity and inclusion.			
The physical setting promotes dialogue and inclusion.			

Note: From *Organizational Learning Capability: Generating and Generalizing Ideas With Impact*, by A. K. Yeung, D. Ulrich, S. W. Nason, & M. A. Von Glinow, 1999, New York, NY: Oxford University Press. Copyright 1999 by Oxford University Press. Adapted with permission.

employees and works with talent acquisition alliances to promote the hiring of women and minorities ("Kellogg Company," 2011). According to Carol Stewart, president and chief executive officer of Kellogg Canada, "The corporate culture is all about the people—we are very people-driven and relationship-oriented" rather than bottom-line-oriented (para. 3). In Stewart's view, retention means locating and hiring employees whose passions and values match those of the company's ("Kellogg Company," 2011).

As part of the governance structure for diversity, Kellogg formed a Global Learning and Insights Community (GLIC) in 2011, composed of the top 150 Kellogg executives around the world ("Kellogg's 2011 Corporate Responsibility Report," 2012). The company further strengthened the relationship of diversity to governance in 2012 by tying diversity and inclusion performance to the compensation reviews of its senior leaders ("Kellogg's 2011 Corporate Responsibility Report," 2012).

Since the capacity for change is at the centerpiece of HR/diversity transformation, we now move from assessment of individual and organizational readiness to the process of building organizational capacity and creating a long-term plan for cultural transformation.

Creating Capacity for Transformational Change

Undertaking diversity transformation is a particular problem since diversity still remains a controversial, highly political, and contested area. In some organizations, discussions of race, gender, sexual orientation, and other ascriptive differences may even be viewed as taboo (Harper & Hurtado, 2007). In the realm of organizational politics, diversity constitutes a political position, and when an issue is identified as political, change often will be less likely to occur because of conflict and resistance (Kezar, 2008). Emotional resistance arises when organizational actors believe change implies that previous behaviors or attitudes were inadequate or wrong (Schein, 2009).

The process of *reculturing*, or changing what is valued in organizational culture, must first involve stakeholders in reciprocal dialogue or making sense and then solidify changes through concrete task or role realignment rather than simply relying on attitudinal shifts (Beer, Eisenstat, & Spector, 1990a; Fullan, 2002). The timing and pace of such change efforts must be calibrated to particular organizational realities and can alternate between relatively long periods of incremental change and occasional reorientations or dramatic revolutions that involved rapid, discontinuous shifts in strategy, distribution of power, core structures, and control systems (Tushman & Romanelli, 1985). We also indicated earlier the importance of a phase-based approach, such as through the sequential or complementary implementation of phases or tracks like the management skills track, team-building track, strategy-structure track, and the rewards track (Kilmann, 1984).

Internal acceptance of diversity change efforts is affected by contextual factors such as leadership support, bifurcated organizational structures, bureaucratic processes, cultural awareness, and organizational climate. External environmental factors that have an impact on the urgency of change include economic, regulatory, and competitive pressures. In higher education, accreditation serves as a powerful external factor. The situational context affects the speed of adopting change and the acceptance of the need for change by organizational stakeholders.

Mapping the Phases of Diversity Organization Development

As a model for systemic diversity organization development, we build upon the foundational principles provided by Lewin's three-step model of change: unfreezing, moving, and refreezing (Burnes, 2009). Lewin's seminal work in the field of organization development identified the importance of destabilizing or unfreezing equilibrium before moving from old patterns of behavior to new modes of interaction (Burnes, 2009). After moving to new models, organizations must take steps to refreeze the culture to ensure that behaviors will not revert to earlier, regressive tendencies (Burnes, 2009; Evans & Chun, 2012). We amplify Lewin's theory with reference to other leading theorists (e.g., Bridges, 2003; Brockbank, 2009; Ruben, 2009; Schein, 2009; Ulrich, Allen, Brockbank, Younger, & Nyman, 2009) and then specifically address the partnership of HR and diversity in each of these phases.

In the first phase of unfreezing the culture in the change process, HR and diversity leaders must work to build awareness in terms of the business case for diversity. A primary focus needs to be on organizational learning initiatives that surface and unpack assumptions and prevailing cultural norms that inhibit acceptance of differences. This period involves ending the status quo, which for some individuals means losing and letting go (Bridges, 2003). It also means taking account of the threat that diversity change represents. In this critical phase of preparation, strategies for input, dialogue, and discussion can include creating focus groups to discuss the change, holding town hall meetings and communication forums, and developing collaborative alliances across employment groups and hierarchical divides. Planning for the development of a diversity strategic action plan will provide a broad framework for the change effort. Diversity councils can play a leading role in ensuring the participation of employees at all levels of the organization and across decentralized or dispersed units and divisions. Psychological safety is an important facet of the unfreezing process to allow employees to share input and feedback without anger, defensiveness, or retribution.

The second stage requires creating the motivation for change through employee engagement and developing responses and commitment to organizational direction based on new information. As a transition between the status quo and the new phase, this phase can mean the difference between success and failure in organizational change efforts. In effect, the intermediate phase between the old and the new is a "neutral zone" when leadership must define what is over and what needs to be left behind (Bridges, 2003, p. 4). In the neutral zone, reorientation and redefinition occur in a period of repatterning when leaders need to expect and accept signs of grieving, compensate for the losses, and let people take a piece of the old with them (Bridges, 2003). HR/diversity leaders can create organizational interventions to trigger repatterning processes, develop transition teams to discuss pending changes, and model new behaviors and mind-sets in experiential organizational learning programs.

Once the neutral zone is crossed, a new beginning becomes possible and cannot be forced but must be encouraged, reinforced, and supported (Bridges, 2003). The third stage involves stabilizing and integrating the change in organizational processes and practices (Ruben, 2009; Schein, 2009). Progression to this stage can only occur if the organization is prepared in the neutral zone by acknowledging psychological losses, clearly presenting the need for the change, and strengthening intragroup connections (Bridges, 2003). HR leaders can solidify the change by fostering intragroup communication through cross-functional task forces and teams and by developing policies, practices, and reward systems that formalize the new processes, behaviors, and performance objectives.

In embarking on the three-step process of organizational change, HR/diversity strategy must integrate with external requirements and the internal business strategy to define the culture needed to realize diversity capability (Brockbank, 2009). A clear read of cultural interactions is necessary. In effect, HR and diversity leaders need to ask, How will people behave differently in the future if diversity capability is executed at an ideal level? Or, to put it another way, what behavior will the organization need more of, and what will it need less of? (Brockbank, 2009).

An example of an institutional response to this question can be found in an approach developed by HR at the Massachusetts Institute of Technology that clarifies foundational diversity behaviors supporting an inclusive workplace (Table 4.1). It describes the essential workplace dynamics that affect individuals as they perform their work (Norton & Fox, 1997).

The approach adopted by MIT solidifies the observation that many diversity programs have failed because they only emphasize awareness and understanding differences rather than teaching skills and behaviors needed to relate effectively in the workplace (Hemphill & Haines, 1997). We would recommend further amplification of MIT's taxonomy of workplace behaviors to take into account the extensive literature on subtle forms of discrimination, including microinequities or small, recurring, and cumulative messages, conduct, and behaviors that marginalize diverse individuals.

TABLE 4.1
Creating an Inclusive and Supportive Environment

Diversity Behavior	*Description*	*Examples of Observable Behaviors*
Listening to Understand	Listening with an open mind to fully understand all aspects of a situation	• Seeking multiple points of view during problem investigation • Using open-ended questions • Asking about a situation before characterizing it • Listening carefully to the person speaking until he/she feels understood • Seeking suggestions and ideas from staff
Seeking Multiple Points of View	Understanding that our perspective is not the only one when looking at a situation, issue, or problem	• Soliciting other relevant points of view • Inviting employees from other parts of the organization to staff meetings • Engaging in collaborative learning • Using cross-functional teams for project and other assignments
Giving and Receiving Feedback	Inviting and giving feedback	• Communicating clearly, directly, and honestly • Giving feedback to employees when the impact of their words or actions differ from their intent • Inviting feedback about the impact of your words and/or actions • Receiving feedback without defensiveness • Giving direct feedback about behavior and/or performance • Thanking people for direct feedback to you

TABLE 4.1 (Continued)

Diversity Behavior	Description	Examples of Observable Behaviors
Enhancing Inclusion	Helping employees feel included and involved	• Integrating newly hired employees into the department • Increasing the diversity in all work groups • Discussing diversity issues at a staff/team meeting • Integrating work/life considerations into work priorities • Establishing and implementing an effective meeting process and managing it • Increasing face-to face interactions with employees • Speaking up when people are excluded
Addressing Inappropriate Workplace Behavior	Acknowledging inappropriate behavior; communicating expectations and consequences for repeated behavior	• Setting group processes and norms that foster trust and respect • Taking action when issues of disrespect happen • Stopping disrespectful jokes or language • Proactively address[es] and resolves conflict

Note: From *Creating an Inclusive and Supportive Environment*, n.d., http://hrweb.mit.edu/diversity/affirmative-action-plan-admins/resources. Copyright 2013 by Massachusetts Institute of Technology. Reprinted with permission.

As another example of unfreezing, moving, and then refreezing cultural norms, consider the affirmative expectations for employee behaviors from Hewlett Packard, the world's largest information technology company: "Our aspiration is that the behaviors and actions that support diversity and inclusion will come from the conviction of every HP employee—making diversity and inclusion a conscious part of how we run our business throughout the world" ("HP: Our Vision and Strategy," 2013). This aspirational statement underscores the company's expectation that conviction and consciousness of the importance of diversity will be reflected in each employee's interactions with clients.

Barriers to Collaboration

Creation of new mental models for diversity is a challenge that presents considerable difficulty yet must be addressed head-on. HR and diversity professionals are faced with persistent organizational defensive routines—actions, policies, or practices that prevent organizational members from experiencing embarrassment or a threat relating to diversity and discovering the causes of the embarrassment or threat (Argyris, 1995). Such defensive routines prevent anxiety-producing identity change and preserve collective and individual self-esteem (see Brown & Starkey, 2009).

One of the main problems relating to defensive routines about diversity is that they are not discussable. HR professionals face a double bind: If they do not discuss them, they will continue to proliferate, but if they do, the individuals who bring them up may get in trouble (Argyris, 1986). Ironically, defensive routines related to diversity can persist in a defensive loop, reinforced and protected by HR professionals who prefer that they be eliminated but cannot discuss their covert protection (Argyris, 1986). Mixed messages may also characterize interactions relating to diversity: sending messages that are inconsistent such as high-level statements about the value of diversity and then not supporting diversity in the hiring process (Argyris, 2002). This inconsistency itself can become organizationally nondiscussable and result in forms of diversity as lip service or mere window dressing without changing the existing culture (Aguirre & Martinez, 2007; Argyris, 2002).

What are the characteristics of organizational learning programs that overcome defensive routines related to diversity? These programs must avoid the phenomenon of single-loop learning (correcting errors or behaviors without altering underlying values) and initiate double-loop learning (correcting errors or behaviors by changing governing values and then succeeding actions; Argyris, 2002). Take, for example, the successful diversity organizational learning effort represented by the Campus Diversity Initiative (CDI) sponsored by the James Irvine Foundation involving 28 independent colleges and universities in California. This initiative was designed to strengthen diversity efforts and increase the success of historically underrepresented students and monitor success using a collaborative organizational learning model (Smith & Parker, 2005).

The CDI project demonstrates the value of a system-level framework for diversity organizational learning. The CDI framework is guided by principles that can be applied in other contexts including (a) a focus on organizational issues (e.g., mission, needs, culture) rather than project-specific concerns, (b) examination of success and problems in results and processes, (c) exploration of possibilities for taking risks and learning from these opportunities, and (d) identification of stages of organizational development in relation to diversity (Smith & Parker, 2005). The use of a meta-framework *depersonalizes* the learning process and facilitates double-loop learning by focusing attention on the organization and its culture rather than on the values and assumptions of individual actors. And such a framework clearly addresses the business case for why a shift in cultural values is important to overall organizational success. Then the question of "What's in it for me?" becomes "What's in it for us?"

When HR leaders undertake the difficult task of changing mental mind-sets in support of diversity, they must also understand the differing standpoints of differently positioned social actors in the workplace (Oliha & Collier, 2010). Members of minority and majority groups differ in their view of the organization's state of diversity, equity, and inclusion (Oliha & Collier, 2010). Consider, for example, the variance between minority and majority groups relating to the value of race-based Affirmative Action plans. A research study involving a laboratory and a field component examined the relation between individuals who held modern racism (MR) beliefs (the belief that racial minorities are no longer subject to discrimination and receive unfair advantage in contemporary society) and collective relative deprivation (CRD) beliefs (the belief that Whites are disadvantaged relative to racial minorities) in relation to their perceptions of race-based Affirmative Action plans (AAP; Shteynberg, Leslie, Knight, & Mayer, 2011). The results of this study revealed that individuals who hold relatively high MR or CRD beliefs perceive greater disadvantage to Whites in organizations with race-based AAPs, as compared to race-neutral equal employment opportunity (EEO) policies. These researchers suggest that organizations may be able to minimize backlash through training programs aimed at changing Whites' MR and CRD beliefs. Such change could be approached by reducing perceptions of White disadvantage coupled with an emphasis on a climate in which diversity is valued and seen as a valuable resource (Shteynberg et al., 2011). Furthermore, race-neutral language that emphasizes equal opportunity to succeed will likely reduce backlash to EEO policies and AAPs in organizations with race-neutral policies (Shteynberg et al., 2011).

A significant longitudinal study based on 708 cases with a minimum of 25 years of data per case from the Equal Employment Opportunity Commission (EEOC) sheds further light on effective approaches to diversity training (Kalev, Dobbin, & Kelly, 2006). The study found that diversity training programs that addressed managerial stereotyping and targeted individual bias or network isolation are less effective than programs that establish accountability for diversity results through structures such as affirmative action plans, diversity staff, and diversity task forces (Kalev et al., 2006). In essence, White males report being tired of being cast as oppressors and made to feel guilty in diversity discussions (Hemphill & Haines, 1997). Researchers in this study also found that interactions with responsibility structures did render training, evaluation, networking, and mentoring more effective, with modest increased effects when the training is associated with regulatory requirements for federal contractors (Kalev et al., 2006). Programs disconnected from everyday practice often have no impact.

From a positive perspective, organizational learning programs need to recognize the role of "White men as champions" (Cross, 2000), and emphasize that simply being a member of a dominant group does not mean that all members have power, equal opportunities, or are accepted by the group. White women also can share dominant-group attitudes and behaviors relating to race, while minority men can share dominant group attitudes toward gender (Cross, 2000). When diversity initiatives only involve minorities, such efforts can be perceived as outside the mainstream of organizational culture in areas that have limited social capital and are undervalued (Aguirre & Martinez, 2007). Engagement of the leadership of majority group members is an important component of diversity initiatives and organizational learning programs.

In the effort to change mental mind-sets, diversity intervention strategies that begin with a case study scenario that allows participants to contextualize a situation with actual events and then enables participants to engage within a defined context will lead to greater success (Oliha & Collier, 2010). Participants can identify different voices and social conditions, recognize conflicting factors in the struggle over the meaning of diversity and what diversity initiatives should accomplish, and identify strategies that incorporate divergent voices applied to a wide variety of settings (Oliha & Collier, 2010). Such approaches that probe for understanding through discussion will be more likely to minimize resistance and defensiveness.

For HR leaders, awareness of the common pitfalls of diversity training is critical since such programs can increase rather than diminish resistance. Some of these pitfalls include divisive, counterproductive programs led by inexperienced trainers; blaming or stereotyping of White males; raising and then disappointing minority expectations; and bringing out sensitive, personal issues in hostile public settings (Hemphill & Haines, 1997).

Challenges and Opportunities

As described in this chapter, organizations face a considerable gauntlet of challenges in implementing effective double-loop organizational learning programs that address and reshape cultural norms and assumptions about diversity. HR and diversity leaders bear the difficult and sometimes thankless responsibility of cracking the code of predominant behaviors to develop approaches that will align internal culture with external realities. They can be assisted in this effort by synergy across all levels of the organization, including the active endorsement and advocacy of senior leadership and the participation of cross-functional alliances, councils, and employee resource groups. Instead of a patchwork of disparate, piecemeal efforts, HR and diversity leaders must instigate coordinated, systemic change.

Readiness is a key consideration of the change process. Leaders must gauge when and whom to engage and the pace of such engagement. Organizational learning programs need to provide nonthreatening opportunities to frame and articulate the undiscussable in acceptable organizational terms. As co-owners with line managers of the organizational capability of diversity, HR and diversity leaders must develop successful strategies that enhance their partnership with line management. In the final analysis, line managers play an instrumental role in the implementation of processes that enhance inclusion in the day-to-day working environment. In the next chapter, we discuss the development of a concrete plan to build and implement a successful and effective HR talent architecture for diversity.

Strategic and Tactical Questions for Further Discussion

The following questions focus on the organizational learning process as well as formal and informal practices that address behavioral interactions related to diversity.

1. What types of organizational learning programs for diversity have been successful in your organization? Which have been less successful? Why?
2. If you could design a new organizational learning program for diversity, what specific approaches could you use to ensure double-loop learning?
3. How has diversity backlash manifested itself in your organizational culture? What specific organizational development interventions could address it?
4. In what ways could HR leaders in your organization enhance their role as change agents for diversity?

5. Has your organization sought to address behaviors for diversity in formal systems such as evaluations, reward systems, or training programs? If so, how effective have these programs been in changing day-to-day climate and interactions? If not, what are the barriers to creating such programs?

Case Study 6: Integrating HR and Diversity Governmental Strategy at the U.S. Office of Personnel Management

In 2010 John Berry, director of the U.S. Office of Personnel Management (OPM), and Christine Griffin, deputy director, initiated a workgroup to examine how diversity and inclusion could be applied to the federal government. In June 2010 a separate initiative was begun by the Human Capital Shared Interest Group (HC SIG) to further collaboration among human capital management professionals. Angela Bailey, deputy associate director of recruitment and hiring at OPM, asked HC SIG to conduct a diversity and inclusion study of federal agencies and corporations that identified best practices in the field.

HC SIG (2011) published a study of 12 of the best performing agencies and corporations in terms of diversity and inclusion practices. The study concluded that diversity should be broadly defined including, but not limited to, legally protected groups. It cited leading best practices in a number of areas: committed leadership, rigorous management, integrated infrastructure, aligned culture and systems, intensive communications, targeted diversity policy and initiatives, and metrics and accountability.

In 2010 a new office of diversity and inclusion was created at OPM, reporting to Berry with Veronica Villalobos as its first director. Villalobos had formerly worked at the U.S. EEOC as the director of the Office of Equal Opportunity and was one of the EEOC's first honor program attorneys. Villalobos was charged with providing a framework for all federal agencies to promote a diverse and inclusive federal workforce.

Nancy Kichak, associate director of human resource policy at OPM, describes the newly formed Office of Diversity and Inclusion as an important impetus for building a coordinated diversity and inclusion strategy:

> I think what is driving us to focus on this in a way that it hasn't been focused upon before [is] to create a separate office to do policies and work plans for the governmentwide initiative. . . . And it's the leadership committing to building that office and listening to what that office has to say that is driving the preliminary success. (N. Kichak, personal communication, August 30, 2012)

Meanwhile, the new work group formed by Berry and Griffin at OPM brought together 30 federal agencies and 50 participants to develop a more coordinated and aligned diversity and inclusion effort in the federal government. Members of the work group immediately realized that HR needed to be more heavily involved in the diversity and inclusion process in view of its significant role in recruitment, hiring, professional development, succession planning, and work/life programs. While the EEOC was doing an excellent job, its responsibilities were focused on the enforcement of federal antidiscrimination laws. The work group formulated a draft of a Diversity and Inclusion Strategic Plan, which was submitted to the White House.

The Evolution of Executive Order 13583

President Barack Obama not only endorsed the work group's draft of the strategic plan but also decided to issue an executive order that established a coordinated governmental initiative for promoting diversity and inclusion in the federal workforce (White House, 2011). Obama had already issued two prior executive orders that strengthened diversity in the federal government:

1. Executive Order No. 13518 (2009), Employment of Veterans in the Federal Government, directed federal agencies to create a Veterans Employment Initiative.
2. Executive Order No. 13548 (2010), Increasing Federal Employment of Individuals With Disabilities, built on President Clinton's Executive Order No. 13163 (2000), Increasing the Opportunity for Individuals With Disabilities to be Employed in the Federal Government, which called for an additional 100,000 individuals with disabilities to be employed by the federal government over five years.

Executive Order No. 13583 addresses structural and programmatic changes in executive departments and agencies of the federal government designed "to develop and implement a more comprehensive, integrated, and strategic focus on diversity and inclusion as a key component of their human resource strategies" (White House, 2011). According to Villalobos, the alliance of HR strategies with diversity and inclusion is specifically focused upon the creation of "high-performing organizations for the 21st century," workplaces that attract, develop, and retain diverse and talented employees (V. Villalobos, personal communication, September 11, 2012). This alliance was solidified by the requirement that each agency's chief human capital officer is the responsible official for enhancing the goals of the Government-wide Diversity and Inclusion Strategic Plan in collaboration with the agency's chief diversity officer and director of equal opportunity.

The Government-wide Diversity and Inclusion Strategic Plan, issued after the executive order in 2011, describes the business imperative for inclusion in three areas:

1. workforce diversity: attaining a high-performing workforce by recruiting from diverse, qualified applicants
2. workplace inclusion: cultivating a culture of fairness, collaboration and flexibility that fosters retention and the contributions of individuals who maximize their potential
3. sustainability: developing strategies and structures that equip leaders to manage diversity, be accountable, develop measurable strategies, and institutionalize an inclusive culture (U. S. OPM, Office of Diversity and Inclusion, 2011)

Executive Order No. 13583 called for the government-wide plan to be updated every four years. In addition, it specified that federal agencies should develop a diversity and inclusion strategic plan within a 120-day time frame that addresses recruiting, hiring, training, developing, promoting, and retaining a diverse workforce.

The Rapid Development of Agency Plans

Given the short time frame for agencies to develop diversity and inclusion plans, in November 2011, OPM (2011) issued "Guidance for Agency-Specific Diversity and Inclusion Plans" to assist agencies in the development of their individual agency plans. This guidance called for greater collaboration between HR programs, equal opportunity programs, and diversity and inclusion efforts in each agency. The document gives examples of priorities, actions, measurements, and sample practices for each goal.

Villalobos saw the effort as not just a way to diversify the workforce but as one directed toward building innovation in the workplace. In this light, agency administrators were encouraged to be mindful of their efforts to accomplish three things: diversify, include, and sustain. Under a broad definition of *diversity*, Villalobos provided specific guidelines for agency practices and actions to support the three goals. Diversifying the workforce requires robust outreach including, for example, veterans and those with disabilities. Inclusion practices involve professional development and leadership programs throughout the employment cycle including mentoring, succession planning, and work/life and onboarding practices. Sustainability of diversity efforts can be promoted by leveraging the use of employee resource and affinity groups, creating diversity and inclusion councils, and ensuring that diversity requirements are reflected in performance plans.

Executive Order No. 13583 was signed in August 2011, and agency strategic plans were submitted in March 2012. As the first plans reached her desk, Villalobos saw the need for a greater focus on the inclusion and sustainability aspects:

> We are also asking agencies through inclusion to think of it as an opportunity to develop each employee to their full potential, and so we are saying it is not about any one group. It's about making sure everyone feels included; everyone feels considered; they experience the workplace as fair. . . . And one of the things I tell folks is that if agencies truly had robust succession plan where people feel like that they were being considered, [that] they were on a deep bench of talent and gaps were being filled in, I think that would go a long way to make people feel included in the workplace. And then the last question is: Is it sustainable? We want to make sure that it is not just an initiative of today. I tell everyone, "Don't call yourself an initiative, don't call yourself an effort." We don't call HR the HR initiative or the EEO initiative, right? So this is diversity and inclusion and we want to make sure that this is a practice that continues throughout government service long after we're all gone.

Villalobos created feedback assistance tables and brought a cluster of three agencies at a time to OPM's innovation labs—a technology hub for innovative problem solving located in OPM's subbasement (Kolawole, 2012). The innovation lab was designed to provide a space to work on human-centered design and solve the "wicked problems" facing government. As the clusters began to meet, the participants realized they really did have innovative practices that looked bland when put into writing. Villalobos provided the agency participants with written feedback, and they now check back quarterly.

The next step is for the agencies to report on progress using the metrics designed by the Office of Diversity and Inclusion. The metrics include representation based on race, ethnicity, national origin, gender, sexual orientation, veterans' status, and disabilities; career progress; attrition rates; and scores for inclusive workplace practices on the Federal Employment Viewpoint Survey, a tool that measures employees' perceptions of their agencies. Finally, the metrics measure agency progress on actions taken to make diversity and inclusion sustainable at each agency. Villalobos is in the process of creating infographs on key variables agencies can provide their own leadership that include demographic comparisons to the civilian labor force.

Future Directions

The coordinated diversity and inclusion strategy at OPM relies on the coordination of the HR office, the Diversity and Inclusion Office, and the EEO office—what some describe as a three-legged stool. In essence, the model at the government-wide level with the chief human capital officer as the responsible official for workforce strategy working in collaboration with the director of diversity and the director of EEO is replicated in every agency. Kichak said that this collaborative organizational arrangement has its own challenges.

> It does take a willful effort to make sure that since the HR office does the hiring and the D&I [diversity and inclusion] office has a policy lead . . . that they stay integrated and on the same mission. . . . The organizational structure does create some barriers; but if you work together and you develop a team, these barriers can be overcome. . . . I think the closeness of these organizations is growing.

Yet she said she sees the purposeful intent of this integration:

> Diversity is the cornerstone of all HR strategic planning. Because we believe that in order to get the best which is our goal, that [diversity] has to be recognized and achieved also. In other words, best is not just the person with the best academic credentials, best is the workforce that represents America.

Villalobos similarly described her vision for government-wide diversity as "a federal workplace that looks like America and that is solving a lot of the challenges we have through the use of different lines of innovation." She views the principal challenges as sustaining diversity and inclusion efforts and integrating the work of the HR, diversity, and EEO offices:

> For me, the most important thing is how are we going to make it sustainable; how do we ensure that this is not just the flavor of the month? And how do we ensure that HR, EEO, and Diversity and Inclusion really work together to provide the best service for the whole agency? Because when we work together, I think we can show the value added so much better.

References

Aguirre, A., Jr., & Martinez, R. O. (2007). *Diversity leadership in higher education* (ASHE-ERIC Higher Education Reports, Vol. 32, No. 3). San Francisco, CA: Jossey-Bass.

Argyris, C. (1986). Reinforcing organizational defensive routines: An unintended human resources activity. *Human Resource Management, 25*(4), 541–555.

Argyris, C. (1995). Action science and organizational learning. *Journal of Managerial Psychology, 10*(6), 20–26.

Argyris, C. (2002). Double-loop learning, teaching, and research. *Academy of Management Learning & Education, 1*(2), 206–218.

Beer, M., Eisenstat, R. A., & Spector, B. (1990). Why change programs don't produce change. *Harvard Business Review, 68*(6), 158–166.

Bridges, W. (2003). *Managing transitions: Making the most of change* (2nd ed.). Cambridge, MA: Perseus.

Brockbank, W. (2009). *Tool 2.5 external environment.* Retrieved from http://www.transformHR.com

Brown, A. D., & Starkey, K. (2009). Organizational identity and learning: A psychodynamic perspective. In W. W. Burke, D. G. Lake, & J. W. Paine (Eds.), *Organization change: A comprehensive reader* (pp. 481–511). San Francisco, CA: Wiley.

Burnes, B. (2009). Kurt Lewin and the planned approach to change: A reappraisal. In W. W. Burke, D. G. Lake, & J. W. Paine (Eds.), *Organization change: A comprehensive reader* (pp. 226–254). San Francisco, CA: Wiley.

Creating an inclusive and supportive environment. (n.d.). Retrieved from Michigan Institute of Technology Human Resources website: http://hrweb.mit.edu/diversity/affirmative-action-plan-admins/resources

Cross, E. Y. (2000). White men as champions. *Diversity Factor, 8*(3), 2–7.

Edmondson, A. C. (2012). *Teaming: How organizations learn, innovate, and compete in the knowledge economy.* San Francisco, CA: Jossey-Bass.

Evans, A., & Chun, E. B. (2012). *Creating a tipping point: Strategic human resources in higher education.* San Francisco, CA: Jossey-Bass.

Executive Order No. 13163. (2000). Increasing the opportunity for individuals with disabilities to be employed in the federal government. *Federal Register, 65*(146). Retrieved from http://www.gpo.gov/fdsys/pkg/FR-2000-07-28/pdf/00-19322.pdf

Executive Order No. 13518. (2009). Employment of veterans in the federal government. *Federal Register, 74*(218). Retrieved from http://www.gpo.gov/fdsys/pkg/FR-2009-11-13/pdf/E9-27441.pdf

Executive Order No. 13548. (2010), Increasing federal employment of individuals with disabilities. *Federal Register, 75*(146). Retrieved from http://www.gpo.gov/fdsys/pkg/FR-2010-07-30/pdf/2010-18988.pdf

Fullan, M. (2002). The change leader. *Educational Leadership, 59*(8), 16–20.

Harper, S. R., & Hurtado, S. (2007). Nine themes in campus racial climates and implications. In S. R. Harper & L. D. Patton (Eds.), *Responding to the realities of race on campus: New Directions for student services* (pp. 7–24). San Francisco, CA: Jossey-Bass.

Hemphill, H., & Haines, R. (1997). *Discrimination, harassment, and the failure of diversity training: What to do now.* Westport, CT: Greenwood.

HP: Our vision and strategy. (2013). Retrieved from http://www8.hp.com/us/en/hp-information/about-hp/diversity/vision.html

Hubbard, E. E. (2004). *The manager's pocket guide to diversity management.* Amherst, MA: HRD Press.

Human Capital Shared Interest Group. (2011). *Becoming more competitive: How diversity and inclusion can transform your organization.* Retrieved from http://www.actgov

.org/knowledgebank/whitepapers/Documents/Forms/FIFO.aspx?rootFolder=%
2Fknowledgebank%2Fwhitepapers%2FDocuments%2FShared%20Interest%20
Groups%2FHuman%20Capital%20SIG&FolderCTID=&View={31DBB49B
-5ACC-4CA6-B253-B31A78703B8F}

Kalev, A., Dobbin, F., & Kelly, E. (2006). Best practices or best guesses? Assessing the efficacy of corporate Affirmative Action and diversity policies. *American Sociological Review, 71*(4), 589–617.

Kellogg Company's 2010 corporate report on diversity and inclusion. (2011). Retrieved from http://kelloggdiversityandinclusion.com/docs/2010_DandI.pdf

Kellogg's 2011 corporate responsibility report. (2012). Retrieved from http://www.kelloggcompany.com/content/dam/kelloggcompanyus/corporate_responsibility/pdf/2011CR/2011_Kelloggs_CRR.pdf

Kezar, A. J. (2008). Understanding leadership strategies for addressing the politics of diversity. *Journal of Higher Education, 79*(4), 406–441.

Kilmann, R. H. (1984). *Beyond the quick fix: Managing five tracks to organizational success.* San Francisco, CA: Jossey-Bass.

Kolawole, E. (2012). Office of personnel management's "innovation lab" a portal to Silicon Valley. *Washington Post.* Retrieved from http://articles.washingtonpost.com/2012-08-02/national/35490359_1_web-site-silicon-valley-new-leadership

Norton, J. R., & Fox, R. E. (1997). *The change equation: Capitalizing on diversity for effective organizational change.* Washington, DC: American Psychological Association.

Oliha, H., & Collier, M. J. (2010). Bridging divergent diversity standpoints & ideologies: Organizational initiatives and trainings. *International Journal of Diversity in Organisations, Communities & Nations, 10*(4), 61–73.

Ruben, B. D. (2009). *Understanding, planning, and leading organizational change: Core concepts and strategies.* Washington, DC: National Association of College and University Business Officers.

Schein, E. H. (2004). *Organizational culture and leadership* (3rd ed.). San Francisco, CA: Jossey-Bass.

Schein, E. H. (2009). The mechanisms of change. In W. W. Burke, D. G. Lake, & J. W. Paine (Eds.), *Organization change: A comprehensive reader* (pp. 78–88). San Francisco, CA: Wiley.

Shteynberg, G., Leslie, L. M., Knight, A. P., & Mayer, D. M. (2011). But Affirmative Action hurts *us!* Race-related beliefs shape perceptions of White disadvantage and policy unfairness. *Organizational Behavior and Human Decision Processes, 115*(1), 1–12.

Smith, D. G., & Parker, S. (2005). Organizational learning: A tool for diversity and institutional effectiveness. In A. J. Kezar (Ed.), *Organizational learning in higher education* (pp. 113–126). San Francisco, CA: Jossey-Bass.

Tushman, M. L., & Romanelli, E. (1985). Organization evolution: A metamorphosis model of convergence and reorientation. In B. Staw & L. L. Cummings (Eds.), *Research in Organizational Behavior* (Vol. 7). Greenwich, CT: JAI Press.

Ulrich, D., Allen, J., Brockbank, W., Younger, J., & Nyman, M. (2009). *HR transformation: Building human resources from the outside in.* New York, NY: McGraw-Hill.

U.S. Office of Personnel Management. (2011). *Guidance for agency-specific diversity and inclusion strategic plans.* Retrieved from http://www.opm.gov/diversityandinclusion/reports/DIAgencySpecificStrategicPlanGuidance.pdf

U. S. Office of Personnel Management, Office of Diversity and Inclusion. (2011). *Government-wide diversity and inclusion strategic plan 2011.* Retrieved from http://archive.opm.gov/diversityandinclusion/reports/GovernmentwideDIStrategicPlan.pdf

White House. (2011). *Executive order 13583—Establishing a coordinated government-wide initiative to promote diversity and inclusion in the federal workforce.* Retrieved from   http://www.whitehouse.gov/the-press-office/2011/08/18/executive-order -establishing-coordinated-government-wide-initiative-prom

Yeung, A. K., Ulrich, D., Nason, S. W., & Von Glinow, M. A. (1999). *Organizational learning capability: Generating and generalizing ideas with impact.* New York, NY: Oxford University Press.

5

CREATING THE HR TALENT
INFRASTRUCTURE
FOR DIVERSITY

Diversity is a visible, ongoing commitment that over time becomes so clear that we don't have to announce as a separate priority; . . . that's the ultimate. As you know we have a long journey to go before we get there, but it just becomes so clear in everything we do and the expectations of . . . HR professionals, that it just becomes second nature; it becomes a part of who we are. (Andy Brantley, chief executive officer, College and University Professional Association for Human Resources)

We turn now to how to build an HR infrastructure for the new talent frontier that will secure sustainable competitive advantage in a global economy. This chapter examines ways to strengthen the confluence of integrated HR and diversity practices in a comprehensive talent management and talent sustainability strategy. What differentiates our model from other talent management approaches is the systematic integration of diversity and HR strategy throughout the talent continuum.

Above all, talent management needs to be tied to business strategy and to build organizational capacity. To achieve competitive success through talent requires a fundamental alteration in how employers think about the workforce and the employment relationship (Pfeffer, Hatano, & Santalainen, 2005). Rather than viewing people as commodities to be replaced, talent management is a core business practice that must be ingrained as an active mind-set among leaders at all levels in the organization (Pfeffer et al., 2005; Silzer & Dowell, 2010).

The perfect storm arising from the rapidly accelerating forces of change in the global marketplace underscores the necessity of marrying the *functionality* of rigorous talent processes with *vitality* or emotional commitment by management to create a dynamic talent management process (Ready & Conger, 2007). Organizations must leverage the cultural differential, that is, the collective leadership and cultural aptitudes of the organization, such as the ability to manage change, build teams, and instigate organizational learning

(Petrick, Scherer, Brodzinski, Quinn, & Ainina, 1999). Yet a survey of executives from 40 companies conducted in 2005 found that virtually all felt they had an insufficient talent pipeline of high-potential employees to fill leadership roles (Ready & Conger, 2007). More than half the specialists polled found they had difficulty keeping executive leaders' attention on talent issues (Ready & Conger, 2007).

Cohesive, integrated talent management systems can unlock and build upon the cultural differential and nurture the diverse talent resources of an organization. To do so, HR and diversity leaders must be the architects and catalysts for a change strategy that embeds diversity in organizational structures, programs, policies, processes, and reward systems. HR systems knit together the functional repertoire of soloistic HR/diversity practices to create integrated processes that transcend divisional and departmental lines, separate lines of business, and the geographic dispersion of organizational units.

As a starting point, organizational mindfulness is needed to build capacity for ongoing learning about how decision making takes place and ways to advance participation and improve inclusive excellence (Sturm, 2006). This mindfulness extends beyond the business case for diversity to an action-oriented agenda that critically assesses how decision making occurs and the participation of diverse employees in formulating policy. HR is a champion of inclusive excellence when it evaluates how organizational processes unfold and the ways diverse talent is recognized, valued, supported, and included.

In this regard, consider the insights of Joe Santana, senior director of diversity for the United States between 1998 and 2012 at Siemens Corporation, a global electronics and electrical engineering firm with 60,000 employees nationally in multiple divisions in four major sectors. When Santana came on board as the first diversity officer, he noted that different diversity efforts were under way in different parts of the company. He saw it as his role to create a strong partnership with HR as the functional process owner of recruitment, training, and development to make changes across the company spectrum and to make sustainable changes in underlying processes.

Santana developed a model to measure progress that measured something different from most other models and focused on two essential questions: How am I addressing the challenges that I need to address relative to my goals? How am I transforming the actual underlying process so that challenge in the future will be addressed by the underlying process rather than an external intervention?

He recognized that he might need to jump-start the process with a diversity program that would train people on a specific issue as a quick fix for a present problem. But Santana clearly identified the need for integration of diversity and HR programs as follows:

> The real challenge and the real goal was actually to incorporate elements of diversity training and development inside the curriculum of the organization, inside the curriculum of management and leadership development, inside the employee orientation, inside the project management training and development and by doing that, making it a permanent part of the curriculum . . . but making it more sustainable and more permanent and also including it as a line item in the diversity and inclusion budget.

Santana cautions against diversity practices and programs as a "prosthetic to make a process that needs to be changed without changing it," just as a patient might go to a doctor for knee issues and receive a leg brace without the underlying issue being addressed. Such approaches are not sustainable because they don't "position the organization for continuing transformation, because no transformation was actually begun," he said.

This chapter focuses on how to create a sustainable architecture for an integrated HR/diversity talent management program that is connected to the overall business strategy and provides a demonstrable return on investment (ROI). This architecture is not static, but represents the dynamic intersection of HR and diversity in organizational processes, policies, and day-to-day workplace interactions.

The Talent Management Platform

Talent management represents the framework of systems, processes, workplace climate, and organizational culture that support the recruitment, retention, and development of employees. In essence, talent management addresses how talent is nurtured, motivated, and engaged in the employment continuum. In no other sphere is the synchronization and integration of HR and diversity practices more critical for organizational performance and results. And in a time of budgetary restraint, talent that builds the organizational capability of innovation is a driver of competitive advantage that differentiates an organization. As leading theorist Edward Lawler (2008) puts it, "Every aspect of the organization is obsessed with talent and talent management" (p. 10). He identifies HR as the most important staff group in the talent equation, since it is versed in business strategy, organizational change, organization design, and talent management (Lawler, 2008).

Integrated talent management systems address the employee value proposition, the key factors that contribute to employee retention,

Figure 5.1 Seven Drivers for Performance-Driven Engagement

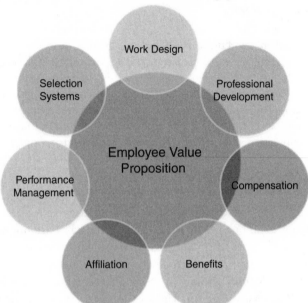

Note: From "Seven Drivers for Performance-Driven Engagement: Performance Increases When We Help Employees Find Ways to Perform Better and Earn Rewards That They Value," by G. Ledford, March 27, 2012, *IndustryWeek,* http://www.industryweek.com/companies-amp-executives/seven-drivers-performance-driven-engagement?page=2.

including compensation, benefits, work content, career development, and affiliation with the organization (Ledford, 2002, 2003). Figure 5.1 identifies seven primary levers for performance-driven engagement that also include performance management and selection systems. Although the average company spends 20 times as many dollars on benefits as compared to compensation, direct compensation including cash incentives and performance management are the most powerful levers to heighten employee engagement (Ledford, 2012).

Talent management also encompasses conflict management systems, work/life benefits, and rewards and recognition programs. The principle that a comprehensive talent management strategy will facilitate the attainment of diversity and inclusion is at the core of our argument for an integrated HR and diversity strategy (Chun & Evans, 2009). A report based on research and interviews with 100 leaders across all organizational sectors in the United Kingdom found that diversity needs to be threaded throughout all talent management functions, enabling organizations to draw on the talents and skills of their employees and respond with resilience to the challenges of the recession and remain focused on the future for recovery (McCartney & Worman, 2010).

The results of a survey of nearly 1,000 firms assessing HR's impact in the latest recession found talent management to have the greatest impact on HR's effectiveness (Lawler, Jamrog, & Boudreau, 2011). Similarly, a post-recession workplace survey of over 350 governmental and private sector organizations concluded that employers are seeking to leverage creativity through attracting and retaining high-quality talent (Society for Human Resource Management, 2010a). Global corporations, in particular, have begun to pay systematic attention and devote organizational resources to talent pipelines and the creation of talent pools.

Yet demonstrating the financial and organizational impact of talent management programs that leverage HR and diversity still remains a challenge for most organizations. In this regard, a survey of 402 HR professionals that compared workplace diversity practices between 2005 and 2010 found a drop in the number of organizations collecting return on investment (ROI) data from 14% in 2005 to 8% in 2010 (Society for Human Resource Management, 2010b). The survey reported the following as the most important outcomes of diversity workplace practices: (a) improved public image, (b) reduced costs from lower turnover and increased productivity, (c) improved financial results, (d) decrease in litigation and complaints, and (e) retention of a diverse employee population (Society for Human Resource Management, 2010b). Practices that address workplace diversity were more prevalent in large organizations with 500 or more employees, and in government agencies, publicly owned for-profit companies, and nonprofit organizations as compared to privately owned for-profit firms (Society for Human Resource Management, 2010b).

The ROI of integrated HR and diversity talent management programs is linked to improved financial performance. In support of this thesis, a study of 22 global companies that included 450 chief executive officers (CEOs) as well as line managers and HR professionals, found that companies scoring in the top third of the survey with a higher talent score on 10 key dimensions earned significantly higher profits per employee (Guthridge & Komm, 2008). This correlation was particularly striking in three dimensions: managing cultural diversity, creating globally consistent talent evaluation processes, and the mobility of global leaders (Guthridge & Komm, 2008). As Deborah Dagit, chief diversity officer (CDO) from 2001 to 2012 at Merck, said, "I think there is no mystery behind why diversity and talent are being integrated with each other, because that's where you get the most traction in terms of the business benefit."

A five-level taxonomy for measuring the ROI of integrated HR and diversity talent management programs can be adopted using the model developed by Hubbard (2008):

- Level 1: Intangible measures that cannot be converted to monetary values (organizational capabilities)
- Level 2: Compliance. Focus on recruitment and retention with attention to equal employment opportunity and Affirmative Action
- Level 3: Inclusion. Efforts that enhance the work environment through infrastructure and improved capability for diversity
- Level 4: Strategic performance. Measures that reflect the impact on business needs
- Level 5: Diversity/HR return on investment. Anticipated profitability of investments in diversity initiatives

This hierarchical model addresses the benefits from integrated HR and diversity initiatives that rise above compliance efforts to permeate the strategic performance of an organization. These benefits result in the creation of a high-performance workplace.

Talent Sustainability

Talent sustainability is essential to build an organization that will last. In an era of ferocious competition, it represents the ability to sustain and optimize the talent resources needed for long-term organizational growth and success. Talent sustainability is the new "organizational prize," shifting the strategic HR paradigm from traditional financial outcomes as measures of the effectiveness of HR processes to a focus on processes, resources, and talents that support sustainability (Boudreau, 2003, p. 5). The importance of talent sustainability has gained increasing attention as organizations seek to ensure the stability of their talent base through HR initiatives that solidify employee commitment and engagement.

The nature of talent sustainability is captured in the metaphor of "clock building, not time telling" introduced by Jim Collins and Jerry Porras (Collins & Porras, 1994, p. 199). Their study of 18 visionary U.S.-based companies led to the evolution of this distinction. Whereas a time teller could look at the sun and stars and state the exact time and date, *clock building* means creating an organization that will adapt through multiple generations of leaders and is not built around a single great leader, idea, or program (Collins & Porras, 1994).

How do HR and diversity leaders engage in clock building rather than time telling when it comes to talent sustainability? They elevate talent management and talent sustainability to the forefront of organizational consideration, and they ensure that diversity is an inextricable component of the talent process, not a fad or momentary addition to existing strategy. HR and diversity leaders must also develop strategic approaches to talent sustainability that help an organization in its decision-making processes.

In this regard, Boudreau (2003) describes talent sustainability as a "decision science" (p. 40) that emphasizes the connection between talent and sustainable strategic success. He notes that sustainable talent development is at the core of critical organizational dilemmas that include

- sustainable trust between companies and investors rather than unsustainable exploitation
- demands for fairness in executive pay
- the emergence of diversity and inclusion and the need for sustainable relationships with suppliers, customers, and employees
- sustainable employment relationships based on mutual respect and security
- consequences of offshore work for local economies

All these critical dilemmas are endangered by a lack of talent sustainability. If diverse talent resources are eroded through lack of attention to a respectful, inclusive workplace environment, an organization may lose the creative talent essential for innovation.

Talent sustainability roles include executive leaders who serve as talent orchestrators, line managers who act as talent influencers, and HR, which represents a talent accelerator (Walsh, 2008). Senior executives orchestrate talent through personal involvement in leading talent management processes that optimize human capital, while line managers influence talent development as coaches and guides by providing opportunities for growth (Walsh, 2008). Ideally, HR processes serve as talent accelerators through the channels of professional development, succession planning, and total rewards.

Take PepsiCo's leading-edge talent sustainability strategy that has four planks: talent acquisition that offers a consistent candidate experience, talent management and development for all levels of employees, an accessible learning environment through PepsiCo University, and an inclusionary culture that supports the behaviors needed to assist present and future talent (Church, 2010, Church & Waclawski, 2010). PepsiCo's career growth model involves five critical components for developing talent: proven results required to get in the game, leadership capability, functional excellence, knowing the business cold, and critical experiences in different sectors (Church & Waclawski, 2010).

According to PepsiCo chairperson and CEO Indra Nooyi, talent sustainability is focused on "creating meaningful employment opportunities in the communities where we operate and developing our associates while fostering a diverse and inclusive workplace" (Nooyi, 2009, para. 3). Since she joined PepsiCo in 2006 as only the fifth CEO since the merger of the Pepsi-Cola Company and Frito-Lay, Inc., Nooyi has emphasized a multicultural, multigenerational, global approach to talent sustainability. Allan Church, vice president of talent and organization and management development for PepsiCo, believes that HR processes, metrics, and behaviors are drivers that reinforce an engaging environments and help employees deliver sustainable "performance with purpose" (Church, 2010, p. 13). As a result, the annual performance review system demonstrates a commitment to values by equally balancing people and business results: 50% people, 50% business. Nooyi said that as part of talent sustainability, "Another crucial element of our promise is our commitment to invest in our associates so they can succeed and develop the skills needed to drive our sustainable growth" (Nooyi, 2009, para. 10).

Talent Segmentation

Talent segmentation refers to the ability to differentiate between the types of talent available in an organization, align talent with strategic objectives, and prepare the organization for future talent needs. Different taxonomies describe the relative talent potential of individuals, including critical talent, or key contributors, who can make the most significant impact on current and future organizational performance, and high potential talent, or individuals with the capacity, motivation, and ability to advance to more senior positions in the organization (Church & Waclawski, 2010; Walsh, 2008).

Yet one of the dangers of a talent segmentation approach is the continued selection of members of dominant groups for choice roles based on the similarity-attraction paradigm. HR and diversity leaders need to collaborate to ensure that talent pipelines offer opportunities to diverse individuals. Our interviews with senior diversity leaders in the private sector revealed that succession planning and active identification of diverse high talent potentials are an active focus. For example, Shirley Davis, vice president of global diversity and inclusion at the Society for Human Resource Management, developed an equitable mechanism for succession planning and talent segmentation while working in a previous private sector leadership role. Instead of preselecting individuals for the succession planning pipeline, a general announcement to the whole organization stated that HR and the leadership team were seeking the talent of the future. Individuals could apply for consideration and had to meet requirements based on performance review ratings, competencies, and leadership ability. This process, she found, enhanced transparency, helped to rule out "cherry picking" and subjectivity, and brought to light "hidden gems" and "unsung heroes" in the organization.

Global and Local: The Talent Challenge

One of the preeminent challenges in large multinational corporations is to maintain a global HR talent focus while strengthening local resources in different geographic locations to serve global customers (Ready & Conger, 2007). How can a unitary focus on diversity and talent be maintained across multiple geographies, multiple sectors, and multiple divisions?

The World Bank, for example, has developed a concerted HR and diversity strategy for the rotation of personnel from an individual's country of origin to other locations for a three-, five-, and seven-year term. Julie Oyegun, CDO from 2001 to 2012, explained the revival of this strategy as a recommendation of her office to HR. She asked herself, "Were we becoming a series of regional development banks or were we one coherent World Bank?" Since the World Bank delivers services to nations with the lowest, middle-income, and emerging economies, these countries benefit from the specialized thematic knowledge of individuals who have worked in different sectors and can bring the knowledge of these sectors to their next assignment. The rotation involves three years to master a role, with a move at five years to another region. If by seven years an individual has not moved, the internal market may not be working, and help may be needed to transfer the individual. The rotation strategy strengthens knowledge management, addresses diversity and inclusion, and solves a global business problem.

As a second example, IBM's Workforce Management Initiative (WMI) was designed to create a globally integrated approach to talent management as sophisticated and analytically sound as the company's approach to finance, technology, operations, and customers (Boudreau, 2010). The WMI was built on the notion of an on-demand workplace—an integrated talent supply chain with four primary goals:

- establish a common language or expertise taxonomy to describe talent resources
- develop an optimal workforce management strategy linked to overall business strategy
- create an inventory of talent resources stored in a central repository
- enable capacity planning that matches resource supply against demand (Boudreau, 2010)

The WMI creates workforce optimization through four core disciplines: talent and mobility (with a common taxonomy and profiles for sources of labor), resource management (an inventory of skills and talent), supplier management (supplier strategy aligned with resource management), and learning (skills development). A new HR organizational design placed HR leaders in "dual-hatted"(p. 48) roles of leading a major HR functional area such as compensation or benefits and at the same time support a large IBM business area as business partner. This organizational structure built a stronger connection between day-to-day planning at the operational business level and central HR functions with a total investment of $230 million over a five-year period, IBM received $1.5 billion in benefits from the WMI, with $453 million added to the bottom line (Boudreau, 2010).

These examples illustrate global talent strategies based on integrated HR and diversity principles that deliver value across different countries and regions. A visionary global company separates operating practices that vary in different countries from core values and purposes that are universal and enduring for the organization (Collins & Porras, 1994). Given this paradigm, the value of integrated HR and diversity practices transcends specific local operations and is infused throughout global organizational strategy.

The Loss of Diverse Talent

If managing cultural diversity is integrally connected with successful talent strategy and in turn with financial performance, why do organizations fail to capitalize on this connection? Our interviews with CDOs reveal two troubling patterns: the rapid turnover in CDO roles because of layoffs, downsizing, and political pressures, and the predominant racialization of the CDO role. Among the 12 private sector CDOs we approached for this study, three had just left their high-profile positions for unidentified reasons. In another case, a CDO who had been profiled as one of the top diversity leaders in a leading magazine suddenly retired because of a reorganization in which her functions were assimilated under talent management. The suddenness of these changes suggests a lack of value accorded to the diversity function as well as the commoditization of individuals in these roles.

Our observations were not limited to the diversity area. Another prominent HR leader in a global corporation whom we contacted had just been leveraged out of her global HR and diversity role. This leader described a situation similar to those we chronicled in a previous interview study that we conducted in higher education (Chun & Evans, 2012). She described the chilling rapidity of her exit and of learning about her own demise secondhand.

One CDO told us that in the top 50 companies for diversity identified by *DiversityInc* magazine over the past two years, almost 75% of CDOs have left their positions. This CDO noted, "When you start to see that kind of pattern, you kind of go, how committed are these organizations, and what are they really trying to accomplish?" To be effective, a CDO needs to be in place for about four years. Yet, as this CDO explained, "Some companies . . . get very impatient or some companies tend to look at inclusion and diversity [as] being a way to drive PR or branding." Or these companies may be seeking quick wins and not seeking to address cultural issues that were roadblocks. The CDO observed the frequency with which people are plucked from a business and told, "Hey, you look like you could do this job because you're a woman, or you're a minority, go do it."

Similarly, T. Hudson Jordan, former global director of diversity at several major corporations, including Pitney Bowes, Toyota, and Time Warner, described the rapid turnover in diversity roles and the lack of integration between diversity and talent management efforts:

> Turnover in the space can be high, because the role is tough. Those that are the most effective have to possess similar leadership qualities as any mission critical role to the organization. That person has to have credibility both internally and externally. The role can be seen as taxing as one can sometimes hit their head against the wall.

The almost exclusive placement of minorities and particularly African Americans in CDO positions suggests an underlying pattern of racialization that pertains to this role. In support of this thesis, Collins's (1997) study of Black corporate executives in Chicago between 1986 and 1992 found that of the 76 executives she interviewed, 51 held Affirmative Action positions. Collins surmised that Black executives remained in racialized positions because of White corporate leadership's need to (a) protect their share of the Black consumer market, (b) help conform to federal legislation, (c) reduce external pressure from the Black community, and (d) maintain racial harmony in the company. While these positions often have high-ranking titles, they may have little actual power, constituting what Collins calls "a race-related mobility trap for black managers" (Collins, 1997, p. 82).

This pattern tends to prevail in higher education as well, where top-ranked positions in doctorate-granting institutions are predominantly held by Whites, 66% by White males. The only exception to this pattern is the CDO position, with 70.8% of these positions held by African Americans (see Chun & Evans, 2012). Clearly, the Society for Human Resource Management's effort to implement professional standards for the diversity and inclusion field as shown in Case Study 2 in Chapter 1 will be instrumental in establishing the CDO role as a cornerstone of the organization.

The Value of a Talent Compact

To overcome the perception of diversity as a sideline in talent management strategy, we suggest the adoption of a talent compact as a vehicle for articulating an organization's commitment to diversity in its talent practices (Ready, 2009). The dual hallmarks of a talent compact are promises made and promises kept (Ready, 2009). *Promises made* refers to the organization's sense of purpose, its promise to deliver on its brand, and the opportunities it provides for talent development; *promises kept* refers to the organization's culture and climate that enables it to fulfill its promises (Ready, 2009). Promises made and promises kept require the day-to-day integration of HR and diversity approaches that not only attract new talent but ensure the retention of diverse talent through career growth, participation in decision making, and a culture of inclusion.

In fact, a talent compact is built on a "value chain" perspective, a promise in terms of the values, heritage, and reputation of a company or institution (McCarthy, 2012). It evokes a powerful set of emotions that affect how individuals interact with an organization (McCarthy, 2012). To build this powerful, emotional contract, we introduce six guiding principles for a talent compact that solidifies integrated HR/diversity talent practices:

1. Talent and diversity are inseparable; talent requires diversity, and diversity is not attained without talent. Diversity is not an additive component of a talent management strategy, something nice to have but not essential.
2. In a global society, diverse talent is not a luxury but a necessity.
3. The concept of inclusive excellence as an alloy between inclusion and excellence is a fundamental precept of the new talent compact.
4. Since talent management is not the sole responsibility of HR and is co-owned with HR by line managers, talent management must be integrated into the cultures of supervision and management.
5. The organization is optimized when diversity and talent are combined and suboptimized when they are not.
6. Without attention to the integration of diversity and talent management, organizations will never reach a critical mass of diverse talent and will only promote the revolving door.

These precepts can form the framework for "an architecture of inclusion" that is composed of the organization's multilevel decisions, underlying structures, and cultural norms (Sturm, 2006). As a foundation for this architecture, the HR mission, vision, and values statements offer the opportunity to join the purposes of HR and diversity in workforce practices, structures, and norms. The potential impact of the value statements in a talent compact lies in their power as markers or signposts that shape the formulation of an action-oriented talent management agenda.

The HR Vision, Mission, and Values Statements

The HR mission, vision, and values statements can serve to affirm the organization's commitment to the link between diversity and talent management. These statements crystallize the talent compact or the psychological contract with employees. Yet, surprisingly, in the course of our interviews of HR and diversity leaders, we found that a number of these leaders could not explicitly recall their organization's HR mission statement or how it relates to diversity. Such mission statements may be seen as vague rhetoric, divorced from reality, or simply too complicated to remember. Perhaps HR mission, vision, and values statements need to become more personal and more appealing to the individual employee. They need to capture what HR can do to improve the day-to-day experiences of diverse and talented employees. Or to return to Jac Fitz-enz's (2009) statement that there is no god-given right for HR to exist, how does HR articulate that right and include the diversity talent imperative in its mission statement?

Some organizations have created separate mission and vision statements for diversity and inclusion or, alternatively, incorporated diversity into the overall organizational mission statement. HR departments in governmental agencies and institutions of higher education are more likely to have incorporated diversity into their mission statements, often in response to compliance mandates. Such references typically are framed in terms of workforce diversity such as the state of Oregon's HR mission statement that emphasizes efforts to "attract, hire, develop and retain a diverse, competent and motivated workforce" ("About Us," n.d., para. 1). This statement references the core value of diversity and states the need to "respect and honor each person's individual dignity" (para. 5).

Mention of inclusion as an organizational goal in HR mission statements is even rarer, suggesting again the typical bifurcation of diversity and HR functions. Examples appear more prevalent in higher education such as Colorado College's HR mission statement that commits to "fostering a campus community of performance excellence and inclusiveness by providing high quality service and leadership" ("Colorado College: HR Mission and Initiatives," n.d.) and the University of North Carolina at Greensboro's HR mission statement that refers to "the creation of an inclusive, collaborative, and responsive university by attracting, retaining, and developing a diverse community of talented individuals in support of the university's mission" ("Human Resources," n.d.). The omission of inclusion from HR mission statements overlooks the multidimensionality of talent as well as the organizational support needed for diverse talent to flourish. All in all, HR mission statements need to present a minimal structure that avoids excessive requirements but leaves the door open for multiple interpretations in an organizational context (Barrett, 2012).

Systematic Gap Analysis

The next step in assessing the talent management platform is to conduct a gap analysis that addresses the degree of integration of HR and diversity talent management programs. Recall the assessment profile of organizational readiness for integration provided in Chapter 4 (pp. 98–99). We now examine key indicators of the level of current HR/diversity integration in talent management programs that will help identify gaps in current practices and areas for future development. The depth, breadth, and consistency of an organization's synergistic HR/diversity talent practices can vary considerably among organizations and even in companies or practices located in a single employer. The assessment in Exercise 5.1 will help assess key facets of HR/diversity integration in the talent equation and provide clear perspectives on the extent, level, and importance given to this effort.

EXERCISE 5.1
Integrated HR and Diversity Talent Strategy

1. What level of importance is diversity given in the organization's talent strategy?

2. What explicit facets of the talent strategy are focused on diversity?

3. What types of partnerships exist between the HR and diversity functions in talent acquisition?

EXERCISE 5.1 (Continued)

4. What types of organizational or structural barriers make it more difficult for HR and diversity functions to collaborate in the talent management space?

5. What kind of diversity training is offered in the talent acquisition and management process?
   Is it required? (Y/N) _____

6. What type of diversity training are HR leaders expected to take?

7. Is HR's role in the talent management process articulated in the organization's diversity strategic plan?

8. Is diversity embedded as a core focus in HR's talent management policies? (Y/N) _____ Which policies?

(Continues)

EXERCISE 5.1 (Continued)

9.   What are the metrics that measure integrated HR and diversity work in the talent area?

10.   In what specific areas of talent management does the organization need to enhance the integration of HR and diversity?

Identification of areas that may require organizational attention in this assessment will provide the groundwork for a comprehensive planning process. Our interviews indicate that the alliance between HR and diversity talent practices can vary on a continuum from tentative and embryonic programs to consciously strategic, phased approaches. To overcome the tendency to fragmentation and piecemeal efforts, a systematic talent framework needs to encompass structural, procedural, and behavioral change. In essence, it is broad and deep in terms of its level of implementation and penetration of organizational culture and practices.

Developing a Strategic HR/Diversity Talent Planning Process

We now introduce a planning framework that gauges gaps in talent needed for specific organizational needs, addresses talent acquisition through sourcing practices, and provides ongoing talent development and succession planning.

For planning purposes, four categories of strategic talent need to be considered: leadership talent, talent for strategic functions, talent for strategic geographies, and talent for strategic technologies (Avedon & Scholes, 2010). Diverse talent plays a role in each of these categories. In leadership talent, organizations need to create a leadership brand in which external demands drive leadership delivery (Ulrich, 2012). This outward-facing requirement means that organizations cannot afford to perpetuate majority-male-dominated leadership cultures that do not reflect a diverse base of consumers. Talent for strategic functions requires building a diverse talent base that will create new knowledge and spark innovation. And talent for strategic geographies necessarily involves the need for diverse talent to serve in emerging markets and rapidly developing economies. Talent for strategic technologies will also benefit from the wealth of diverse talent in the evolution of new technological platforms and solutions that enhance organizational advantage.

In all these areas of talent focus, talent reviews can serve as a way to create talent pools or feeders for diverse talent. These reviews can benefit from the following seven lessons or principles: (a) focus as much on development as assessment, (b) include the individual in the planning process, (c) emphasize dialogue rather than the format of the review process, (d) link to strategic plans, (e) value current contributions as well as future potential, (f) hold line leadership accountable for the management of talent pools, and (g) focus on follow-up and review of the effectiveness of talent pools (Dowell, 2010). Because of the integral relation of diversity to talent management strategy, the HR/diversity planning process necessarily includes the development of aggressive recruiting and hiring practices to build a pipeline of diverse and talented individuals and to create partnerships with line managers to promote job satisfaction, psychological empowerment, and career development over the long term.

Our HR/diversity talent management model includes four critical phases: talent mapping through predictive workforce analytics, talent identification and acquisition, enhancing structural and behavioral components of inclusive talent support, and inclusive talent development that will enhance contributions to organizational capabilities.

Talent Mapping Through Predictive Workforce Analytics

The first step in talent mapping involves assessment of the strategic sectors of talent need and the current demographic makeup of the talent spectrum. The mapping process will reveal areas of historic underrepresentation of women and minorities and demographic distribution by type of position. Research has shown, for example, that women and minorities have difficulty attaining positions they have been excluded from in the past (Konrad & Pfeffer, 1991). In addition to demographic data, key elements for consideration in the talent mapping process are salary, grade level, scope of responsibility, credentials including education and experience, and career progression.

The next step in talent mapping involves identifying areas of future talent need and planning for how these needs will be met. As we have seen in Case Study 3 in Chapter 2, predictive workforce analytics is a key factor in the development of an enterprise-wide diversity talent strategy at Ingersoll Rand, a global manufacturing company. As the case study reveals, organizations must adopt a proactive talent approach that anticipates future needs rather than reacting only as vacancies occur. Time is of the essence in the talent mapping process; global corporations must be prepared for the launch of products or services in emerging markets.

Talent Identification and Acquisition

The second phase of the talent planning process focuses on identifying where the best talents are internally and developing external outreach strategies to attract minorities, women, and other diverse groups to the organization. The internal talent process needs to include individuals who may not have risen to organizational attention previously but perhaps have been hampered by lack of supervisory support or opportunities to demonstrate their expertise.

The external talent acquisition process requires aggressive and creative recruitment practices to address underrepresentation, anticipate workforce needs, and develop diverse talent streams that fulfill strategic functions. Strategies that enhance diversity recruitment include development of broader job requirements to recognize diverse and nontraditional backgrounds, formation of diverse search committees, and accenting the positive attributes of organizational affiliation including talent development and total rewards programs and an inclusive work environment.

Since hiring is a two-way process of attracting qualified and talented individuals to an organization, hiring managers need to create a welcoming atmosphere throughout the screening process. Too often the focus of searches seems to be on disqualifying or eliminating candidates rather than on identifying the candidates' strengths and attributes that will contribute to organizational success.

Enhancing Structural and Behavioral Components of Inclusive Talent Support

Once talented and diverse individuals join an organization, the battle is only half won. To avoid the continuously revolving door, organizations must provide a welcoming climate characterized by inclusive workplace practices and a supportive infrastructure. From an overall perspective, a sustainable competitive advantage can be attained through integrated workplace practices that include employment security, selectivity in recruiting, competitive wages, incentive pay, employee ownership, information sharing, participation and empowerment, self-managed teams, promotion from within, training and skill development, symbolic egalitarianism, cross-utilization, and cross training (Pfeffer et al., 2005). As a result, HR and diversity leaders must coordinate vigorous efforts to ensure resource allocation for professional development, monitor equity in performance reviews, build career ladders, and design effective total rewards programs.

Yet persistent organizational barriers may preclude the realization of optimal workplace practices. These barriers are often subtle but may have a significant impact on the success of women, minorities, and other diverse individuals (see Chun & Evans, 2012; Evans & Chun, 2007). Such workplace barriers include the following:

- Failure to empower and include in decision making. While diverse individuals may hold high-ranking positions, they may lack the authority associated with these positions as well as the power to gain the compliance of subordinates.
- Differing expectations. Minorities and women may be subjected to differential standards compared to similarly situated majority males. Pfeffer's (2010) research on promotion and advancement underscores the weak link between performance and job outcomes, indicating that "performance doesn't matter that much for what happens to most people in most organizations" (p. 22). This weak link permits differential treatment and subjective assessments that can be influenced by in-group preferences and exercise of the similarity-attraction paradigm, which refers to preferences given by organizational decision makers to members of their own racial or ethnic group that produce different outcomes for different groups (see Chun & Evans, 2012).
- Lack of support. Lack of support can be reflected in the differential authority level granted to similar positions in the organizational hierarchy. Mechanisms of exclusion for diverse individuals may involve limited budget allocations and restricted decision making and job discretion that make diverse individuals more subject to criticism and attack and biased attributions (see Ragins, 1997).
- Stereotyping and organizational fit. Stereotyping of diverse employees can involve differential assessment of capabilities through biased interpretation. One of the prevailing assumptions about minorities and women, for example, is incompetence. This phenomenon can result in subjective performance evaluations that reflect such biases and may minimize actual accomplishments.
- Isolation and soloing. The lack of diversity in different strata of the workplace can result in isolation and soloing for women, minorities, and other protected class members. And where diversity resides in an organization also can influence and limit organizational success for diverse individuals. As Smith and Elliott (2002) point out, the

"sticky floor" (p. 274) or concentration of minorities at lower levels of the organization can limit authority chances for minorities. Similarly, the dominance of majority groups at higher levels of the organization can increase the chances of authority gain for majority group members.

Inclusive Talent Development

The case studies in this book illustrate how global corporations build inclusive talent pipelines through affinity groups, mentoring opportunities, networking opportunities, and succession planning to foster the career progression of diverse talent. Another important component of an inclusive talent development process is the need to provide constructive and supportive feedback. Even more than their majority group counterparts, diverse employees need to understand the unwritten rules of an organization and how to navigate within the existing infrastructure. Without adequate feedback, diverse individuals can operate in a vacuum like a plane flying without a gyroscope (Pettigrew & Martin, 1987). Because of the limited tolerance for mistakes and the stereotypes applied to women and minorities such as weakness, incompetence, and lack of initiative, diverse individuals may have to work harder to prove their worth and justify their contributions (see Chun & Evans, 2012).

In closing this chapter, we conclude that all is not rosy in the global talent arena. In some organizations, CDOs have been seen as expendable or as a cost to be minimized in light of dwindling financial returns. If the guardians of diversity are not protected, then certainly other diverse employees in an organization are at risk. Nonetheless, the synergistic relationship of HR and diversity represents an investment that will yield not only financial benefits but organizational results. An organization will be more effective when it manages its talent proactively and protectively. Talent must be viewed as a sustainable resource, a message that employees will absorb and gauge based upon the tangible actions of organizational leadership.

Moving from consideration of the essential components of an inclusive talent management strategy and structure, we provide the framework for the development of an HR/diversity strategic plan in Chapter 6. Such a plan will operationalize the principles discussed here and provide specific performance indicators that will guide organizational progress in the evolution of an integrated HR and diversity strategy.

To close, we provide a case study involving a comprehensive effort to strengthen HR professionals' diversity competencies and contributions through an initiative undertaken by the College and University Professional Association for Human Resources (CUPA-HR). Finally, consider the following questions in light of the goals of a sustainable, inclusive talent strategy that strengthens employee engagement and retention.

Strategic and Tactical Questions for Further Discussion

1. What are the financial and organizational risks of not developing an integrated HR/diversity talent management strategy?
2. How can organizations prepare to develop a concerted HR/diversity strategy?
   a. What structural changes may be needed?
   b. How do organizational learning programs contribute to this preparation?
3. What specific measures can an organization use to measure its success in building inclusiveness in all phases of its talent management strategy?
4. What strategies will help overcome behavioral barriers to inclusive talent development?
5. How can organizations identify hidden talent gems, individuals with creative and innovative capabilities who have been traditionally overlooked, isolated, or even marginalized?
6. What steps can an organization take to strengthen its talent compact with its employees?

Case Study 7: Launching a Transformative Diversity Initiative in the Largest HR Professional Association in Higher Education

In July 2010 Andy Brantley, CEO of CUPA-HR, met with its 15-member national board of directors to consider an agenda item on diversity and inclusion. As the largest HR organization in higher education with 1,898 member institutions and 14,500 representations from these institutions, CUPA-HR had never previously developed a formal position statement or program that identified the leadership role of HR professionals in diversity and inclusion.

Brantley, though, had a different vision. From his perspective, HR professionals need to know how HR plugs in to diversity on their campuses, regardless of what their institutions do. Most HR professionals have viewed their diversity responsibilities as limited to compliance and affirmative action reporting. By contrast, Brantley and the national board wanted to define an agenda for this national organization that clearly articulates HR's role in the attainment of diversity and inclusion on college and university campuses. Although Brantley believed that CUPA-HR members might want to become more engaged, he surmised that members might also assume diversity was being handled by another office on campus.

And this whole issue of the broader diversity and inclusion, "oh that's some-one else's responsibility on campus," "you know there's an associate provost," or "you know student life is taking care of that" or whatever. As opposed to . . . and that is one of the challenges . . . is that lots of student life organiza-tions on campus have really put together some stellar programs and services in support of a more diverse student population but that's where it ends. (A. Brantley, personal communication, August 6, 2012)

He also realized there was a lack of understanding by HR professionals on where to begin and what contributions they could make.

But as it related to HR leadership roles in creating a more diverse, inclu-sive environment, what we found was that for many HR professionals on campus, it wasn't a matter of not wanting to be more fully engaged or not seeing HR as being part of diversity and inclusion effort, but the lack of understanding of some clear actions that HR could take in support of cam-puswide diversity and inclusion efforts.

One of the barriers he perceived was the tendency of HR profession-als to worry about the views of senior leadership and whether "they get it" in relation to the need for diversity and inclusion. Instead, he believed HR leaders on campus needed to make a start and begin the incremental change that would eventually lead to diversity transformation. His focus was action-oriented.

We can have an impact every single day if we choose to have an impact. And the more that we as HR professionals choose to focus on the areas and ways that we can have an impact every single day, [these strategies] are the key to our ultimate success and our ultimate relevance on campus. And so continuing to educate and to help our colleagues across the country be aware of that and not get bogged down in the perspective that senior leadership [on campus] doesn't get it or not is, I think, the most important thing.

But what concrete actions could the national board take to emphasize the shared institutional responsibility for diversity among HR professionals and make it an intentional commitment?

First Steps

At the national board of directors meeting, the first hurdle to overcome was to reach a common definition of *diversity* from the perspective of HR profes-sionals on campus. After about an hour of writing down ideas and sharing differing individual perspectives, the board members felt they needed outside assistance from an expert to move beyond words to the actions they felt were necessary.

The board asked Alma Clayton-Pedersen, former vice president for education and institutional renewal at the Association of American Colleges and Universities (AAC&U), who had just retired, to help them with this process. They adopted the definitions of *diversity* and *inclusion* AAC&U had created through months of dialogue with people from campuses across the country. Board members also decided they would check back after a year to see if the definitions needed revision.

A small task force met with Clayton-Pedersen to develop a position statement about why diversity is important for HR and for higher education and to create the first set of action statements that move the position statement into action. The position statement clearly articulated HR's unique position and responsibility to provide leadership in diversity. As Brantley explained:

> So as part of this effort on behalf of CUPA-HR, we as a national board and national office adopted a strategic priority that clearly defines this as not just an initiative for CUPA-HR or just an initiative for our education of HR professionals but truly something that we emphasize as a way for HR to make our D&I [diversity and inclusion] efforts a core part of HR's role on campus, in other words, a key piece of the culture within HR as it relates to the larger organization.

Between late October 2010 and early July 2011, a systematic plan for input by CUPA-HR's membership was launched. While the first step of the process was to create the position statement and action plan, the second step was to gather feedback at the four regional conferences in the spring of 2011. Dialogue and input were generated at preconference sessions at each of these meetings. Then the full membership of CUPA-HR was addressed through several communications. As step three of the process, the position statement and program were vetted in July 2011 with the association leadership program attended by representatives from each of the 41 CUPA-HR chapters.

After gathering feedback from its constituencies, CUPA-HR leadership began working on a plan for the official launch of the position statement and action plan at the annual national conference in September 2012. The theme of the national conference held in Orlando, Florida, was "Inclusion Cultivates Excellence," and all concurrent session presenters who submitted proposals were asked to incorporate some aspect of diversity and inclusion into their presentations. Working with CUPA-HR's Corporate Advisory Council, private sector diversity and inclusion experts from the firms represented on the council led a diversity-related concurrent session to share best practices in the private sector.

CUPA-HR decided to launch collaborative partnerships with other organizations as part of its diversity and inclusion initiative. A partnership was formed with the Council of Higher Education Associations (CHEMA), representing more than 40 management-related associations in higher education, and the National Association of Diversity Officers in Higher Education. Brantley chaired the Diversity and Inclusion Committee at CHEMA and that group developed guiding principles for diversity and inclusion that were subsequently adopted by many of its associations.

Brantley sums up the diversity progress made by CUPA-HR as a journey shared by the member institutions and the HR departments and professionals at those institutions: "So much of this we have embarked on, we are emphasizing—it is a journey for CUPA-HR as an organization. It's a journey for each one of us as individuals. It's a journey for our institutions, and HR at those institutions."

Challenges and Open Questions

Looking toward the future of the diversity and inclusion initiative, the primary challenges facing CUPA-HR are limited resources and a hefty to-do list of many important priorities for higher education. In 2011 alone, CUPA-HR added 163 more institutions with 1,400 more representatives. To strengthen its global focus, CUPA-HR recognizes the strategic importance of international outreach. Without a defined outreach program, CUPA-HR already has 20 international institutions and 100 representatives among its members and is seeking to broaden this focus. An international higher education symposium was included in the 2012 national preconference in Boston to help CUPA-HR decide on an action plan.

Another project under way is to develop a new learning model for CUPA-HR that includes culture competence, or what Brantley defines as "key actions that are demonstrated to help ensure that the person gives more than lip service to a concept."

Among CUPA-HR's 29 staff, no single position is devoted to diversity, but Brantley anticipates reassessing roles and ensuring that diversity and inclusion become a clearer part of one of the staff roles. In Brantley's view, the changing landscape in higher education is challenging CUPA-HR to "create the opportunities for institutions to plug into this, and find the places that make this relevant for their campus, and heighten awareness." HR professionals need to have examples of to-dos, one or two things they can do immediately, while recognizing that every institution is at a different place on the diversity spectrum. These to-dos can serve as the building blocks for future growth and long-term change.

To keep the momentum going, the next decision point is to determine what two or three initiatives would build on CUPA-HR's diversity and inclusion program and best serve HR professionals as leaders in the process of diversity transformation on their campuses. And given the limited resources available to CUPA-HR, Brantley believes this decision must be made very carefully.

References

About us. (n.d.). Retrieved from Oregon Department of Transportation website: http://www.oregon.gov/EMPLOY/HR/Pages /about_us.aspx

Avedon, M. J., & Scholes, G. (2010). Building competitive advantage through integrated talent management. In R. Silzer & B. E. Dowell (Eds.), *Strategy-driven talent management: A leadership imperative* (pp. 73–122). San Francisco, CA: Jossey-Bass.

Barrett, F. J. (2012). *Yes to the mess: Surprising leadership lessons from jazz.* Boston, MA: Harvard Business School Press.

Boudreau, J. W. (2003). *Sustainability and the talentship paradigm: Strategic human resource management beyond the bottom line.* Retrieved from http://digitalcommons .ilr.cornell.edu/cgi/viewcontent.cgi?article=1039&context=cahrswp

Boudreau, J. W. (2010). *IBM's global talent management strategy: The vision of the globally integrated enterprise.* Retrieved from http://www.shrm.org/education/ hreducation/documents/boudreau_ibm%20case%20study%20with%20 teaching%20notes_final.pdf

Chun, E., & Evans, A. (2009). *Bridging the diversity divide: Globalization and reciprocal empowerment in higher education* (ASHE-ERIC Higher Education Reports, Vol. 35, No. 1). San Francisco, CA: Jossey-Bass.

Chun, E., & Evans, A. (2012). *Diverse administrators in peril: The new indentured class in higher education.* Boulder, CO: Paradigm.

Church, A. H. (2010). *Talent sustainability defined.* Retrieved from http://www.hci .org/files/field_slides/July%2027%202010%20final.pdf

Church, A. H., & Waclawski, J. (2010). Take the Pepsi challenge: Talent development at PepsiCo. In R. Silzer & B. E. Dowell (Eds.), *Strategy-driven talent management: A leadership imperative* (pp. 617–640). San Francisco, CA: Jossey-Bass.

Collins, J., & Porras, J. I. (1994). *Built to last: Successful habits of visionary companies.* New York, NY: HarperCollins.

Collins, S. (1997). *Black corporate executives: The making and breaking of a Black middle class.* Philadelphia, PA: Temple University Press.

Colorado College: HR mission and initiatives. (n.d.). Retrieved from http://www .coloradocollege.edu/offices/humanresources/mission.dot

Dowell, B. E. (2010). Managing leadership talent pools. In R. Silzer & B. E. Dowell (Eds.), *Strategy-driven talent management: A leadership imperative* (pp. 399–438). San Francisco, CA: Jossey-Bass.

Evans, A., & Chun, E. B. (2007). *Are the walls really down? Behavioral and organizational barriers to faculty and staff diversity* (ASHE-ERIC Higher Education Reports, Vol. 33, No. 1). San Francisco, CA: Jossey-Bass.

Fitz-enz, J. (2009). Disruptive technology for human resources. *Employment Relations Today, 35*(4), 1–10.

Guthridge, M., & Komm, A. (2008). *Why multinationals struggle to manage talent: A survey shows a strong correlation between financial performance and best practices for managing talent globally.* Retrieved from http://www.talentnaardetop.nl.kpnis.nl/uploaded_files/document/2008_Why_multinationals_struggle_to_manage_talent_M.pdf

Hubbard, E. E. (2008). *The diversity discipline: Implementing diversity work with a strategy, structure and ROI measurement focus.* Petaluma, CA: Global Insights.

Human resources. (n.d.). Retrieved from University of North Carolina at Greensboro website: http://web.uncg.edu/hrs/

Konrad, A. M., & Pfeffer, J. (1991). Understanding the hiring of women and minorities in educational institutions. *Sociology of Education, 64*(3), 141–157.

Lawler, E. E., III. (2008). *Talent: Making people your competitive advantage.* San Francisco, CA: Jossey-Bass.

Lawler, E. E., III, Jamrog, J., & Boudreau, J. (2011). Shining light on the HR profession. *HR Magazine, 56*(2), 38–41.

Ledford, G. E., Jr. (2002, October). *Attracting, retaining, and motivating employees: The rewards of work framework.* Paper presented at a meeting of the College and University Professional Association for Human Resources, Dallas, TX.

Ledford, G. E., Jr. (2003). The rewards of work framework: Attracting, retaining and motivating higher education employees. *CUPA-HR Journal, 54*(2), 22–26.

Ledford, G. (2012, March 27). Seven drivers for performance-driven engagement: Performance increases when we help employees find ways to perform better and earn rewards that they value. *IndustryWeek.* Retrieved from http://www.industryweek.com/companies-amp-executives/seven-drivers-performance-driven-engagement?page=2

McCarthy, K. T. (2012). Value chain focus: The human touch. In A. Tavis, R. Vosburgh, & E. Gubman (Eds.), *Point counterpoint: New perspectives on people & strategy* (pp. 31–32). Chicago, IL: Society for Human Resource Management.

McCartney, C., & Worman, D. (2010). *Opening up talent for business success: Integrating talent management and diversity.* Retrieved from http://www.cipd.co.uk/hr-resources/research/talent-business-success-integrating-talent-management-diversity.aspx

Nooyi, I. (2009). *Letter from Indra Nooyi.* Retrieved from http://pepsicoindia.co.in/purpose/performance-with-purpose/letter-from-indra-nooyi.html

Petrick, J. A., Scherer, R. F., Brodzinski, J. D., Quinn, J. F., & Ainina, M. F. (1999). Global leadership skills and reputational capital: Intangible resources for sustainable competitive advantage. *Academy of Management Executive, 13*(1), 58–69.

Pettigrew, T. F., & Martin, J. (1987). Shaping the organizational context for Black American inclusion. *Journal of Social Issues, 43*(1), 41–78.

Pfeffer, J. (2010). *Power: Why some people have it and others don't.* New York, NY: HarperCollins.

Pfeffer, J., Hatano, T., & Santalainen, T. (2005). Producing sustainable competitive advantage through the effective management of people. *Academy of Management Executive, 19*(4), 95–106.

Ragins, B. R. (1997). Diversified mentoring relationships in organizations: A power perspective. *Academy of Management Review, 22*(2), 482–521.

Ready, D. (2009). Forging the new talent compact. *Business Strategy Review, 20*(2), 4–7.

Ready, D. A., & Conger, J. A. (2007). Make your company a talent factory. *Harvard Business Review, 85*(6), 68–77.

Silzer, R., & Dowell, B. E. (2010). Strategic talent management matters. In R. Silzer & B. E. Dowell (Eds.), *Strategy-driven talent management: A leadership imperative* (pp. 3–72). San Francisco, CA: Jossey-Bass.

Smith, R. A., & Elliott, J. R. (2002). Does ethnic concentration influence employees' access to authority? An examination of contemporary urban labor markets. *Social Forces, 81*(1), 255–279.

Society for Human Resource Management. (2010a). *The post-recession workplace: Competitive strategies for recovery and beyond survey report.* Retrieved from http://www.shrm.org/Research/SurveyFindings/Documents/SHRM%20Post%20Recession%20Workplace_FINAL-sm.pdf

Society for Human Resource Management. (2010b). *Workplace diversity practices: How has diversity and inclusion changed over time? SHRM poll.* Retrieved from http://www.shrm.org/Research/SurveyFindings/Articles/Pages/WorkplaceDiversityPractices.aspx

Sturm, S. (2006). The architecture of inclusion: Advancing workplace equity in higher education. *Harvard Journal of Law & Gender, 29*(2), 247–334.

Ulrich, D. (2012). Counterpoint. In A. Tavis, R. Vosburgh, & E. Gubman (Eds.), *Point counterpoint: New perspectives on people & strategy* (p. 13). Chicago, IL: Society for Human Resource Management.

Walsh, R. (2008). *Talent sustainability: Frameworks and tools for developing organizational capacity.* Retrieved from http://www.ccl.org/leadership/pdf/community/TalentSustainabilityWalsh.pdf

6

BUILDING THE HR/DIVERSITY
STRATEGIC PLAN

Valuing the differences is the essence of synergy—the mental, the emotional, the psychological differences between people. (Covey, 1989, p. 277)

As the capstone of our argument for systematically integrated HR and diversity practices, we introduce the collaborative HR/Diversity Strategic Plan. The strategic alliance between HR and diversity in the organizational planning process could be considered the equivalent of organizational heresy, since it bridges two traditionally separate fiefdoms. While many organizations today have diversity strategic plans, collaboration with HR as a strategic partner usually occurs only in defined areas such as in recruitment and appointment practices.

Why is an HR/Diversity Strategic Plan a leading best practice? In a study of the implementation of equity issues at 14 California higher education institutions, researchers identified weak contextual links that hindered the success of diversity initiatives. A glaring weakness that offset one institution's strengths was the lack of a strategic plan, making it difficult to connect the effort with the institution's overall efforts. Another institution was reluctant to study whether inequities even existed on campus (Kezar et al., 2008).

In another study of eight multinational corporations in a midwestern state, all the diversity managers agreed that having a strategic plan was a critical factor in the success of diversity initiatives since the plan provides guidance, avoids one-shot initiatives, and prevents shortsightedness (Wentling, 2004). As these examples demonstrate, the written plan helps stakeholders link their individual and collective efforts to organizational purposes. It also identifies areas of improvement that are needed and steps to take to address gaps or deficits.

The HR/Diversity Strategic Plan creates the capacity for revitalization and a "management reset" (Lawler & Worley, 2011) by supporting flatter, more flexible, and less hierarchical organizations that enhance the abilities of employees and management to cope with a high competitive environment

(Beer, Eisenstat, & Spector, 1990). Such revitalization is painful: it demands changes in assumptions and behaviors that employees may find threatening; it challenges the power and status bestowed by hierarchy upon employees; it calls into question the subjective sense of competence among some employees (Beer et al., 1990).

Although few, if any, examples exist of blended HR/diversity plans, the benefits to be gained by such synergistic planning are substantial and demonstrable. Recall the importance of reciprocal empowerment in creating the conditions for a culture of inclusion. When the workplace offers psychological safety, diverse and talented employees can express their own identity freely, and their contributions are unhampered by repressive control. When behavioral barriers are removed, a level playing field for all organizational members fosters empowerment, creativity, and innovation. Organizational effectiveness, improved financial performance, and differentiation in a competitive marketplace are the outcomes of a high-performance workplace characterized by respect and inclusion. Conversely, devaluing employees and treating them as dispensable commodities erodes employee commitment and abridges the talent compact.

In the development of an integrated HR/Diversity Strategic Plan, we build on Hubbard's (2004) four strategic planks: workforce diversity, structural diversity, behavioral diversity, and business diversity. This multidimensional framing provides a clear structure for setting goals, measurement of progress, and assessment of accountability across organizational divisions, lines of business, and hierarchies.

Workforce diversity. Representational diversity is the most common component of diversity strategic plans and is the area where HR and diversity programs most commonly intersect. It focuses on recruitment and retention.

The first hurdle for most organizations is to identify areas of underrepresentation for women, minorities, disabled people, and veterans, particularly with respect to Affirmative Action requirements for federal contractors. Organizations that prepare annual Affirmative Action plans for the federal government must assess structural imbalances based on the availability of minority and female workers in a given job group with incumbency in the workforce. Legislation has added federal civil rights protection for gender expression. And some states, cities, and counties have developed legislative protections for sexual orientation and gender expression. Without the attainment of the protected characteristics of race, ethnicity, gender, disability, and sexual orientation, attainment of genuine diversity will not be possible (see Evans & Chun, 2007).

The second objective of the HR/Diversity Strategic Plan is to focus on the overall characteristics of the workforce to encompass "the situational identities" of employees, such as generational differences, marital status, religion, and so forth (Hubbard, 2004, p. 27). This objective focuses essentially on inclusion and reinforces the self-determination necessary for the attainment of reciprocal empowerment.

Structural diversity. Hubbard's (2004) notion of structural diversity is interactional in nature, bridging levels of hierarchy and lines of business to create an infrastructure that promotes diversity. This infrastructure involves flattening the organization and a greater dependence on team-based interactions. A contemporary structural practice in multinational corporations is the use of dispersed, global work teams that work together virtually. Such teams help ensure consistency across countries in each step of the value chain, ensuring cross-functional and cross-border coordination (Gupta & Cao, 2005). These teams can enhance the quality and level of organizational outcomes by coalescing differences and contributions in service of an overarching goal (Hickman & Creighton-Zollar, 1998). In fact, diverse work teams may represent one of the most natural vehicles for incorporating diversity in 21st-century organizations (Hickman & Creighton-Zollar, 1998).

Looking into the future, the luxury of hierarchical, stratified, and solo leadership practices may be eclipsed by dynamic, interactive ways of interacting that permit rapid innovation, promote employee empowerment, and benefit from diverse contributions.

By extension, the leadership tier also involves more team-based interactions. The evolution of intergroup leadership—boundaryless leadership that bridges different social identity groups in the service of the organization's vision—is symptomatic of a shifting leadership focus (Ernst & Yip, 2009). This revolutionary reconceptualization of leadership to be more inclusive, context bound, collective, and collaborative has begun to replace hierarchical models based on control, power, and individualism (Kezar & Carducci, 2009). Although historically a great deal of emphasis has been placed on individual charisma in leadership roles, the synergy arising from diverse leadership teams accelerates innovation. In this regard, a study by Frank Barrett (2012) compares leadership to jazz improvisation in which a small group of players reach transcendental heights when they forget themselves and truly "achieve the groove" (p. 33). Similarly, Jim Collins's (2001) description of the level 5 leader emphasizes a concern for the organization and its future over individual impact. Such leaders build greatness through a "paradoxical combination of personal humility plus professional will" (p. 70).

In our view, however, structural diversity exceeds interactional diversity and also includes the body of policies and procedures that govern employment processes. These policies apply throughout the employment continuum and describe requirements for talent acquisition, performance evaluation, compensation, promotion, and termination. In considering structural interactions, supervisor-subordinate demography is also an essential component for consideration. Since workplace climates vary considerably in organizational units, those in HR and diversity need to collaborate to ensure equitable organizational processes and outcomes. This facet of interactional diversity has been overlooked in most organizations. Without adequate attention from HR and diversity professionals, diverse individuals may be left to cope singlehandedly with subtle forms of exclusion and marginalization.

Behavioral diversity. Behavioral diversity addresses the subtle components of day-to-day interactions in the workplace that are driven by underlying beliefs, normative assumptions, and value systems of employees. Traditionally, measures of behavioral diversity have relied on climate and attitudinal surveys to identify workplace barriers to diversity. In this regard, HR departments in many organizations offer formal and informal programs to ameliorate the barriers faced by diverse employees including mediation, conflict resolution, informal procedures for reporting grievances and complaints, employee relations, exit interviews, organizational learning programs, and mentoring. Partnership of HR with the diversity office strengthens these programs by providing a more explicit focus on the retention of diverse employees and by increasing awareness of the contemporary forms of second-generation subtle discrimination, such as microinequities, that have arisen in the post–Civil Rights era.

Business diversity. Business diversity takes into account supplier diversity, the development of services and/or products for a diverse consumer clientele, shifts in governmental relationships, and geographic diversity in terms of markets, business norms, and social relationships (Hubbard, 2004). Civic and community engagement represent a central focus of business diversity, which is closely tied to financial performance, branding of image and products, and consumer relations.

Sample HR/Diversity Strategic Planning Template

The HR/Diversity Strategic Plan performs five primary functions: it establishes the goals for integrated HR and diversity progress, it sets the bar for attainment of these goals through performance indicators that measure short- and long-term progress, it presents a specific time frame and accountability framework for identified goals, it establishes resource allocations, and it communicates the value of concerted HR and diversity programs to the organization as a whole. The plan's strategic value lies in its framework for comparative longitudinal evaluation. Each year's report will serve as a comparison with prior years to measure the pace and degree of organizational progress.

To begin the planning process, we introduce high-performance indicators that will assist in the evaluation of system dynamics. In essence, the technique of system dynamics addresses the complexity of how these systems interact and evaluates problems and obstacles that may be structural, procedural, cultural, or behavioral (Moore & Antao, 2007). We present an inventory of qualitative and quantitative performance indicators for the sectors of workforce, structural, behavioral, and business diversity. This inventory represents a metaview of the key components to be incorporated into the HR/Diversity Strategic Plan. Naturally, the precise selection of performance indicators will vary depending on the particular structure, purpose, and type of organization. Across all organizational types, however, a tiered analysis by authority level will facilitate a clear evaluation of the organizational infrastructure for diversity. Levels for a tiered employment analysis typically include the following:

- executive
- managerial
- supervisory
- administrative
- trades
- entry level

For organizations with union contracts for specific job groups, the terms and conditions of these agreements need to be factored into the analysis for each of the four strategic sectors. The template in Table 6.1 provides the basis for metrics that can be linked to necessary financial and resource investments and will ultimately include an HR/Diversity return on investment (ROI) dashboard.

Measuring HR/Diversity ROI

The next step in the HR/Diversity strategic planning process is to use the analysis of performance indicators to project costs and benefits. The benefits or ROI for each performance measure can be expressed in specific terms, whether the impact is on revenue enhancement or reduction; workforce outcomes, such as reduced turnover and increased productivity or job satisfaction; or risk avoidance. For example, Lawrence Baytos (1995) has developed a list delineating the potential profit impact of each diversity-related programmatic variable. Sample outcomes in his analysis include lower turnover, reducing the cost of replacement; reduced equal employment opportunity claims and compliance sanctions; and reduced legal costs. We propose a

TABLE 6.1
Performance Indicators by Sector for the HR/Diversity Strategic Plan

Workforce	Indicators	Structural	Indicators	Behavioral	Indicators	Business	Indicators
Affirmative Action plan	Representation of women and minorities by job group compared to availability in recruitment area	Policies	Specific policies that address interrelation of HR/diversity processes including hiring, performance evaluation, compensation, promotion, and employment protections	Climate surveys and culture audit	Responses on level of inclusion from diverse groups analyzed by divisions and units; study of cultural norms	Supplier diversity	Policy and action plan with goals for supplier diversity; percentage of total spending on diverse supplier contracts; average spending level per diverse supplier
Disability analysis	Percentage of workforce with identified disabilities; reasonable accommodation requests; workplace accessibility	Organizational design	Flattened reporting structures and span of control; intergroup leadership; use of diverse, multicultural, multinational team-based structures; representative participation in decision making groups	Organizational learning programs	Required diversity programs; diversity competency programs; managerial and supervisory training on diversity; intergroup dialogue	Business planning for diversity	New business development; outreach programs for diverse market sectors and consumers

TABLE 6.1 (Continued)

Workforce	Indicators	Structural	Indicators	Behavioral	Indicators	Business	Indicators
Veterans' status analysis	Percentage of veterans in workforce; use of veterans' preference in hiring process	Promotional opportunities	Posting requirements and availability of channels for internal promotion, advancement, and lateral transfers	Exit interview programs	Analysis of reasons by demographic group and organizational sectors	Community engagement	Financial and resource investment in external community programs serving diverse constituencies
Affinity groups	Availability of affinity groups; organizational sponsorship	Internal mentoring programs	Evaluation of formal and informal programs and outcomes	Safety zones	Creation of safe spaces and zones	Multicultural marketing	Content of ads; website and external outreach in foreign languages
Compensation analysis	Analysis of wage ratios between women/men, minorities/nonminorities in each job family; wage compression between supervisor/subordinates	Communication forums	Programs and vehicles designed to provide information and elicit employee feedback such as town halls, listening posts, newsletters	Integrated employee relations programs	Mediation and conflict resolution programs for informal resolution of issues; employee assistance programs	Professional development	Training offered on supplier diversity; business norms; intercultural communication; languages
Internal promotions	Demographic analysis by organizational tier	Succession planning	Leadership programs to enhance diversity in leadership pipeline and bridge vertical tiers			Geographic rotation in job assignments	Planned job rotations to foster cross-cultural learning

(Continues)

TABLE 6.1 (Continued)

Workforce	Indicators	Structural	Indicators	Behavioral	Indicators	Business	Indicators
Supervisor/ subordinate demography	Demographic analysis related to organizational process outcomes such as performance evaluation	Cross-training	Training to bridge horizontal job sectors and offer additional job mobility				
Turnover	Demographic analysis by turnover reason	Performance evaluation	Diversity as a dimension				
		Rewards and recognition	Team-based awards; recognition for collaboration				
		Diversity Council	HR/diversity leadership				

matrix that reflects the specific deliverables of integrated HR and diversity processes and identifies the strategic, workforce, and financial impact of this collaboration (see Table 6.2).

Since most organizations do not give credit for prevention, quantifiable evidence (e.g., a decline in equal employment opportunity claims, decreased turnover of protected class members) combined with qualitative improvements (e.g., climate survey responses, focus groups) will strengthen the demonstrated ROI of concerted HR/diversity programs.

Another way of conceptualizing the ROI of synergistic HR/diversity programs is in terms of value-added results—outcomes, accomplishments, services, and products that result from specific activities (Hubbard, 1999). As a joint activity between HR and diversity, brainstorming a list of value-added results can serve as a simple yet powerful tool for demonstrating the benefits of HR/diversity collaboration (see Table 6.3).

	TABLE 6.2 **HR/Diversity ROI Dashboard Example**			
Dimension	*Performance Indicator*	*Strategic Impact*	*Individual Impact*	*Financial Impact*
Policies	Specific policies that address the interrelation of HR/diversity processes including hiring, criteria for evaluation of performance, compensation, promotion, and articulation of employment protections	Greater consistency and equity across divisions, sectors, and lines of business; specific reference to the value of diversity and inclusion in organizational processes; clear accountability structure with employment protections; branding of organization as a best place to work	Enhanced knowledge and ability to navigate within policy framework; increased job satisfaction because of inclusive and equitable workplace practices	Reduced equal employment opportunity claims and grievances; avoidance of litigation; increased retention and reduced turnover through clearly articulated organizational processes

TABLE 6.3 Sample Checklist of Value-Added Outcomes		
Value-Added Outcomes	*Qualitative Results*	*Quantitative Results*
Reduced turnover of women and minorities	Job retention	Reduction in number of searches (calculated at average cost per search)
Documented increase in cultural competence through organizational learning programs	Decreased workplace conflicts; enhanced customer relations	Improvement in diverse markets (calculated by increases in revenue; diverse populations accessed)
Required managerial training on diversity	Decrease in workplace complaints; enhanced retention; increase in diverse hires	Reduction in legal costs for defending discrimination complaints; increased retention of diverse employees
Improved ratings on workplace climate survey	Enhanced retention and job satisfaction	Reduced turnover costs
Improved career success/ psychosocial support resulting from diversified mentoring program	Internal promotions	Salary savings from reducing external recruitments/postings

Creating Organizational Synergy

The HR/Diversity Strategic Plan describes the talent infrastructure that enables organizations to maximize their human capital resources. As such, it is a critical component of sense making, in terms of helping employees understand organizational objectives and make progress over a multiyear period toward defined goals. It serves as a communication tool for disseminating information, criteria, and expected results. It also defines the espoused values of the organization—what is considered important and what behaviors, actions, and outcomes are desired and rewarded. And it is built from the input of stakeholders whose participation ensures their commitment to desired outcomes.

Communication about the plan and its goals needs to be timely, consistent, targeted for specific audiences, unbiased and modest, and use testimonials from specific individuals with high credibility (Hubbard, 1999). Based on over a decade of observation of 100 companies, Kotter (1995) has identified key steps to transformation that include establishing a sense of urgency, forming a powerful guiding coalition, empowering others to act on the vision, creating short-term wins, and institutionalizing new approaches by anchoring them in the culture. In this light, HR/diversity leaders must strategize on how to create a guiding coalition for the HR/Diversity Plan that will inspire employees' commitment to its goals.

Final Considerations

The HR/Diversity Strategic Plan is emblematic of the principle of execution as learning, reinforcing the way the organization changes and learns. Once a collaborative plan is developed, sustaining progress over a multiyear period is a critical test of its ongoing value to the organization. Consistent with Collins's (2001) flywheel concept, establishing milestones for specific time periods for each quadrant (workforce, structural, behavioral, business) will help ensure steady progress. Recommended action steps in plan implementation include the following:

- Create diverse, cross-functional teams of stakeholders at all organizational levels to address specific plan objectives.
- Ensure alignment with the organization's overall strategic plan.
- Assess goal attainment in each plan quadrant using quantitative and qualitative measures that demonstrate the ROI of integrated HR and diversity processes.
- Collaborate with partners and allies who can lend credence and instrumental support to this effort.
- Strengthen community outreach on issues of hiring, workforce development, and professional development.
- Develop seminars, workshops, and organizational interventions to reinforce desired goals.
- Monitor success of line managers in implementation of integrated HR/diversity strategies.
- Create a joint HR/diversity recognition program.
- Benchmark against best practices in the industry/field.
- Share success stories, first-person testimonials, and anecdotes that concretely demonstrate the value of HR/diversity partnership.

Summarizing the need for a customer-oriented diversity change process, Ricardo Forbes, chief diversity officer for the Baptist Health System in Southeast Florida, indicates that "inclusive adoption at all levels of the organization" needs to be based upon an implementation strategy "triggered from a position of recognition that the changes are rooted in the organization's operational culture of doing the right thing for the population served."

Strategic and Tactical Questions for Further Discussion

The following questions address the extent that an organization has developed the planning mechanisms for HR and diversity strategy and the potential vulnerability when these practices are not synchronized.

1. What mechanisms for input are most effective for the development of a HR/Diversity Strategic Plan? What methods can be used to facilitate collaborative planning?
2. In what ways has your organization strengthened accountability for HR/diversity integration?
3. What are the areas of greatest organizational vulnerability if HR and diversity programs are not synchronized?
4. What are the most difficult factors to measure? The least difficult?
5. How can an organization strengthen rewards and recognition for collaborative HR/diversity achievement?

Finally, we include two case studies that address the development of integrated HR and diversity approaches in complex, decentralized organizations: Walmart, the world's largest retailer, and Kent State University, a public research university with eight regional campuses.

Case Study 8: Building an Integrated HR/Diversity Strategy at Walmart

Walmart is the world's largest retailer with more than 10,000 stores and 2.2 million associates in 27 countries. About 1.4 million associates work in the United States. Walmart's workforce is highly diverse with 813,000 female associates, over 272,000 African American associates, over 174,000 Hispanic associates, over 44,000 Asian and 6,000 Pacific Islander associates, and over 14,000 American Indian and Alaska Native associates ("2012 Workforce Diversity," n.d.). Walmart's employee population has grown rapidly with an increase of 22% from 1.8 million employees in 2005 to 2.2 million in 2011. In 2011 the company generated net sales of $443.8 billion ("2012 Annual Report," 2012).

Walmart's workforce is predominantly female: in the United States, women make up 57% of the workforce, topping retail industry averages of 49% ("2011 Workforce Diversity," n.d.). One of the predominant challenges Walmart has faced relates to women's upward mobility and pay.

A class-action suit filed against Walmart that sought billions of dollars on behalf of 1.5 million female workers was dismissed by the U.S. Supreme Court in 2011 by a margin of 5 to 4. The judges did not decide whether Walmart had discriminated against the women but ruled against on the issue of whether the case qualified as a class-action suit. The plaintiffs offered testimony from William T. Bielby, a sociologist with a specialization in social framework analysis, who argued that localized compensation and promotion decisions could be vulnerable to stereotypes arising from gender bias (Liptak, 2011). According to conservative justice Antonin Scalia, the testimony offered by sociologist William Bielby was "worlds away from significant proof" that Walmart had "operated under a general policy of discrimination" (Liptak, 2011).

Despite these legal challenges, Walmart has steadily increased the representation of minority and female officials and managers. Between 2007 and 2011, the percentage of minority officials and managers increased from 21.3% to 26.7% , and female managers and officials increased from 38.8% to 41.3% ("2011 Workforce Diversity," n.d.). Of Walmart's U.S. officers, 26% are women compared with an average of 14% in Fortune 500 companies ("Accelerating Our Diversity and Inclusion Journey," n.d.). A growing percentage of women are represented on Walmart's board of directors, rising to 20% as compared to an overall average of 15% in Fortune 500 companies. With the addition of Marissa Mayer to the board of directors in April 2012, female board representation now stands at 23.5%.

Walmart has made significant progress with women and minorities at the store level in the United States. From 2008 to 2013 the number of female store managers has increased by 42%, and the number of minority store managers has increased by 32%. A store manager is similar to a chief executive officer in terms of the scale and scope of responsibilities that involve oversight of several hundred associates, direct profit and loss accountability, and responsibility for a fuel station, pharmacy, deli, bakery, grocery, and general merchandise.

At the next level of operation, market managers have responsibility for multiple stores and oversee 10 to 12 stores. The number of female market managers has increased by 92%, and the number of minority market managers has increased by 61% over the same five-year time period. Building the pipeline to managerial positions, 12,000 women and 8,500 minorities have completed the management training program over the past five years.

Walmart has taken an active stance in countering claims of discrimination and adopted an aggressive diversity program that identifies specific areas of progress for women and minorities. Mike Duke, Walmart's chief executive officer, formed the President's Global Council of Women Leaders in 2009 of 16 senior-level women. Half the group are international employees and half are from the United States. In addition, the Women's Economic Empowerment Initiative is another major effort that will create opportunities for women-owned businesses by sourcing $20 billion over the next 5 years. Other programs centered on women's advancement at Walmart include the Women's Officer Caucus, which mentors future women leaders; the Women in Retail Associate Resource Group; and Women's Leadership Councils in each country, which are designed to accelerate the advancement and retention of women in each international market.

Enter Sharon Orlopp, Global Chief Diversity Officer

In January 2011 Sharon Orlopp began her role as global chief diversity officer and senior vice president of corporate HR at Walmart. She had risen quickly within the corporate hierarchy from her initial hire as vice president for HR at Sam's Club in 2003 to senior vice president of HR for Sam's Club in 2004. Orlopp reports to Susan Chambers, executive vice president of HR, who reports to Mike Duke.

Because of the organizational structure with diversity reporting through HR, the diversity and HR functions are closely aligned. Every quarter a trio of representatives from HR, diversity, and business leadership meet with the Compensation, Nominating, and Governance Committee of Walmart's board to discuss diversity outcomes. Walmart's diversity strategic plan identifies business leaders and HR leaders as key owners of the diversity plans in their business units. This strategy of ownership allows business and HR leaders to customize diversity and inclusion plans to their areas of the business.

In 2004 Walmart established the Diversity Goals Program that created the foundation for educational awareness and accountability and involves 60,000 individuals, including all members of management in the field and stores as well as positions at the director's level and on up in the home office. The program links diversity outcomes and compensation, since 10% of managerial performance evaluation ratings is linked to diversity and inclusion, and 15% of bonus components can be withheld if diversity goals are not fulfilled. Specific requirements of the program include mentoring at least two associates and attending or participating in at least one diversity event a year.

Walmart measures its diversity progress through core metrics in three domains: workforce, workplace, and marketplace. Workforce metrics address representation and talent acquisition. Workplace metrics include retention and inclusion. Inclusion is measured by an associate survey conducted annually and includes questions that provide an inclusion index. Marketplace metrics involve a review of supplier diversity and the representation of individuals providing goods and services to Walmart.

According to Orlopp, "Everything we do has a diversity lens on it." Diversity is an integral part of strategic HR planning, which encompasses recruiting, training, on boarding, and retention. Orlopp characterizes the relationship between HR and diversity as "extremely strong and very solid," since many of the individuals have worked in both areas (S. Orlopp, personal communication, September 25, 2012).

Orlopp views the partnership of these two areas as imperative to the business and directly tied to the work of Walmart's business leaders. She describes the business case for integrated diversity and HR programs as "all about the best talent and customer relevance—stores and products [that] are relevant to customers." As a result, the role of HR and diversity is focused on supporting the work of the business leaders:

> Whether we're in HR or in diversity, our goal is to ensure that business leaders are also the ones that are driving diversity and inclusion. It's not viewed as an HR initiative or a diversity initiative; it's really imperative to the business. Our business leaders tend to tackle it from two perspectives, first is that it's all about talent and having the best talent. The second is it's about customer relevance and ensuring that our stores and products are relevant to our customers. Our customers are very diverse. So the business case is critical. HR and diversity are great strategic partners to the business, ensuring that the business leaders are bought in . . . throughout the organization.

One of the core training programs required of all business leaders and associates is micromessaging and microinequities. HR leaders are actively involved as champions in Walmart's seven associate resource groups of individuals with common interests and backgrounds.

Future Directions

As Orlopp looks into the future, she sees three key areas of a diversity focus for Walmart: communications, education, and community. From a communications perspective, she plans an increased focus on communicating diversity initiatives and results, internally and externally. Walmart's Workforce Diversity Reports and annual Diversity and Inclusion Diversity Reports are examples of this broad communication strategy.

In the area of education, Orlopp believes that diversity and inclusion have the greatest impact through affective and emotional understanding when there is an "aha moment that touches our hearts." These defining moments enable employees to see diversity and inclusion through a different lens. As she explains, "Once your heart is touched, behaviors change."

Her efforts in experiential diversity learning at Sam's Club included the development of diversity immersion trips for associates. These immersion trips focus on historical events as well as the current diversity context. The signature journey was a two-day trip to Montgomery, Alabama, where associates visited the Rosa Parks Museum, Martin Luther King's church and parsonage, the Interpretive Center (focused on the voting rights march), and the Southern Poverty Law Center. Other immersion outings included a trip focused on the Hispanic and Latino communities where associates visited the border wall between Mexico and the United States, and a San Francisco trip focused on disabilities that included tours of the Lighthouse for the Blind, the Center for Independent Living, and the specific location of the disability rights sit-ins. Walmart associates have described these trips as "life changing."

Orlopp is seeking to scale diversity immersion training to the entire company. As she explains, "What we are wrestling with is how to do these types of experiences in a cost-effective manner on a large-scale basis. We are teaching others how to fish." As an opportunity for associates to create their own inclusion experiences, for example, all American diversity museums are listed on the company intranet.

From a community perspective, Walmart has launched an ambitious youth mentoring program focused on eighth graders to encourage them to graduate from high school and college. The mentoring program began with 25 students and has now grown to include 1,700 students. Orlopp draws on the notion of a "Big Hairy Audacious Goal" to describe the strategic and emotionally compelling future goal of reaching one million students (Collins & Porras, 1994, p. 9). Eighth graders are targeted because the future pathway of these students is set as they choose their track of classes in high school—either college preparatory or noncollege preparatory classes. Orlopp concludes: "We have not completely figured out how to do this—one of the neat things about Walmart is that we think big and set big goals. We will connect with many external and internal partners to determine how to achieve this huge goal."

Case Study 9: Creating a Division of Diversity, Equity, and Inclusion at Kent State University

Kent State University is a large public research university with eight campuses in northeast Ohio; the main campus is located in Kent. Over 42,000 students are enrolled in the eight-campus system, and 36,521 students are undergraduates. In terms of campus diversity, about 11.8% of undergraduate students are minorities, and 60% are women, while at the graduate level 7.6% are minority, and 67% are women. The university also employs 633 tenured and tenure-track faculty, 1,283 part-time faculty, and 2,736 classified and unclassified employees. Women represent 60% of the workforce, while minorities represent 12%.

With the departure of a vice provost for diversity in 2009, president Lester Lefton created the Commission on Inclusion to analyze the state of diversity at Kent State and provide recommendations about changes that needed to occur. The commission submitted 15 recommendations, including the creation of the position of a chief diversity officer reporting directly to the president. Other recommendations of the commission were

- implementation of a university-wide accountability system for diversity progress for all administrative and academic units;
- incorporation of an inclusive excellence component in each senior leader's performance review;
- creation of an ongoing presidential advisory committee to monitor progress on the commission's recommendations;
- recruitment, promotion, and retention of diverse faculty and staff;
- support and enhancement of recruitment, retention, and scholarship programs for first-generation, underrepresented student populations; and
- identification and dissemination of a Kent State mission and vision statement on inclusive values.

In response to the commission's recommendations, Alfreda Brown was hired in October 2009 as vice president of diversity, equity, and inclusion.

Pragmatic Challenges in Launching a Diversity Division

When she joined the university, Brown realized she needed to create and develop the infrastructure for Kent State's first Division of Diversity, Equity, and Inclusion (DDEI). As a newcomer to Kent State, Brown saw the state of diversity as "in flux," with a great deal to be done and many initiatives that needed to be introduced. While the university had data on diversity, an overall assessment of diversity and metrics to gauge progress had not yet been developed. Furthermore, Brown observed that a common understanding of the meaning of diversity had not been reached. She noted that discussions of inclusive excellence, a concept widely used in higher education to describe the fusion of diversity and quality, seemed disconnected from campus life.

As a result, Brown sought to operationalize the principles of inclusive excellence in the creation of the DDEI. With responsibility for overseeing all of Kent State's diversity programs, DDEI includes the Student Multicultural Center, the Women's Center, and precollege and Upward Bound programs. The division also has responsibility for diversity initiatives in faculty recruitment and retention, diversity and equal opportunity training, and collaborative oversight of the Lesbian, Gay, Bisexual, Transgender, and Queer Center. The units within the new division had few staff: the Women's Center and Student Multicultural Center were each run by one person. Furthermore, both facilities needed refurbishing, and the Upward Bound program had been affected by cuts in grant funding.

An immediate challenge facing Brown was to make the case for and obtain the financial resources to staff DDEI as well as to find the right talent for positions. Once she gained the needed support and executive commitment, she created a staffing structure of 12 people with a focus on diversity planning, assessment, and research management. Since Brown's goal was to institute a diversity scorecard, she needed a professional skilled in diversity research and assessment as a key staff member on her team. In addition to a new assistant vice president for diversity assessment and strategic planning, she also hired an assistant vice president for pipeline initiatives, a faculty recruitment and retention manager, and an equal opportunity and diversity training manager.

Initial Steps

As one of her first initiatives, Brown undertook a talking tour, meeting with each vice president and dean with a list of 10 questions. She found wide variation among these leaders in their definitions of *diversity* as well as their expectations for diversity progress. Brown used the meetings to learn about the senior leaders' perspectives as well as to share her plan to implement a diversity scorecard framework with a dashboard of indicators that would provide an annual assessment of diversity progress. In Brown's view, getting acceptance from constituents and building sustainable coalitions were critical to the success of DDEI programs. As she explained, "If you care about stakeholders and what is important to them, then they have a tendency to care about what you are doing" (A. Brown, personal communication, January 30, 2013).

Since infusing diversity means expanding ways of circulating information and developing diverse communication strategies (Ahmed, 2012), Brown talked to constituents, visited the regional campuses, and reviewed reports from the Commission on Inclusion and other smaller committees. An African American female, Brown learned on the tour that some individuals thought she had been hired to focus only on the progress of African Americans and that diversity initiatives were focused only on race or gender. She explained that her primary focus was on three groups: Latino/Latina, African American, and Native American (AALANA) because of their relative lack of representation. She also learned that the AALANA student graduation rates were only 37%, and she felt she needed to work on strengthening a sense of community on the campus for underrepresented student populations.

Although Brown wished to implement a climate study, she found some initial reluctance among stakeholders to pursue it. As a result she postponed this initiative until 2013 and used other opportunities to gain insight into the needs and perceptions of employees at the eight campuses. She brought the commission back together to recognize their work, provide an updated status on their recommendations, and hold an appreciation reception on their behalf. This step was important, since the responsibility for ensuring the success for implementation of the commission's recommendations was now under new leadership.

Several members from the Commission on Inclusion were also members of the University Diversity Advisory Council (UDAC), which was renamed the University Diversity Action Council to emphasize its focus on action rather than advice. Using the recommendations from the commission as a foundation for a new diversity plan, within 6 months she had put together a small group to develop an Equity Action Plan for Kent State's eight campuses.

To create an infrastructure for strategic diversity planning, Brown reconvened the Commission on Diversity and Inclusion and changed its name to the University Diversity Action Committee (keeping the acronym UDAC) to focus on action rather than advice. UDAC members served as liaisons to their areas and were empowered to be the voice of diversity. The members pooled their expertise to provide input to the plan and communicated with their respective constituencies. Within 6 months, Brown had put together a small group of committee members to develop an Equity Action Plan.

The Equity Action Plan

The name Equity Action Plan was chosen by Alfreda Brown to designate the new diversity strategic plan and ensure that considerations for transformative changes are grounded in fairness, justice, and integrity. Brown believes that "equity considerations are informed by historical and cultural circumstances and through individual and collective responsibility." As a result, equity "has become the catalyst of the action plan and is established through open engagement of ideas and fairness of thought and action" ("Charting Our Future; Division of Diversity Equity and Inclusion, Equity Action Plan, Fall 2012–Spring 2017," 2012, p. 7, hereafter cited as "Charting Our Future").

As a five-year blueprint for Kent State's evolution in relation to diversity and equity, the plan draws on research by Darryl Smith (2004) of Claremont

Graduate University and is framed around four dimensions: institutional climate, culture, and community relationships; student access, recruitment, retention, and success; education and scholarship; and institutional accountability. The plan is not designed as an addendum to the university's strategic plan but rather as "a living particle of Kent State's core—its values, its practices, and its vision of a transformative future" ("Charting Our Future," 2012, p. 6). To emphasize this alignment, Brown developed a strategy map to link the university's key themes and projects with the DDEI's directions, themes, projects, and goals.

Brown developed the diversity scorecard as an empirical tool for gauging diversity progress. The scorecard presents longitudinal metrics on access, retention, and excellence for student, faculty, and staff in AALANA groups. It was presented to the board of trustees as part of a report on the division's progress in December 2012.

One of the major objectives highlighted in the report was the need to increase faculty diversity. Since AALANA tenure and non-tenure-track faculty representation had remained at roughly 5% for a period of six years, Brown set a goal for 9% of new hires for this group.

To accelerate progress in minority faculty hiring, Brown developed a number of strategies to incentivize faculty outreach and hiring. She instituted a program of incremental funding for tenure-track AALANA hires, providing up to $15,000 per year for six years to the hiring dean. To obtain this funding, the dean is required to provide a success plan for the new faculty hire, which includes mentoring, research support, and help in acclimating the faculty member to the university environment. If the new faculty member does not attain tenure or leaves before attaining tenure, the funds must be repaid. To date, Brown has provided funding for three individuals, with two more faculty hires in the pipeline.

As a second major strategy, Brown took several deans with her to conferences to recruit and interview diverse candidates, resulting in three new hires. Furthermore, she built a database of AALANA researchers, mostly individuals who are either close to completing their doctorates or are postdoctorates, to strengthen the faculty recruitment pipeline.

Future Objectives

In moving forward with the Equity Action Plan, Brown foresees a primary challenge as keeping the assessment process going until it is "reasonably successful, but clearly understood" as a campus priority. She envisions a future when such an assessment will not be needed and when the meaning of inclusion is widely understood. When the campus reaches that point, she said, "Inclusive excellence would work automatically." She concluded the Equity

Action Plan with an essay titled "A Philosophical Declaration: The Academic Need for Inclusive Excellence in Action" in which she crystallizes her vision for the future of diversity at Kent State University by linking behaviors and a welcoming environment to the attainment of inclusive excellence ("Charting Our Future," 2012):

> Inclusive excellence is revealed when diversity becomes a natural process, a welcomed aspect of institutional will and vitality. Inclusive excellence in action is an essential element of an institution's brand. It promotes an environment that conveys the power of inclusion in a matter of fact acceptance, without biases, hindrances, or intolerant behaviors. Inclusive excellence in action dwells within a place where diversity is not only honored, but also expected.

References

Accelerating our diversity and inclusion journey: 2011 diversity and inclusion report. (n.d.). Retrieved from http://www.walmartstores.com/sites/diversity-and-inclusion-report/2011/

Ahmed, S. (2012). *On being included: Racism and diversity in institutional life.* Durham, NC: Duke University Press.

Barrett, F. J. (2012). *Yes to the mess: Surprising leadership lessons from jazz.* Boston, MA: Harvard Business School Press.

Baytos, L. M. (1995). *Designing & implementing successful diversity programs.* Upper Saddle River, NJ: Prentice Hall.

Beer, M., Eisenstat, R. A., & Spector, B. (1990). Why change programs don't produce change. *Harvard Business Review, 68*(6), 158–166.

Charting our future: Division of Diversity Equity and Inclusion, Equity Action Plan, Fall 2012–Spring 2017. (2012). Unpublished manuscript, Kent State University, Kent, Ohio..

Collins, J. (2001). *Good to great: Why some companies make the leap . . . and others don't.* New York, NY: HarperCollins.

Collins, J., & Porras, J. I. (1994). *Built to last: Successful habits of visionary companies.* New York, NY: HarperCollins.

Covey, S. R. (1989). *The 7 habits of highly effective people: Powerful lessons in personal change.* New York, NY: Simon & Schuster.

Ernst, C., & Yip, J. (2009). Boundary-spanning leadership: Tactics to bridge social identity groups in organizations. In T. L. Pittinsky (Ed.), *Crossing the divide: Intergroup leadership in a world of difference* (pp. 73–86). Boston, MA: Harvard Business School Press.

Evans, A., & Chun, E. B. (2007). *Are the walls really down? Behavioral and organizational barriers to faculty and staff diversity* (ASHE-ERIC Higher Education Reports, Vol. 33, No. 1). San Francisco, CA: Jossey-Bass.

50 years of helping customers save money and live better: Walmart 2012 annual report. (2012). Retrieved from http://www.walmartstores.com/sites/annual-report/2012/ WalMart_AR.pdf

Gupta, A. K., & Cao, Q. (2005). A strategic embeddedness analysis of global business teams: Directions for future research. In D. L. Shapiro, M. A. Von Glinow, & J. L. C. Cheng (Eds.), *Managing multinational teams: Global perspectives* (Vol. 18, pp. 233–248). San Diego, CA: Elsevier.

Hickman, G. R., & Creighton-Zollar, A. (1998). Diverse self-directed work teams: Developing strategic initiatives for 21st century organizations. *Public Personnel Management, 27*(2), 187–200.

Hubbard, E. E. (1999). *How to calculate diversity return on investment.* Petaluma, CA: Global Insights.

Hubbard, E. E. (2001). *Measuring diversity results* (Vol. 1). Petaluma, CA: Global Insights.

Hubbard, E. E. (2004). *The manager's pocket guide to diversity management.* Amherst, MA: HRD Press.

Kezar, A., & Carducci, R. (2009). Revolutionizing leadership development: Lessons from research and theory. In A. Kezar (Ed.), *Rethinking leadership in a complex, multicultural, and global environment: New concepts and models for higher education* (pp. 1–38). Sterling, VA: Stylus.

Kezar, A. J., Glenn, W. J., Lester, J., & Nakamoto, J. (2008). Examining organizational contextual features that affect implementation of equity initiatives. *Journal of Higher Education, 79*(2), 125–159.

Kotter, J. P. (1995). Leading change: Why transformation efforts fail. *Harvard Business Review, 73*(2), 59–67.

Lawler, E. E., III, & Worley, C. G. (with Creelman, D.). (2011). *Management reset: Organizing for sustainable effectiveness.* San Francisco: Jossey-Bass.

Liptak, A. (2011, June 20). Justices rule for Wal-Mart in class-action bias case. *New York Times.* Retrieved from http://www.nytimes.com/2011/06/21/business/21bizcourt .html?pagewanted=all&_r=0

Moore, A. P., & Antao, R. S. (2007). *Modeling and analysis of information technology change and access controls in the business context.* Retrieved from http://www.sei .cmu.edu/reports/06tn040.pdf

Smith, D. G. (2004), *The campus diversity initiative: Current status, anticipating the future.* Retrieved from https://folio.iupui.edu/bitstream/handle/10244/43/ CDIStatusandFuture2004.pdf?sequence=12012

Walmart: Accelerating our diversity and inclusion journey: 2011 diversity and inclusion report. (2011). Retrieved from http://www.walmartstores.com/sites/diversity -and-inclusion-report/2011/

Wentling, R. M. (2004). Factors that assist and barriers that hinder the success of diversity initiatives in multinational corporations. *Human Resource Development International, 7*(2), 165–180.

7

SYNTHESIS AND RECOMMENDATIONS

And so a good way to look at organizational health . . . is to see it as the multiplier of intelligence. . . .
Most organizations exploit only a fraction of the knowledge, experience, and intellectual capital that
is available to them. (Lencioni, 2012, p. 11)

In this summary chapter, we offer perspectives gained from our analysis of the progress of synergistic HR/diversity talent management programs found from research, case studies, and interviews of HR and diversity thought leaders. Since integration of HR and diversity talent strategy still remains relatively new, we have focused on the principle of execution as learning as organizations innovate, experiment, and develop sustainable, inclusive talent approaches (Edmondson, 2012). The broad thesis that underpins this book is that common themes and challenges characterize the development of integrated HR/diversity talent practices. These themes transcend specific organizational environments—private, public, governmental, nonprofit, and higher education. What may be different about these environments is the level of recognition HR has attained as a strategic partner as well as the perceived urgency and pace of integrative HR/diversity efforts.

As modern organizations have grown larger and older, they must devote an increasing portion of their resources to integrative services, and these services keep the organization from falling apart (Bergquist, 1993). Economist Kenneth Boulding (1969) referred to an "integrative system" or what he calls "integry" (p. 1), the aspects of a social system that address relationships of status, community, identity, legitimacy, trust, and their interrelationships. A transformational HR/diversity strategy reinforces the organizational talent infrastructure as an integrative system that supports the principles of reciprocal empowerment. Such a system nurtures diverse talent, overcomes oppressive practices of marginalization, and creates a culture of inclusive, democratic participation. It positions diversity as a central organizational concern that is critical to effective modern management practices. And this pathway will lead to organizational health, a state reached when management, strategy, and culture fit together with minimal politics and confusion (Lencioni, 2012).

Keeping in mind the 10 predominant themes in HR/diversity transformation discussed in Chapter 1, we reflect further on specific approaches that will assist the process of execution as learning in the attainment of integrated HR/diversity strategy. Our focus in presenting these recommendations is on development of the mind-set and conditions that will help leaders jump-start change, overcome organizational inertia and resistance, maintain momentum, and build collaborative stakeholder input into the change process.

1. Accept the reality of the situation and believe it can be overcome. This principle embodies what Jim Collins (2001) termed the *Stockdale paradox*, named after Admiral James Stockdale who was held captive for eight years during the Vietnam War and was tortured more than 20 times. In contrast to the optimists in that situation who thought they would be out by Christmas each year, Stockdale began with the discipline of confronting the brutal facts and combining it with the unwavering faith that the circumstances could be overcome (Collins, 2001). As organizations operationalize plans to create inclusive talent practices, they must begin with the brutal facts of turnover of diverse employees, inequitable working conditions, compensation disparities, and microclimates of fear and even repression. Specific indicators of progress can include the resolution of complaints and grievances through HR's mediation and conflict resolution processes as well as systemic policy changes that address areas of organizational concern such as protections against retaliation. And presidents and chief executive officers (CEOs) need to be realists who do not take yes for an answer when working with members of their executive team who may avoid presenting bad news (Martin & Samels, 2009).

2. Build success by beginning in small, isolated units or departments. Based on the results of a study of six major corporations conducted by Beer, Eisenstat, and Spector (1990), starting renewal at the top of an organization is a high-risk proposition. These researchers recommend sparking change through separate divisions or plants, which represent small, peripheral, isolated units rather than large operations. Use Collins's (2001) flywheel principle, which emphasizes small, sustained efforts to push the flywheel of change rather than expecting a single miracle moment.

3. Develop a small cadre of influential stakeholders from all levels of the organization to spearhead the integration of HR and diversity work. According to the 80/20 principle, a minority of efforts can create the majority of results (Koch, 1998). The small cadre of stakeholders can be a cross-section of individuals from different organizational units and of differing employment types that represent the diversity of the organization. Insights from a pioneering study of grassroots leadership in five academic institutions undertaken by

Adrianna Kezar and Jaime Lester (2011) found that grassroots efforts may often be independent of top-down efforts, and that convergence is frequently limited. To overcome this tendency, navigate bureaucratic inertia related to HR/diversity integration using a workgroup of stakeholders that bridge subcultures, organizational hierarchies, and employment types.

Throughout the case studies, we have seen examples of how representative groups of stakeholders can help drive HR/diversity change efforts. Such groups can be at the leadership level, such as Sodexo's Diversity Leadership Council chaired by the CEO, or representative of the specific constituency affected, such as Massachusetts Institute of Technology's faculty-led Initiative for Faculty Race and Diversity. Although the collective impact of multiple organizational units and powerful constituencies can be substantial, effective leadership is still needed to ensure that holding meetings and covering familiar ground is not a substitute for action-based outcomes.

4. Focus on the emotional undertones that accompany diversity discussions to take the temperature of the organization. The key to developing a successful organizational learning strategy is to recognize the power of emotion in overcoming cultural barriers to diversity. HR/diversity leaders need to appeal to the emotional side by illustrating problems and issues in dramatic, concrete terms (Heath & Heath, 2010). As a result, systemic professional development initiatives cannot simply take diversity constructs and present them in a didactic manner. Persuasion needs to begin by dealing with the emotional elephant, the underlying assumptions, presuppositions, and behaviors related to intergroup relations and acceptance of difference.

If Kilmann's concept of tracking introduced in Chapter 1 (p. 17) is correct, then an emotional track for diversity change is needed. HR leaders must be able to diagnose emotional blockages in the lifeblood of an organization and develop strategies that will shift affective undercurrents. As discussed in Chapter 3, diversity emotional intelligence emerges as an essential competency for HR and diversity leaders in terms of their own self-awareness, self-management, and relationship management.

5. Obtain a stable configuration of staffing and resources for diversity efforts. The struggle to garner sufficient resources for diversity efforts has resulted from the fact that diversity efforts are often perceived as peripheral programs rather than essential practices. The instability of resources devoted to diversity and high turnover of staff noted in this study can place program outcomes in doubt. While organizational cutbacks have resulted in the consolidation of HR and diversity offices in a number of settings, such consolidation needs to preserve the vital role of diversity and inclusion as a key component of organizational processes. We have emphasized that diversity is not a quick fix; on average, it may take four or five years to build an effective HR/diversity strategy that shifts predominant cultural assumptions and norms. If funding is not stable over a multiyear period, and the turnover of chief diversity officers is rapid, the continuity of diversity programs will be jeopardized. Recall the testimonial of a CDO who noted that over the past two years almost 75% of the CDOs in the top 50 companies cited for diversity by *DiversityInc* magazine have left (see Chapter 5, p. 128). This pattern was replicated in our interview sample, suggesting that diversity is still not seen as peripheral rather than integral to organizational mission. In budget-cutting exercises, this approach inevitably results in downsizing diversity staff.

   6. Rethink and rebuild systematic HR processes for diversity from the ground up. The lack of systematization of HR processes in terms of diversity represents a significant deficit for organizations seeking to develop a competitive talent strategy. This deficit is observable in the omission of diversity from HR mission statements and strategic planning. We were surprised by the fact that most interviewees, including HR leaders, could not recall or cite their HR mission statement and any reference it might contain to diversity. From the standpoint of the nuts and bolts of HR processes, no mention was made of the role of diversity in job descriptions. And relatively few organizations require or provide more than occasional professional development in diversity competency for HR professionals. The assumption still prevails that diversity work is the realm of the CDO and remains only ancillary to HR's responsibilities. As Andy Brantley, CEO of the College and University Professional Association, emphasized in Case Study 7 in Chapter 5, HR professionals tend to worry about the views of senior leadership in relation to the need for diversity and inclusion and may lack understanding about where to begin and what contributions they can make.

   7. Retain some degree of centralization and oversight of component HR/ diversity programs. One of the great benefits of retaining some degree of centralization in the oversight of HR and diversity processes in large organizations is the ability to shape policy direction and ensure consistency and equity in practices across dispersed units, departments, and sectors. Centralized HR and diversity offices can create templates and models for smaller and medium-size units to emulate, provide consulting guidance, develop a common metrics, and assess progress in meeting defined goals.

   The creation of the Office of Diversity and Inclusion in the federal government's Office of Personnel Management in 2010 is a case in point. Following President Barack Obama's Executive Order 13583 that directed federal agencies to implement a strategic focus on diversity and inclusion as a key component of their HR strategies, OPM quickly issued guidelines for government agencies in the development of agency plans with sample practices, actions, and measurements (see Case Study 6).

The result of this effort was the creation of highly developed and leading-edge agency plans such as, for example, the Department of Defense's Diversity and Inclusion Strategic Plan 2012–2017 (2012). The plan provides strategic actions and initiatives in support of three overarching goals and explicitly aligns and connects with other efforts such as the National Military Strategy and the National Security Strategy. It builds on the progress made in the 2009 directive (No. 1020.02) issued by David Chu, undersecretary of defense for personnel and readiness, institutionalizing diversity and establishing policies designed to keep the defense department and its component diversity offices for each military service in alignment (Military Leadership Diversity Commission, 2009). This directive tied the definitions of *diversity* and *diversity management* to the need for the workforce to reach its greatest productive capability (Military Leadership Diversity Commission, 2010).

8. *Encourage positive deviance using a strength-based approach.* The notion of positive deviance specifically focuses on extreme cases of excellence in which employees break through existing norms in honorable ways. Positive deviance focuses on intentions rather than outcomes, is voluntary and discretionary, and involves a significant departure from prevailing norms (Spreitzer & Sonenshein, 2004). Acts of positive deviance are observable exceptions, in which individual differences become a community resource (Pascale, Sternin, & Sternin, 2010). Positive deviance relies on the premise that solutions to difficult problems already exist, have been discovered by members of the community, and these innovators have succeeded despite facing the same barriers as others (Pascale, Sternin, & Sternin, 2010). Applied to the area of strategic HR/diversity implementation, positive deviance means that some units in the organization have undoubtedly already applied and obtained results from these principles. Building positive deviance requires recognizing innovation and the strength it brings to an organization.

9. *Build the concept of disruptive innovation into HR/diversity change processes.* Positive deviance refers to cases when employees with honorable intentions exhibit excellence in efforts that deviate from existing norms. It is closely allied with another important concept—disruptive innovation—which transforms complex, expensive products and services into things that are simple, affordable, and improves the quality of the experience (Richardson, 2011). If the culture of an organization determines the limits and possibilities of strategies, then a disruptive improvement in the area of HR/diversity processes can lead toward significant change (Shugart, 2012).

The concept of disruptive innovation introduced by Clay Christensen and his colleagues focuses on jobs to be done and is action-oriented (Richardson, 2011). Coupled with organizational learning as the engine of change, disruptive innovation can provide a new lens, a deepened way of interacting, or a simple yet creative approach to strengthening diversity outcomes. For example, scholars have described successful strategies for hiring diverse faculty as "interrupting the usual" and found that underrepresented faculty of color are more likely to be hired at predominantly White institutions when an institutional intervention strategy that enhances the traditional search process is used (Smith, Turner, Osei-Kofi, & Richards, 2004). In another example, the intergroup dialogue process introduced at the University of Michigan provides an avenue for disrupting predominant ways of interacting and building meaningful communication across social group boundaries and social identities. Through the improved interactions among small groups of individuals, it can create the sea change necessary for transformative organizational communication.

10. *Provide meaningful incentives for team innovation at all levels of the organization.* Since diverse work teams are the catalyst for inclusion and innovation, a paradigm shift is necessary from a focus on individual achievement to team innovation. Teamwork is not a virtue; it is a strategic choice (Lencioni, 2012). Teamwork strengthens interdependence and requires learning how to make decisions that involve different perspectives (Edmondson, 2012). Furthermore, the creation of expertise silos in organizations can inhibit the teaming necessary to solve global problems (Edmondson, 2012).

Most reward and professional development programs focus on individual learning, not team-based experiential learning. In creating sustainable talent management strategies, organizations need to develop programs that recognize, encourage, and reward the success of diverse work teams.

Looking Ahead

In an era of uncertainty, economic instability, and rapid global change, talent represents the differentiating factor in organizational success. Organizations can no longer afford to overlook the importance of creating the conditions that will allow the creativity and innovation of talent to thrive. When HR and diversity talent strategies are systematically integrated throughout an entire organization, this synergy enhances the organizational capacity for innovation. The case studies presented in this book suggest that organizations are at different phases in the process of implementing a phase-based approach to diversity, establishing solid metrics, and developing a clear accountability structure to support longitudinal progress.

Although the need for strategic HR may appear self-evident, some sectors such as higher education have been slower in recognizing the relation of strategic HR to organizational and financial performance. In our view, if HR continues to function at a transactional level, the vision of a comprehensive talent management strategy cannot be attained. Diversity also struggles to be recognized as a core and mainstream function that is tied to strategic planning and overall organizational objectives. The rapid turnover among chief diversity officers in some organizations as described in Chapter 5 suggests a tendency to view diversity as peripheral and outside the mainstream of strategic organizational concern. Such turnover and lack of strategic focus seriously undermine the potential for the creation of sustainable talent management practices.

We have noted the reluctance of some HR professionals to take a leadership role in diversity, either because of a lack of assigned responsibility for this function, lack of executive support, or even the belief that diversity is not a core HR issue. The relatively late emergence of HR's role in the diversity arena has delayed the incorporation of diversity into organization-wide processes, policies, systems, and structures. By contrast, diversity leaders interviewed for the study have taken the lead in conceptualizing and implementing systematic diversity talent practices. As institutional change agents, HR leaders need to play an instrumental role in coleading diversity transformation and helping to shift the normative assumptions, attitudes, and patterns of behaviors in relation to diversity within the organizational culture. In this regard, Andy Brantley foresees that HR leaders "can have an impact every single day if we choose to have an impact" (see Chapter 5, p. 140). To help guide such a transformation, HR leaders must also draw upon the diversity competencies, intercultural sensitivity, and diversity emotional intelligence that will build organizational capacity for diversity.

Given the changing global landscape and demands of the knowledge economy, the structures of top-down, command-and-control leadership that led to success in the industrial era no longer suffice. The power of diverse team-based models is necessary to provide flexibility and nurture innovation. Furthermore, when organizations function as *egosystems* rather than *ecosystems*, they forfeit the ability of contributors to work synergistically to pursue valuable institutional goals (Crocker & Garcia, 2010). Reciprocal empowerment and psychological safety are important characteristics of a workplace that allows individuals to have a voice in decision making, obtain the resources to perform their work, and retain the ability to determine and express their own identities. Organizations that have crossed the talent frontier actively embrace the concept of full participation—enabling individuals to thrive, engage meaningfully, and collaborate in reciprocal, coequal ways (see Sturm, Eatman, Saltmarsh, & Bush, 2011). In such organizations, diversity and inclusion become strengths rather than points of vulnerability for organizations seeking to build a high-performance workplace. The return on investment from such talent approaches includes lower turnover, enhanced retention, and increased employee commitment and job satisfaction.

Early recognition of the pivotal role of talent in organizational success has led global corporations to focus on building diverse talent pipelines, succession planning programs, and leadership opportunities that build innovative capacity and ensure readiness for growth. Similarly, the leading HR and diversity professional associations have developed programs that solidify diversity and inclusion standards for the profession and recognize HR/diversity attainment in member organizations. Federal and state governments are making significant strides in building workforce representation to mirror the demographics of the American population.

From an architectural standpoint, we have discussed the barriers created by bifurcated structures and bureaucratic hurdles that hinder the attainment of strategic talent capabilities. By contrast, an integrated platform for talent management creates the infrastructure needed for a high-performance workplace. Total rewards programs offer the opportunity for integration of diversity and inclusion into formal organizational processes. For example, diversity has become a criterion for evaluation in managerial reviews and is linked to executive and managerial compensation. Progressive organizations are implementing systematic diversity organizational learning programs rather than stand-alone training opportunities and requiring these programs for management. Integrated conflict management systems provide the opportunity to resolve conflicts and problems before they percolate to the top in formal complaints. Employee resource and affinity groups offer employees an avenue for self-expression, group affiliation, and identity development. Reward and recognition structures for diversity solidify desired outcomes and create motivation for change. And through such systemic, comprehensive efforts, an organization can establish and reinforce equity and consistency in HR practices across dispersed and decentralized units, divisions, and lines of business.

A core principle for successful HR and diversity talent strategies is that these strategies ultimately must include all employees, not simply diverse employees. In operationalizing the meaning of inclusion, Veronica Villalobos, director of the Office of Diversity and Inclusion in the U.S. Office of Personnel Management, emphasizes that talent programs include the optimal contributions of all employees: "We always make every effort to gain talent from every group. . . . We always look to retain our talent; we can't afford to make these investments in people and watch them walk out the door. . . . it's really about every single employee."

In our discussion of the discourse of diversity, we have emphasized the importance of a more inclusive definition of *diversity*, one that embraces the multiplicity of characteristics that constitute social and individual identity.

As HR and diversity leaders join to build an integrated, systematic approach to diversity and inclusion, they epitomize what the poet Richard

Blanco, the son of Cuban exiles, describes as "hope—a new constellation waiting for us to map it, waiting for us to name it—together" (as cited in Bruce, 2013, para. 10). The new constellation represents the synergistic work of HR and diversity professionals who collaborate to create the architecture, practices, and workplace environment that enable organizations to cross the new talent frontier in a diverse and interconnected global society. The journey toward this new constellation is under way but will require continued vigilance and sustained organizational attention.

References

Beer, M., Eisenstat, R. A., & Spector, B. (1990). Why change programs don't produce change. *Harvard Business Review, 68*(6), 158–166.

Bergquist, W. H. (1993). *The postmodern organization: Mastering the art of irreversible change.* San Francisco, CA: Jossey-Bass.

Boulding, K. E. (1969). Public choice and the grants economy: The intersecting set. *Public Choice, 7*(1), 1–2.

Bruce, M. (2013). *'One today': Full text of Richard Blanco inaugural poem.* Retrieved from http://abcnews.go.com/Politics/today-richard-blanco-poem-read-barack-obama-inauguration/story?id=18274653

Collins, J. (2001). *Good to great: Why some companies make the leap . . . and others don't.* New York, NY: HarperCollins.

Crocker, J., & Garcia, J. A. (2010). Internalized devaluation and situational threat. In J. J. Dovidio, M. Hewstone, P. Glick, & V. M. Esses (Eds.), *The Sage handbook of prejudice, stereotyping and discrimination* (pp. 395–409). Thousand Oaks, CA: Sage.

Edmondson, A. C. (2012). *Teaming: How organizations learn, innovate, and compete in the knowledge economy.* San Francisco, CA: Jossey-Bass.

Heath, C., & Heath, D. (2010). *Switch: How to change things when change is hard.* New York, NY: Broadway Books.

Kezar, A. J., & Lester, J. (2011). *Enhancing campus capacity for leadership: An examination of grassroots leaders in higher education.* Stanford, CA: Stanford University Press.

Kilmann, R. H. (1984). *Beyond the quick fix: Managing five tracks to organizational success.* San Francisco, CA: Jossey-Bass.

Koch, R. (1998). *The 80/20 principle: The secret to success by achieving more with less.* New York, NY: Doubleday.

Lencioni, P. (2012). *The advantage: Why organizational health trumps everything else in business.* San Francisco, CA: Jossey-Bass.

Martin, J., & Samels, J. E. (2009). *Turnaround: Leading stressed colleges and universities to excellence.* Baltimore, MD: Johns Hopkins University Press.

Military Leadership Diversity Commission. (2009). *The defense diversity working group*. Retrieved from http://diversity.defense.gov/Resources /Commission/ docs/Issue%20Papers/Paper%2007%20-%20Defense%20Diversity%20 Working%20Group.pdf

Military Leadership Diversity Commission. (2010). *Department of defense directive 1020.02: A foundation for effective, accountable diversity management?* Retrieved from http://diversity.defense.gov/Resources/Commission/docs/Issue%20Papers/ Paper%2050%20-%20DOD%20Directive%201020-02.pdf

Pascale, R., Sternin, J., & Sternin, M. (2010). *The power of positive deviance: How unlikely innovators solve the world's toughest problems*. Boston, MA: Harvard Business School Press.

Richardson, J. (2011). Disrupting how and where we learn: An interview with Clayton Christensen and Michael Horn. *Phi Delta Kappan, 92*(4), 32–36, 38.

Shugart, S. M. (2012). *The challenge to deep change: A brief cultural history of higher education*. Retrieved from http://www.scribd.com/doc/120481213/The-Challenge -to-Deep-Change-A-Brief-Cultural-History-of-Higher-Education

Smith, D. G., Turner, C. S., Osei-Kofi, N., & Richards, S. (2004). Interrupting the usual: Successful strategies for hiring diverse faculty. *Journal of Higher Education, 75*(2), 133–160.

Spreitzer, G. M., & Sonenshein, S. (2004). Toward the construct definition of positive deviance. *American Behavioral Scientist, 47*(6), 828–847.

Sturm, S., Eatman, T., Saltmarsh, J., & Bush, A. (2011). *Full participation: Building the architecture for diversity and community engagement in higher education*. Retrieved from http://surface.syr.edu/cgi/viewcontent.cgi?article=1001&context=ia

U.S. Department of Defense. (2012). *Diversity and inclusion strategic plan: 2012–2017*. Retrieved from http://diversity.defense.gov/docs/DoD_Diversity_Strategic_Plan_ %20final_as%20of%2019%20Apr%2012[1].pdf

AUTHORS

Edna Chun and **Alvin Evans** are award-winning authors and HR and diversity leaders with extensive experience in complex, multicampus systems of higher education. Two of their books, *Are the Walls Really Down?: Behavioral and Organizational Barriers to Faculty and Staff Diversity* (San Francisco, CA: Jossey-Bass, 2007) and *Bridging the Diversity Divide: Globalization and Reciprocal Empowerment in Higher Education* (San Francisco, CA: Jossey-Bass, 2009) were recipients of the prestigious Kathryn G. Hansen Publication Award by the College and University Professional Association for Human Resources. Their latest publications include *Diverse Administrators in Peril: The New Indentured Class in Higher Education* (Boulder, CO: Paradigm, 2012) and *Creating a Tipping Point: Strategic HR in Higher Education* (San Francisco: Jossey-Bass, 2012). Chun and Evans have published a number of journal articles in leading professional and diversity journals on talent management and diversity strategies.

Evans serves as associate vice president of HR for Kent State University and Chun is associate vice chancellor for HR at the University of North Carolina at Greensboro.

INDEX

Strategic Diversity Leadership

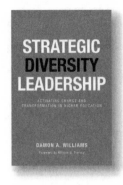

Activating Change and Transformation in Higher Education
Damon A. Williams
Foreword by William G. Tierney

"Williams has done a masterful job of integrating organizational planning savvy with both practitioner wisdom and scholarly research from over four decades of campus diversity initiatives. He keeps his eye firmly on the human side of diversity change and provides a wealth of practical guidance for leaders who see the need to move beyond episodic diversity interventions toward comprehensive institutional engagement and change. I warmly recommend this exceptionally useful book for any educational institution that already sees diversity as an educational value and now wants to reach toward the next and more challenging level of making excellence inclusive."—*Carol Schneider, President, Association of American Colleges and Universities (AAC&U)*

"In this book, Williams melds a deep understanding of diversity with a sophisticated understanding of the nuances of leadership and organizational change. He delivers a blueprint of approaches to activating diversity plans, creating meaningful chief diversity officer roles, fostering accountability, and avoiding the pitfalls of leading change efforts on college and university campuses. This is an important book, which harnesses research and theory to lead real world change."—*Molly Corbett Broad, President, American Council of Education*

22883 Quicksilver Drive
Sterling, VA 20166-2102   Subscribe to our e-mail alerts: www.Styluspub.com

Also available from Stylus

The Chief Diversity Officer

CHIEF
DIVERSITY
OFFICER

Strategy, Structure, and Change Management
Damon A. Williams and Katrina C. Wade-Golden
Foreword by Mark A. Emmert

"*The Chief Diversity Officer* provides an extremely thorough and thoughtful overview of the importance of the evolving role and responsibilities of this position in higher education. This timely volume includes a sophisticated discussion of the structural issues involved in diversity leadership, incorporating both educational theory and practical wisdom and advice. It will be a valuable resource for academic leaders across the country who care about the educational imperatives of diversity in higher education."—*Jonathan Alger, President, James Madison University*

"If you are interested in chief diversity officers, you have to read this book. It will frame how you think about the definition, design, and realities of the CDO role, whether you are a leader in higher education or the corporate sector. Grounded in research, but written for practitioners and scholars alike, this book provides an excellent road map, telling leaders how to develop high impact CDO roles, lead through relationships and influence, get off to a fast start, and the critical principles for leading change. We've waited too long for the *Chief Diversity Officer* and I'm glad it's finally here, very well done!"— *Billy Dexter, Partner Global Diversity Services Practice, Heidrick & Struggles*

"As organizations of all kinds look to engage issues of diversity and inclusion, they often think of creating or recasting the CDO role within their respective organizations. Done correctly, the results can be powerful; done incorrectly, and the fallout can be devastating. *The Chief Diversity Officer* carefully lays out the questions that need to be answered and the critical factors to ensure that the person who is going to assume the role is set up for success. Focused on higher education, but relevant across the board, every HR executive, CEO, or board member who is considering the CDO role in their organization should read this book."—*Dennis Kennedy, Founder & CEO, National Diversity Council*